casenote™ Legal Briefs

CIVIL PROCEDURE

Adaptable to courses utilizing Marcus, Redish and Sherman's
casebook on Civil Procedure

NORMAN S. GOLDENBERG, SENIOR EDITOR
PETER TENEN, MANAGING EDITOR

STAFF WRITERS
CHRIS YOUKER MIAO
PATRICIA P. LAIACONA
KEMP RICHARDSON
RICH LOVICH

ALSO AVAILABLE!
CIVIL PROCEDURE
OUTLINE
This Casenote Legal Briefs volume
is now cross-referenced to the new
Casenote Law Outline
on Civil Procedure
by Profs. Oakley & Perschbacher

PUBLISHED BY CASENOTES PUBLISHING CO., INC. 1640 5th ST., SUITE 208 SANTA MONICA, CA 90401

ISBN 0-87457-163-4

FORMAT FOR THE CASENOTE LEGAL BRIEF

CASE CAPSULE: This boldface section (first three paragraphs) highlights the procedural nature of the case, a short summary of the facts, and the rule of law. This is an invaluable quick-review device designed to refresh the student's memory for classroom discussion and exam preparation.

NATURE OF CASE: This section identifies the form of action (e.g., breach of contract, negligence, battery), the type of proceeding (e.g., demurrer, appeal from trial court's jury instructions) and the relief sought (e.g., damages, injunction, criminal sanctions).

FACT SUMMARY: The fact summary is included to refresh the student's memory. It can be used as a quick reminder of the facts when the student is chosen by an instructor to brief a case.

CONCISE RULE OF LAW: This portion of the brief summarizes the general principle of law that the case illustrates. Like the fact summary, it is included to refresh the student's memory. It may be used for instant recall of the court's holding and for classroom discussion or home review.

FACTS: This section contains all relevant facts of the case, including the contentions of the parties and the lower court holdings. It is written in a logical order to give the student a clear understanding of the case. The plaintiff and defendant are identified by their proper names throughout and are always labeled with a (P) or (D).

ISSUE: The issue is a concise question that brings out the essence of the opinion as it relates to the section of the casebook in which the case appears. Both substantive and procedural issues are included if relevant to the decision.

HOLDING AND DECISION: This section offers a clear and in-depth discussion of the rule of the case and the court's rationale. It is written in easy-to-understand language. When relevant, it includes a thorough discussion of the exceptions listed by the court, the concurring and dissenting opinions, and the names of the judges.

CONCURRENCE / DISSENT: All concurrences and dissents are briefed whenever they are included by the casebook editor.

EDITOR'S ANALYSIS: This last paragraph gives the student a broad understanding of where the case "fits in" with other cases in the section of the book and with the entire course. It is a hornbook-style discussion indicating whether the case is a majority or minority opinion and comparing the principal case with other cases in the casebook. It may also provide analysis from restatements, uniform codes, and law review articles. The editor's analysis will prove to be invaluable to classroom discussion.

CROSS-REFERENCE TO OUTLINE: Wherever possible, following each case is a cross-reference linking the subject matter of the issue to the appropriate place in the *Casenote Law Outline,* which provides further information on the subject.

WINTER v. G.P. PUTNAM'S SONS
938 F.2d 1033 (1991).

NATURE OF CASE: Appeal from summary judgment in a products liability action.

FACT SUMMARY: Winter (P) relied on a book on mushrooms published by Putnam (D) and became critically ill after eating a poisonous mushroom.

CONCISE RULE OF LAW: Strict products liability is not applicable to the expressions contained within a book.

FACTS: Winter (P) purchased The Encyclopedia of Mushrooms, a book published by Putnam (D), to help in collecting and eating wild mushrooms. In 1988, Winter (P), relying on descriptions in the book, ate some wild mushrooms which turned out to be poisonous. Winter (P) became so ill he required a liver transplant. He brought a strict products liability action against Putnam (D), alleging that the book contained erroneous and misleading information that caused his injury. Putnam (D) responded that the information in the book was not a product for purposes of strict products liability, and the trial court granted its motion for summary judgment. The trial court also rejected Winter's (P) actions for negligence and misrepresentation. Winter (P) appealed.

ISSUE: Is strict products liability applicable to the expressions contained within a book?

HOLDING AND DECISION: (Sneed, J.) No. Strict products liability is not applicable to the expressions contained within a book. Products liability is geared toward tangible objects. The expression of ideas is governed by copyright, libel, and misrepresentation laws. The Restatement (Second) of Torts lists examples of the items that are covered by §402A strict liability. All are tangible items, such as tires or automobiles. There is no indication that the doctrine should be expanded beyond this area. Furthermore, there is a strong public interest in the unfettered exchange of ideas. The threat of liability without fault could seriously inhibit persons who wish to share thoughts and ideas with others. Although some courts have held that aeronautical charts are products for purposes of strict liability, these charts are highly technical tools which resemble compasses. The Encyclopedia of Mushrooms, published by Putnam (D), is a book of pure thought and expression and therefore does not constitute a product for purposes of strict liability. Additionally, publishers do not owe a duty to investigate the contents of books that they distribute. Therefore, a negligence action may not be maintained by Winter (P) against Putnam (D). Affirmed.

EDITOR'S ANALYSIS: This decision is in accord with the rulings in most jurisdictions. See Alm v. Nostrand Reinhold Co., Inc., 480 N.E. 2d 1263 (Ill. 1985). The court also stated that since the publisher is not a guarantor of the accuracy of an author's statements, an action for negligent misrepresentation could not be maintained. The elements of negligent misrepresentation are stated in § 311 of the Restatement (Second) of Torts.

[For more information on misrepresentation, see Casenote Law Outline on Torts, Chapter 12, § III, Negligent Misrepresentation.]

NOTE TO STUDENT

OUR GOAL. It is the goal of Casenotes Publishing Company, Inc. to create and distribute the finest, clearest and most accurate legal briefs available. To this end, we are constantly seeking new ideas, comments and constructive criticism. As a user of *Casenote Legal Briefs,* your suggestions will be highly valued. With all correspondence, please include your complete name, address, and telephone number, including area code and zip code.

THE TOTAL STUDY SYSTEM. Casenote Legal Briefs are just one part of the Casenotes TOTAL STUDY SYSTEM. Most briefs are (wherever possible) cross-referenced to the appropriate *Casenote Law Outline,* which will elaborate on the issue at hand. By purchasing a Law Outline together with your Legal Brief, you will have both parts of the Casenotes TOTAL STUDY SYSTEM. (See the advertising in the front of this book for a list of Law Outlines currently available.)

A NOTE ABOUT LANGUAGE. Please note that the language used in *Casenote Legal Briefs* in reference to minority groups and women reflects terminology used within the historical context of the time in which the respective courts wrote the opinions. We at Casenotes Publishing Co., Inc. are well aware of and very sensitive to the desires of all people to be treated with dignity and to be referred to as they prefer. Because such preferences change from time to time, and because the language of the courts reflects the time period in which opinions were written, our case briefs will not necessarily reflect contemporary references. We appreciate your understanding and invite your comments.

A NOTE REGARDING NEW EDITIONS. As of our press date, this Casenote Legal Brief is current and includes briefs of all cases in the current version of the casebook, divided into chapters that correspond to that edition of the casebook. However, occasionally a new edition of the casebook comes out in the interim, and sometimes the casebook author will make changes in the sequence of the cases in the chapters, add or delete cases, or change the chapter titles. Should you be using this Legal Brief in conjuction with a casebook that was issued later than this book, you can receive all of the newer cases, which are available free from us, by sending in the "Supplement Request Form" in this section of the book (please follow all instructions on that form). The Supplement(s) will contain all the missing cases, and will bring your Casenote Legal Brief up to date.

EDITOR'S NOTE. Casenote Legal Briefs are intended to supplement the student's casebook, not replace it. There is no substitute for the student's own mastery of this important learning and study technique. If used properly, *Casenote Legal Briefs* are an effective law study aid that will serve to reinforce the student's understanding of the cases.

SUPPLEMENT REQUEST FORM

At the time this book was printed, a brief was included for every major case in the casebook and for everyy existing supplement to the casebook. However, if a new supplement to the casebook (or a new edition of the casebook) has been published since this publication was printed and if that casebook supplement (or new edition of the casebook) was available for sale at the time you purchased this Casenote Legal Briefs book, we will be pleased to provide you the new cases contained therein AT NO CHARGE when you send us a stamped, self-addressed envelope.

TO OBTAIN YOUR FREE SUPPLEMENT MATERIAL, **YOU MUST FOLLOW THE INSTRUCTIONS BELOW PRECISELY** OR YOUR REQUEST WILL NOT BE ACKNOWLEDGED!

1. Please check if there is in fact an existing supplement and, if so, that the cases are not already included in your Casenote Legal Briefs. Check the main table of cases as well as the supplement table of cases, if any.

2. **REMOVE THIS ENTIRE PAGE FROM THE BOOK.** You MUST send this ORIGINAL page to receive your supplement. This page acts as your proof of purchase and contains the reference number necessary to fill your supplement request properly. No photocopy of this page or written request will be honored or answered. Any request from which the reference number has been removed, altered or obliterated will not be honored.

3. Prepare a STAMPED self-addressed envelope for return mailing. Be sure to use a FULL SIZE (9 X 12) ENVELOPE (MANILA TYPE) so that the supplement will fit and AFFIX ENOUGH POSTAGE TO COVER 3 OZ. **ANY SUPPLEMENT REQUEST NOT ACCOMPANIED BY A STAMPED SELF-ADDRESSED ENVELOPE WILL ABSOLUTELY NOT BE FILLED OR ACKNOWLEDGED.**

4. MULTIPLE SUPPLEMENT REQUESTS: If you are ordering more than one supplement, we suggest that you enclose a stamped, self-addressed envelope for each supplement requested. If you enclose only one envelope for a multiple request, your order may not be filled immediately should any supplement which you requested still be in production. In other words, your order will be held by us until it can be filled completely.

5. Casenotes prints two kinds of supplements. A "New Edition" supplement is issued when a new edition of your casebook is published. A "New Edition" supplement gives you all major cases found in the new edition of the casebook which did not appear in the previous edition. A regular "supplement" is issued when a paperback supplement to your casebook is published. If the box at the lower right is stamped, then the "New Edition" supplement was provided to your bookstore and is *not* available from Casenotes; however, Casenotes will still send you any regular "supplements" which have been printed either before or after the new edition of your casebook appeared and which, according to the reference number at the top of this page, have not been included in this book. If the box is not stamped, Casenotes will send you any supplements, "New Edition" and/or regular, needed to completely update your Casenote Legal Briefs.

ωΛ *NOTE:* **REQUESTS FOR SUPPLEMENTS WILL NOT BE FILLED UNLESS THESE INSTRUCTIONS ARE COMPLIED WITH!**

6. Fill in the following information:

Full title of CASEBOOK ___ **CIVIL PROCEDURE**

CASEBOOK author's name ___ **Marcus, Redish, and Sherman**

Copyright year of new edition or new paperback supplement

Name and location of bookstore where this Casenote Legal Brief was purchased _____

Name and location of law school you attend _____

Any comments regarding Casenote Legal Briefs _____

NOTE: IF THIS BOX IS STAMPED, NO NEW EDITION SUPPLEMENT CAN BE OBTAINED BY MAIL.

PUBLISHED BY CASENOTES PUBLISHING CO., INC. 1640 5th ST, SUITE 208 SANTA MONICA, CA 90401

PLEASE PRINT

NAME _____ PHONE _____ DATE_____

ADDRESS/CITY/STATE/ZIP _____

Announcing the First *Totally Integrated* Law Study System

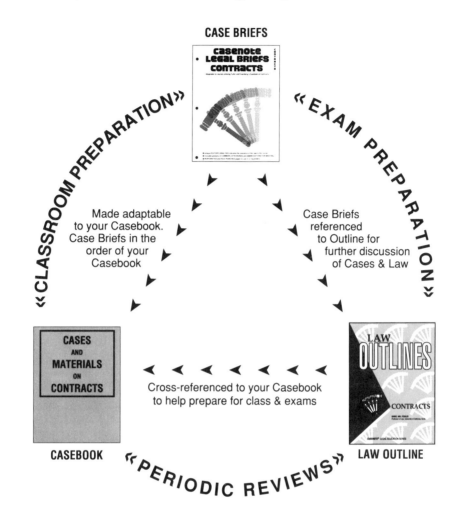

CASE BRIEFS

«CLASSROOM PREPARATION»

«EXAM PREPARATION»

Made adaptable to your Casebook. Case Briefs in the order of your Casebook

Case Briefs referenced to Outline for further discussion of Cases & Law

Cross-referenced to your Casebook to help prepare for class & exams

CASEBOOK

LAW OUTLINE

«PERIODIC REVIEWS»

Casenotes Integrated Study System Makes Studying Easier and More Effective Than Ever!

Casenotes has just made studying easier and more effective than ever before, because we've done the work for you! Through our exclusive integrated study system, most briefs found in this volume of Casenote Legal Briefs are cross-referenced to the corresponding area of law in the Casenote Law Outline series. The cross-reference immediately follows the Editor's Analysis at the end of the brief, and it will direct you to the corresponding chapter and section number in the Casenote Law Outline for further information on the case or the area of law.

This cross-referencing feature will enable you to make the most effective use of your time. While each Casenote Law

Outline focuses on a particular subject area of the law, each legal briefs volume is adapted to a specific casebook. Now, with cross-referencing of Casenote Legal Briefs to Casenote Law Outlines, you can have the best of both worlds – briefs for all major cases in your casebooks and easy-to-find, easy-to-read explanations of the law in our Law Outline series. Casenote Law Outlines are authored exclusively by law professors who are nationally recognized authorities in their field. So using Casenote Law Outlines is like studying with the top law professors.

Try Casenotes new totally integrated study system and see just how easy and effective studying can be.

Casenotes Integrated Study System Does The Work For You!

LAW OUTLINES from CASENOTE™

the Ultimate Outline

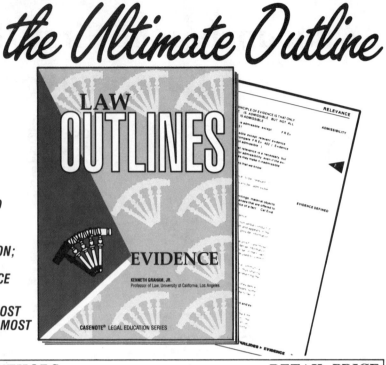

▶ WRITTEN BY NATIONALLY RECOGNIZED AUTHORITIES IN THEIR FIELD.

▶ FEATURING A FLEXIBLE, SUBJECT-ORIENTED APPROACH.

▶ CONTAINS: TABLE OF CONTENTS; CAPSULE OUTLINE; FULL OUTLINE; EXAM PREPARATION; GLOSSARY; TABLE OF CASES; TABLE OF AUTHORITIES; CASEBOOK CROSS REFERENCE CHART; INDEX.

▶ THE TOTAL LAW SUMMARY UTILIZING THE MOST COMPREHENSIVE STUDY APPROACH IN THE MOST EFFECTIVE, EASY-TO-READ FORMAT.

REF #	SUBJECT / AUTHORS	RETAIL PRICE
#5260 —	ADMINISTRATIVE LAW by **Charles H. Koch, Jr.,** Dudley W. Woodbridge Professor of Law, College of William and Mary. **Sidney A. Shapiro,** John M. Rounds Professor of Law, University of Kansas. (1996 w/'98 supp.)	(effective 7/1/98) **$20.95**
#5040 —	CIVIL PROCEDURE by **John B. Oakley,** Professor of Law, University of California, Davis. **Rex R. Perschbacher,** Professor of Law & Associate Dean, Academic Affairs, University of California, Davis. (1996)	**$21.95**
	COMMERCIAL LAW (*see* 5700 SALES ● 5710 SECURED TRANS. ● 5720 NEG. INSTRUMENTS & PMT. SYST.)	
#5070 —	CONFLICT OF LAWS by **Luther L. McDougal, III,** W.R. Irby Professor of Law, Tulane University. **Robert L. Felix,** James P. Mozingo, III, Prof. of Law, Univ. of S. Carolina. (1996)	**$20.95**
#5080 —	CONSTITUTIONAL LAW by **Gary Goodpaster,** Prof. of Law, Univ. of California, Davis. (1997 w/'98 supp.)	**$23.95**
#5010 —	CONTRACTS by **Daniel Wm. Fessler,** Professor of Law, University of California, Davis. (1996)	**$20.95**
#5050 —	CORPORATIONS by **Lewis D. Solomon,** Arthur Selwin Miller Research Prof. of Law, George Washington Univ. AND ALTERNATIVE **Daniel Wm. Fessler,** Prof. of Law, University of California, Davis. BUSINESS VEHICLES **Arthur E. Wilmarth, Jr.,** Assoc. Prof. of Law, George Washington University. (1997)	**$23.95**
#5020 —	CRIMINAL LAW by **Joshua Dressler,** Professor of Law, McGeorge School of Law. (1996)	**$20.95**
#5200 —	CRIMINAL PROCEDURE by **Joshua Dressler,** Prof. of Law, McGeorge School of Law. (1997)	**$19.95**
#5800 —	ESTATE & GIFT TAX by **Joseph M. Dodge,** W.H. Francis Prof. of Law, University of INCLUDING THE FEDERAL Texas at Austin (w/ supp. due Fall 1998) . . . . GENERATION-SKIPPING TAX	**$20.95**
#5060 —	EVIDENCE by **Kenneth Graham, Jr.,** Professor of Law, University of California, Los Angeles. (1996)	**$22.95**
#5400 —	FEDERAL COURTS by **Howard P. Fink,** Isadore and Ida Topper Prof. of Law, Ohio State University. **Linda S. Mullenix,** Bernard J. Ward Centennial Prof. of Law, Univ. of Texas. (1997)	**$21.95**
#5210 —	FEDERAL INCOME TAXATION by **Joseph M. Dodge,** W.H. Francis Professor of Law, University of Texas at Austin (1998).	**$21.95**
#5300 —	LEGAL RESEARCH by **Nancy L. Schultz,** Associate Professor of Law, Chapman University. **Louis J. Sirico, Jr.,** Professor of Law, Villanova University. (1996)	**$20.95**
#5720 —	NEGOTIABLE INST. & PMT. SYST. by **Donald B. King,** Professor of Law, Saint Louis University. **Peter Winship,** James Cleo Thompson, Sr. Trustee Prof., SMU. (1995)	**$21.95**
#5030 —	PROPERTY by **Sheldon F. Kurtz,** Percy Bordwell Professor of Law, University of Iowa. **Patricia Cain,** Professor of Law, University of Iowa (1997)	**$21.95**
#5700 —	SALES by **Robert E. Scott,** Dean and Lewis F. Powell, Jr. Professor of Law, University of Virginia. **Donald B. King,** Professor of Law, Saint Louis University. (1992)	**$20.95**
#5710 —	SECURED TRANSACTIONS by **Donald B. King,** Professor of Law, Saint Louis University. (1995 w/'96 supp.) . . .	**$19.95**
#5000 —	TORTS by **George C. Christie,** James B. Duke Professor of Law, Duke University. **Jerry J. Phillips,** W.P. Toms Professor of Law & Chair, Committee on Admissions, University of Tennessee. (1996 w/'98 supp.)	**$21.95**
#5220 —	WILLS, TRUSTS & ESTATES by **William M. McGovern,** Professor of Law, University of California, Los Angeles. (1996)	**$21.95**

rev. 6/1/98

CASENOTE™ LEGAL BRIEFS

PRICE LIST — EFFECTIVE JULY 1, 1998 • PRICES SUBJECT TO CHANGE WITHOUT NOTICE

Ref. No.	Course	Adaptable to Courses Utilizing	Retail Price
1263	ADMINISTRATIVE LAW	BREYER, STEWART & SUNSTEIN	20.00
1266	ADMINISTRATIVE LAW	CASS, DIVER & BEERMAN	18.00
1260	ADMINISTRATIVE LAW	GELLHORN, B., S., R., S. & F.	18.00
1264	ADMINISTRATIVE LAW	MASHAW, MERRILL & SHANE	19.50
1267	ADMINISTRATIVE LAW	REESE	18.00
1262	ADMINISTRATIVE LAW	SCHWARTZ	19.00
1350	AGENCY & PARTNERSHIP (ENT.ORG)	CONARD, KNAUSS & SIEGEL	22.00
1351	AGENCY & PARTNERSHIP	HYNES	21.00
1690	AMERICAN INDIAN LAW	GETCHES, W. & W.	TBA
1281	ANTITRUST (TRADE REGULATION)	HANDLER, P., G. & W.	18.50
1280	ANTITRUST	AREEDA & KAPLOW	17.50
1283	ANTITRUST	SULLIVAN & HOVENKAMP	19.00
1611	BANKING LAW	MACEY & MILLER	18.00
1303	BANKRUPTCY (DEBTOR-CREDITOR)	EISENBERG	20.00
1305	BANKRUPTCY	JORDAN & WARREN	18.00
1058	BUSINESS ASSOCIATIONS (CORPORATIONS)	KLEIN & RAMSEYER	20.00
1040	CIVIL PROCEDURE	COUND, F., M. & S	21.00
1043	CIVIL PROCEDURE	FIELD, KAPLAN & CLERMONT	21.00
1049	CIVIL PROCEDURE	FREER & PERDUE	17.00
1041	CIVIL PROCEDURE	HAZARD, TAIT & FLETCHER	20.00
1047	CIVIL PROCEDURE	MARCUS, REDISH & SHERMAN	20.00
1044	CIVIL PROCEDURE	ROSENBERG, S. & D.	21.00
1046	CIVIL PROCEDURE	YEAZELL	18.00
1311	COMM'L LAW	FARNSWORTH, H., R., H. & M.	20.00
1312	COMM'L LAW	JORDAN & WARREN	20.00
1310	COMM'L LAW (SALES/SEC.TR./PAY.LAW [Sys.])	SPEIDEL, SUMMERS & WHITE	23.00
1313	COMM'L LAW (SALES/SEC.TR./PAY.LAW)	WHALEY	21.00
1320	COMMUNITY PROPERTY	BIRD	18.50
1630	COMPARATIVE LAW	SCHLESINGER, B., D., H.& W.	17.00
1048	COMPLEX LITIGATION	MARCUS & SHERMAN	18.00
1072	CONFLICTS	BRILMAYER	18.00
1071	CONFLICTS	CRAMTON, C. K., & K.	18.00
1070	CONFLICTS	ROSENBERG, HAY & W.	21.00
1086	CONSTITUTIONAL LAW	BREST & LEVINSON	19.00
1082	CONSTITUTIONAL LAW	COHEN & VARAT	22.00
1088	CONSTITUTIONAL LAW	FARBER, ESKRIDGE & FRICKEY	19.00
1080	CONSTITUTIONAL LAW	GUNTHER & SULLIVAN	21.00
1081	CONSTITUTIONAL LAW	LOCKHART, K., C., S. & F.	19.00
1085	CONSTITUTIONAL LAW	ROTUNDA	21.00
1089	CONSTITUTIONAL LAW (FIRST AMENDMENT)	SHIFFRIN & CHOPER	16.00
1087	CONSTITUTIONAL LAW	STONE, S., S. & T.	20.00
1103	CONTRACTS	BARNETT	22.00
1102	CONTRACTS	BURTON	21.00
1017	CONTRACTS	CALAMARI, PERILLO & BENDER	24.00
1101	CONTRACTS	CRANDALL & WHALEY	21.00
1014	CONTRACTS	DAWSON, HARVEY & H.	20.00
1010	CONTRACTS	FARNSWORTH & YOUNG	19.00
1011	CONTRACTS	FULLER & EISENBERG	22.00
1100	CONTRACTS	HAMILTON, RAU & WEINTRAUB	20.00
1013	CONTRACTS	KESSLER, GILMORE & KRONMAN	24.00
1016	CONTRACTS	KNAPP & CRYSTAL	21.50
1012	CONTRACTS	MURPHY & SPEIDEL	23.00
1018	CONTRACTS	MURRAY	23.00
1015	CONTRACTS	ROSETT	22.00
1019	CONTRACTS	VERNON	21.00
1502	COPYRIGHT	GOLDSTEIN	19.00
1501	COPYRIGHT	NIMMER, M., M. & N.	20.50
1218	CORPORATE TAXATION	LIND, S. L. & R	15.00
1050	CORPORATIONS	CARY & EISENBERG	20.00
1054	CORPORATIONS	CHOPER, COFFEE, & GILSON	22.50
1350	CORPORATIONS (ENTERPRISE ORG.)	CONARD, KNAUSS & SIEGEL	22.00
1053	CORPORATIONS	HAMILTON	20.00
1058	CORPORATIONS (BUSINESS ASSOCIATIONS	KLEIN & RAMSEYER	20.00
1057	CORPORATIONS	O'KELLEY & THOMPSON	19.00
1056	CORPORATIONS	SOLOMON, S., B. & W.	20.00
1052	CORPORATIONS	VAGTS	19.00
1300	CREDITOR'S RIGHTS (DEBTOR-CREDITOR)	RIESENFELD	22.00
1550	CRIMINAL JUSTICE	WEINREB	19.00
1029	CRIMINAL LAW	BONNIE, C., J. & L.	18.00
1020	CRIMINAL LAW	BOYCE & PERKINS	23.00
1028	CRIMINAL LAW	DRESSLER	22.00
1027	CRIMINAL LAW	JOHNSON	21.00
1021	CRIMINAL LAW	KADISH & SCHULHOFER	20.00
1026	CRIMINAL LAW	KAPLAN, WEISBERG & BINDER	19.00
1205	CRIMINAL PROCEDURE	ALLEN, KUHNS & STUNTZ	18.00
1202	CRIMINAL PROCEDURE	HADDAD, Z., S. & B.	21.00
1200	CRIMINAL PROCEDURE	KAMISAR, LAFAVE & ISRAEL	20.00
1204	CRIMINAL PROCEDURE	SALTZBURG & CAPRA	18.00
1203	CRIMINAL PROCEDURE (PROCESS)	WEINREB	19.50
1303	DEBTOR-CREDITOR	EISENBERG	20.00
1300	DEBTOR-CREDITOR (CRED. RTS.)	RIESENFELD	22.00
1304	DEBTOR-CREDITOR	WARREN & WESTBROOK	20.00
1224	DECEDENTS ESTATES (TRUSTS)	RITCHIE, A, & E.(DOBRIS & STERK)	22.00
1222	DECEDENTS ESTATES	SCOLES & HALBACH	22.50
1231	DECEDENTS ESTATES (TRUSTS)	WAGGONER, A. & F.	21.00
	DOMESTIC RELATIONS (see FAMILY LAW)		
3000	EDUCATION LAW (COURSE OUTLINE)	AQUILA & PETZKE	26.50
1670	EMPLOYMENT DISCRIMINATION	FRIEDMAN & STRICKLER	18.00
1671	EMPLOYMENT DISCRIMINATION	ZIMMER, SULLIVAN, R. & C.	19.00
1660	EMPLOYMENT LAW	ROTHSTEIN, KNAPP & LIEBMAN	20.50
1350	ENTERPRISE ORGANIZATION	CONARD, KNAUSS & SIEGEL	22.00
1342	ENVIRONMENTAL LAW	ANDERSON, MANDELKER & T.	17.00
1341	ENVIRONMENTAL LAW	FINDLEY & FARBER	19.00
1345	ENVIRONMENTAL LAW	MENELL & STEWART	18.00
1344	ENVIRONMENTAL LAW	PERCIVAL, MILLER, S. & L.	19.00
1343	ENVIRONMENTAL LAW	PLATER, A., G. & G.	18.00
	EQUITY (see REMEDIES)		

Ref. No.	Course	Adaptable to Courses Utilizing	Retail Price
1217	ESTATE & GIFT TAXATION	BITTKER, CLARK & McCOUCH	16.00
	ETHICS (see PROFESSIONAL RESPONSIBILITY)		
1065	EVIDENCE	GREEN & NESSON	21.00
1066	EVIDENCE	MUELLER & KIRKPATRICK	18.00
1064	EVIDENCE	STRONG, BROUN & M.	23.50
1062	EVIDENCE	SUTTON & WELLBORN	23.00
1061	EVIDENCE	WALTZ & PARK	21.00
1060	EVIDENCE	WEINSTEIN, M., A. & B.	23.50
1244	FAMILY LAW (DOMESTIC RELATIONS)	AREEN	23.00
1242	FAMILY LAW (DOMESTIC RELATIONS)	CLARK & GLOWINSKY	20.00
1245	FAMILY LAW (DOMESTIC RELATIONS)	ELLMAN, KURTZ & BARTLETT	21.00
1246	FAMILY LAW (DOMESTIC RELATIONS)	HARRIS, T. & W.	20.00
1243	FAMILY LAW (DOMESTIC RELATIONS)	KRAUSE, O., E. & G.	25.00
1240	FAMILY LAW (DOMESTIC RELATIONS)	WADLINGTON	21.00
1231	FAMILY PROPERTY LAW (WILLS/TRUSTS)	WAGGONER, A. & F.	21.00
1360	FEDERAL COURTS	FALLON, M. & S. (HART & W.)	20.00
1360	FEDERAL COURTS	HART & WECHSLER (FALLON)	20.00
1363	FEDERAL COURTS	LOW & JEFFRIES	17.00
1361	FEDERAL COURTS	McCORMICK, C. & W.	21.00
1364	FEDERAL COURTS	REDISH & SHERRY	18.00
1089	FIRST AMENDMENT (CONSTITUTIONAL LAW)	SHIFFRIN & CHOPER	16.00
1510	GRATUITOUS TRANSFERS	CLARK, LUSKY & MURPHY	19.00
1650	HEALTH LAW	FURROW, J., J. & S.	18.50
1640	IMMIGRATION LAW	ALEINIKOFF, MARTIN & M.	17.00
1641	IMMIGRATION LAW	LEGOMSKY	20.00
1690	INDIAN LAW (AMERICAN)	GETCHES, W. & W.	TBA
1371	INSURANCE LAW	KEETON	22.00
1372	INSURANCE LAW	YORK, WHELAN & MARTINEZ	20.00
1370	INSURANCE LAW	YOUNG & HOLMES	18.00
1394	INTERNATIONAL BUSINESS TRANSACTIONS	FOLSOM, GORDON & SPANOGLE	16.00
1393	INTERNATIONAL LAW	CARTER & TRIMBLE	17.00
1392	INTERNATIONAL LAW	HENKIN, P., S. & S.	18.00
1390	INTERNATIONAL LAW	OLIVER, F., B., S. & W.	23.00
1331	LABOR LAW	COX, BOK, GORMAN & FINKIN	20.00
1332	LABOR LAW	HARPER & ESTREICHER	21.00
1333	LABOR LAW	LESLIE	19.50
1330	LABOR LAW	MERRIFIELD, S. & C.	20.00
1471	LAND FINANCE (REAL ESTATE TRANS)	BERGER & JOHNSTONE	19.00
1620	LAND FINANCE (REAL ESTATE TRANS)	NELSON & WHITMAN	20.00
1452	LAND USE	CALLIES, FREILICH & ROBERTS	18.00
1421	LEGISLATION	ESKRIDGE & FRICKEY	16.00
1480	MASS MEDIA	FRANKLIN & ANDERSON	16.00
1312	NEGOTIABLE INSTRUMENTS (COMM. LAW)	JORDAN & WARREN	20.00
1541	OIL & GAS	KUNTZ, L., A. & S.	19.00
1540	OIL & GAS	MAXWELL, WILLIAMS, M. & K.	19.00
1560	PATENT LAW	FRANCIS & COLLINS	24.00
1310	PAYMENT LAW [SYST.][COMM. LAW]	SPEIDEL, SUMMERS & WHITE	23.00
1313	PAYMENT LAW (COMM.LAW / NEG. INST.)	WHALEY	23.00
1431	PRODUCTS LIABILITY	OWEN, MONTGOMERY & K.	23.00
1091	PROF. RESPONSIBILITY (ETHICS)	GILLERS	14.00
1093	PROF. RESPONSIBILITY (ETHICS)	HAZARD, KONIAK, & CRAMTON	19.00
1092	PROF. RESPONSIBILITY (ETHICS)	MORGAN & ROTUNDA	14.00
1030	PROPERTY	CASNER & LEACH	22.00
1031	PROPERTY	CRIBBET, J., F. & S.	22.50
1037	PROPERTY	DONAHUE, KAUPER & MARTIN	19.00
1035	PROPERTY	DUKEMINIER & KRIER	19.00
1034	PROPERTY	HAAR & LIEBMAN	21.50
1036	PROPERTY	KURTZ & HOVENKAMP	20.00
1033	PROPERTY	NELSON, STOEBUCK, & W.	21.50
1032	PROPERTY	RABIN & KWALL	21.00
1038	PROPERTY	SINGER	19.50
1621	REAL ESTATE TRANSACTIONS	GOLDSTEIN & KORNGOLD	19.00
1471	REAL ESTATE TRANS. & FIN. (LAND FINANCE)	BERGER & JOHNSTONE	19.00
1620	REAL ESTATE TRANSFER & FINANCE	NELSON & WHITMAN	20.00
1254	REMEDIES (EQUITY)	LAYCOCK	21.00
1253	REMEDIES (EQUITY)	LEAVELL, L., N. & K/F.	22.00
1252	REMEDIES (EQUITY)	RE & RE	24.00
1255	REMEDIES (EQUITY)	SHOBEN & TABB	23.50
1250	REMEDIES (EQUITY)	YORK, BAUMAN & RENDLEMAN	26.00
1310	SALES (COMM. LAW)	SPEIDEL, SUMMERS & WHITE	23.00
1313	SALES (COMM. LAW)	WHALEY	21.00
1312	SECURED TRANS. (COMM. LAW)	JORDAN & WARREN	20.00
1310	SECURED TRANS.	SPEIDEL, SUMMERS & WHITE	23.00
1313	SECURED TRANS. (COMM. LAW)	WHALEY	21.00
1272	SECURITIES REGULATION	COX, HILLMAN, LANGEVOORT	19.00
1270	SECURITIES REGULATION	JENNINGS, M., C. & S.	19.00
1680	SPORTS LAW	WEILER & ROBERTS	18.50
1217	TAXATION (ESTATE & GIFT)	BITTKER, CLARK & McCOUCH	16.00
1219	TAXATION (INDIV. INC.)	BURKE & FRIEL	20.00
1212	TAXATION (FED. INC.)	FREELAND, LIND & STEPHENS	19.00
1211	TAXATION (FED. INC.)	GRAETZ & SCHENK	18.00
1210	TAXATION (FED. INC.)	KLEIN & BANKMAN	19.00
1218	TAXATION (CORPORATE)	LIND, S., L. & R.	15.00
1006	TORTS	DOBBS	20.00
1003	TORTS	EPSTEIN	21.50
1004	TORTS	FRANKLIN & RABIN	18.50
1001	TORTS	HENDERSON, P. & S.	21.50
1000	TORTS	PROSSER, W., S., K. & P.	25.00
1005	TORTS	SHULMAN, JAMES & GRAY	23.00
1281	TRADE REGULATION (ANTITRUST)	HANDLER, P., G. & W.	18.50
1230	TRUSTS	BOGERT, O., H. & H.	21.50
1231	TRUSTS/WILLS (FAMILY PROPERTY LAW)	WAGGONER, A. & F.	21.00
1410	U.C.C.	EPSTEIN, MARTIN, H. & N.	16.00
1223	WILLS, TRUSTS & ESTATES	DUKEMINIER & JOHANSON	20.00
1220	WILLS	MECHEM & ATKINSON	21.00
1231	WILLS/TRUSTS (FAMILY PROPERTY LAW)	WAGGONER, A. & F.	21.00
			(SERIES XLI)

CASENOTES PUBLISHING CO. INC. ● 1640 FIFTH STREET, SUITE 208 ● SANTA MONICA, CA 90401 ● (310) 395-6500

E-Mail Address- casenote@westworld.com
Website-http://www.casenotes.com

NOTES

GLOSSARY

COMMON LATIN WORDS AND PHRASES ENCOUNTERED IN LAW

A FORTIORI: Because one fact exists or has been proven, therefore a second fact that is related to the first fact must also exist.

A PRIORI: From the cause to the effect. A term of logic used to denote that when one generally accepted truth is shown to be a cause, another particular effect must necessarily follow.

AB INITIO: From the beginning; a condition which has existed throughout, as in a marriage which was void ab initio.

ACTUS REUS: The wrongful act; in criminal law, such action sufficient to trigger criminal liability.

AD VALOREM: According to value; an ad valorem tax is imposed upon an item located within the taxing jurisdiction calculated by the value of such item.

AMICUS CURIAE: Friend of the court. Its most common usage takes the form of an amicus curiae brief, filed by a person who is not a party to an action but is nonetheless allowed to offer an argument supporting his legal interests.

ARGUENDO: In arguing. A statement, possibly hypothetical, made for the purpose of argument, is one made arguendo.

BILL QUIA TIMET: A bill to quiet title (establish ownership) to real property.

BONA FIDE: True, honest, or genuine. May refer to a person's legal position based on good faith or lacking notice of fraud (such as a bona fide purchaser for value) or to the authenticity of a particular document (such as a bona fide last will and testament).

CAUSA MORTIS: With approaching death in mind. A gift causa mortis is a gift given by a party who feels certain that death is imminent.

CAVEAT EMPTOR: Let the buyer beware. This maxim is reflected in the rule of law that a buyer purchases at his own risk because it is his responsibility to examine, judge, test, and otherwise inspect what he is buying.

CERTIORARI: A writ of review. Petitions for review of a case by the United States Supreme Court are most often done by means of a writ of certiorari.

CONTRA: On the other hand. Opposite. Contrary to.

CORAM NOBIS: Before us; writs of error directed to the court that originally rendered the judgment.

CORAM VOBIS: Before you; writs of error directed by an appellate court to a lower court to correct a factual error.

CORPUS DELICTI: The body of the crime; the requisite elements of a crime amounting to objective proof that a crime has been committed.

CUM TESTAMENTO ANNEXO, ADMINISTRATOR (ADMINISTRATOR C.T.A.): With will annexed; an administrator c.t.a. settles an estate pursuant to a will in which he is not appointed.

DE BONIS NON, ADMINISTRATOR (ADMINISTRATOR D.B.N.): Of goods not administered; an administrator d.b.n. settles a partially settled estate.

DE FACTO: In fact; in reality; actually. Existing in fact but not officially approved or engendered.

DE JURE: By right; lawful. Describes a condition that is legitimate "as a matter of law," in contrast to the term "de facto," which connotes something existing in fact but not legally sanctioned or authorized. For example, de facto segregation refers to segregation brought about by housing patterns, etc., whereas de jure segregation refers to segregation created by law.

DE MINIMUS: Of minimal importance; insignificant; a trifle; not worth bothering about.

DE NOVO: Anew; a second time; afresh. A trial de novo is a new trial held at the appellate level as if the case originated there and the trial at a lower level had not taken place.

DICTA: Generally used as an abbreviated form of obiter dicta, a term describing those portions of a judicial opinion incidental or not necessary to resolution of the specific question before the court. Such nonessential statements and remarks are not considered to be binding precedent.

DUCES TECUM: Refers to a particular type of writ or subpoena requesting a party or organization to produce certain documents in their possession.

EN BANC: Full bench. Where a court sits with all justices present rather than the usual quorum.

EX PARTE: For one side or one party only. An ex parte proceeding is one undertaken for the benefit of only one party, without notice to, or an appearance by, an adverse party.

EX POST FACTO: After the fact. An ex post facto law is a law that retroactively changes the consequences of a prior act.

EX REL.: Abbreviated form of the term ex relatione, meaning, upon relation or information. When the state brings an action in which it has no interest against an individual at the instigation of one who has a private interest in the matter.

FORUM NON CONVENIENS: Inconvenient forum. Although a court may have jurisdiction over the case, the action should be tried in a more conveniently located court, one to which parties and witnesses may more easily travel, for example.

GUARDIAN AD LITEM: A guardian of an infant as to litigation, appointed to represent the infant and pursue his/her rights.

HABEAS CORPUS: You have the body. The modern writ of habeas corpus is a writ directing that a person (body) being detained (such as a prisoner) be brought before the court so that the legality of his detention can be judicially ascertained.

IN CAMERA: In private, in chambers. When a hearing is held before a judge in his chambers or when all spectators are excluded from the courtroom.

IN FORMA PAUPERIS: In the manner of a pauper. A party who proceeds in forma pauperis because of his poverty is one who is allowed to bring suit without liability for costs.

INFRA: Below, under. A word referring the reader to a later part of a book. (The opposite of supra.)

IN LOCO PARENTIS: In the place of a parent.

IN PARI DELICTO: Equally wrong; a court of equity will not grant requested relief to an applicant who is in pari delicto, or as much at fault in the transactions giving rise to the controversy as is the opponent of the applicant.

IN PARI MATERIA: On like subject matter or upon the same matter. Statutes relating to the same person or things are said to be in pari materia. It is a general rule of statutory construction that such statutes should be construed together, i.e., looked at as if they together constituted one law.

IN PERSONAM: Against the person. Jurisdiction over the person of an individual.

IN RE: In the matter of. Used to designate a proceeding involving an estate or other property.

IN REM: A term that signifies an action against the res, or thing. An action in rem is basically one that is taken directly against property, as distinguished from an action in personam, i.e., against the person.

INTER ALIA: Among other things. Used to show that the whole of a statement, pleading, list, statute, etc., has not been set forth in its entirety.

INTER PARTES: Between the parties. May refer to contracts, conveyances or other transactions having legal significance.

INTER VIVOS: Between the living. An inter vivos gift is a gift made by a living grantor, as distinguished from bequests contained in a will, which pass upon the death of the testator.

IPSO FACTO: By the mere fact itself.

JUS: Law or the entire body of law.

LEX LOCI: The law of the place; the notion that the rights of parties to a legal proceeding are governed by the law of the place where those rights arose.

MALUM IN SE: Evil or wrong in and of itself; inherently wrong. This term describes an act that is wrong by its very nature, as opposed to one which would not be wrong but for the fact that there is a specific legal prohibition against it (malum prohibitum).

MALUM PROHIBITUM: Wrong because prohibited, but not inherently evil. Used to describe something that is wrong because it is expressly forbidden by law but that is not in and of itself evil, e.g., speeding.

MANDAMUS: We command. A writ directing an official to take a certain action.

MENS REA: A guilty mind; a criminal intent. A term used to signify the mental state that accompanies a crime or other prohibited act. Some crimes require only a general mens rea (general intent to do the prohibited act), but others, like assault with intent to murder, require the existence of a specific mens rea.

MODUS OPERANDI: Method of operating; generally refers to the manner or style of a criminal in committing crimes, admissible in appropriate cases as evidence of the identity of a defendant.

NEXUS: A connection to.

NISI PRIUS: A court of first impression. A nisi prius court is one where issues of fact are tried before a judge or jury.

N.O.V. (NON OBSTANTE VEREDICTO): Notwithstanding the verdict. A judgment n.o.v. is a judgment given in favor of one party despite the fact that a verdict was returned in favor of the other party, the justification being that the verdict either had no reasonable support in fact or was contrary to law.

NUNC PRO TUNC: Now for then. This phrase refers to actions that may be taken and will then have full retroactive effect.

PENDENTE LITE: Pending the suit; pending litigation underway.

PER CAPITA: By head; beneficiaries of an estate, if they take in equal shares, take per capita.

PER CURIAM: By the court; signifies an opinion ostensibly written "by the whole court" and with no identified author.

PER SE: By itself, in itself; inherently.

PER STIRPES: By representation. Used primarily in the law of wills to describe the method of distribution where a person, generally because of death, is unable to take that which is left to him by the will of another, and therefore his heirs divide such property between them rather than take under the will individually.

PRIMA FACIE: On its face, at first sight. A prima facie case is one that is sufficient on its face, meaning that the evidence supporting it is adequate to establish the case until contradicted or overcome by other evidence.

PRO TANTO: For so much; as far as it goes. Often used in eminent domain cases when a property owner receives partial payment for his land without prejudice to his right to bring suit for the full amount he claims his land to be worth.

QUANTUM MERUIT: As much as he deserves. Refers to recovery based on the doctrine of unjust enrichment in those cases in which a party has rendered valuable services or furnished materials that were accepted and enjoyed by another under circumstances that would reasonably notify the recipient that the rendering party expected to be paid. In essence, the law implies a contract to pay the reasonable value of the services or materials furnished.

QUASI: Almost like; as if; nearly. This term is essentially used to signify that one subject or thing is almost analogous to another but that material differences between them do exist. For example, a quasi-criminal proceeding is one that is not strictly criminal but shares enough of the same characteristics to require some of the same safeguards (e.g., procedural due process must be followed in a parol hearing).

QUID PRO QUO: Something for something. In contract law, the consideration, something of value, passed between the parties to render the contract binding.

RES GESTAE: Things done; in evidence law, this principle justifies the admission of a statement that would otherwise be hearsay when it is made so closely to the event in question as to be said to be a part of it, or with such spontaneity as not to have the possibility of falsehood.

RES IPSA LOQUITUR: The thing speaks for itself. This doctrine gives rise to a rebuttable presumption of negligence when the instrumentality causing the injury was within the exclusive control of the defendant, and the injury was one that does not normally occur unless a person has been negligent.

RES JUDICATA: A matter adjudged. Doctrine which provides that once a court of competent jurisdiction has rendered a final judgment or decree on the merits, that judgment or decree is conclusive upon the parties to the case and prevents them from engaging in any other litigation on the points and issues determined therein.

RESPONDEAT SUPERIOR: Let the master reply. This doctrine holds the master liable for the wrongful acts of his servant (or the principal for his agent) in those cases in which the servant (or agent) was acting within the scope of his authority at the time of the injury.

STARE DECISIS: To stand by or adhere to that which has been decided. The common law doctrine of stare decisis attempts to give security and certainty to the law by following the policy that once a principle of law as applicable to a certain set of facts has been set forth in a decision, it forms a precedent which will subsequently be followed, even though a different decision might be made were it the first time the question had arisen. Of course, stare decisis is not an inviolable principle and is departed from in instances where there is good cause (e.g., considerations of public policy led the Supreme Court to disregard prior decisions sanctioning segregation).

SUPRA: Above. A word referring a reader to an earlier part of a book.

ULTRA VIRES: Beyond the power. This phrase is most commonly used to refer to actions taken by a corporation that are beyond the power or legal authority of the corporation.

ADDENDUM OF FRENCH DERIVATIVES

IN PAIS: Not pursuant to legal proceedings.

CHATTEL: Tangible personal property.

CY PRES: Doctrine permitting courts to apply trust funds to purposes not expressed in the trust but necessary to carry out the settlor's intent.

PER AUTRE VIE: For another's life; in property law, an estate may be granted that will terminate upon the death of someone other than the grantee.

PROFIT A PRENDRE: A license to remove minerals or other produce from land.

VOIR DIRE: Process of questioning jurors as to their predispositions about the case or parties to a proceeding in order to identify those jurors displaying bias or prejudice.

TABLE OF CASES

Continued on next page

TABLE OF CASES (Continued)

CHAPTER 1
CHOOSING A SYSTEM OF PROCEDURE

QUICK REFERENCE RULES OF LAW

1. **The Trial Process.** A judge may not assume the role of advocate in a trial over which he presides. (Band's Refuse Removal v. Borough of Fair Lawn)

   [For more information on the trial process, see Casenote Law Outline on Civil Procedure, Chapter 9, § I, Overview of the Trial Process.]

2. **Court-enforced Alternatives.** A court may not sanction a party for refusing to settle. (Kothe v. Smith)

   [For more information on court-enforced alternatives, see Casenote Law Outline on Civil Procedure, Chapter 8, § I, Alternatives to Trial.]

BAND'S REFUSE REMOVAL, INC.
v. BOROUGH OF FAIR LAWN

N.J. Super. Ct., App. Div., 62 N.J. Super. 522, 163 A.2d 465 (1960).

NATURE OF CASE: Appeal of order declaring municipal contract void.

FACT SUMMARY: In an action challenging a municipal contract, the judge used the trial as a vehicle for conducting an investigation into the underlying transaction.

CONCISE RULE OF LAW: A judge may not assume the role of advocate in a trial over which he presides.

FACTS: The Borough of Fair Lawn, N.J. (D) awarded a refuse collection contract to Capasso (D). Band's Refuse Removal, Inc. (P) challenged the legality of the contract. At trial, the judge largely took over the prosecution of the case, calling his own witnesses, creating his own issues, and doing his own cross- and direct examination, citing the public importance of the case as justification for this. At the close of the trial, he voided the contract and awarded over $300,000 in damages.

ISSUE: May a judge assume the role of advocate in a trial over which he presides?

HOLDING AND DECISION: (Goldman, J.) No. A judge may not assume the role of advocate in a trial over which he presides. The power of a judge to take an active role in the trial of a case must be exercised with the greatest restraint. While the judge may do this to move a trial along, he may not assume the role of advocate. Courts must both be impartial and give the appearance of impartiality. The conduct of the judge in this instance fell far short of that. He called witnesses not wanted by Band's Refuse (P) and essentially took on the plaintiff's case. This was inappropriate and seriously prejudiced the defense of the case. Reversed.

EDITOR'S ANALYSIS: The rules in this area are quite nebulous. There is no question that a court can actively participate in trials, especially at the federal level. The point at which a judge goes too far will essentially be a matter of degree.

[For more information on the trial process, see Casenote Law Outline on Civil Procedure, Chapter 9, § I, Overview of the Trial Process.]

NOTES:

KOTHE v. SMITH
771 F.2d 667 (2d Cir. 1985).

NATURE OF CASE: Appeal of sanctions levied in medical malpractice.

FACT SUMMARY: A court sanctioned Smith (D) for not settling in what the court believed to be a timely fashion.

CONCISE RULE OF LAW: A court may not sanction a party for refusing to settle.

FACTS: Kothe (P) sued Smith (D) for medical malpractice. At a pretrial conference, the judge expressed a view that the value of the case was $20,000 to $30,000 and urged settlement. Smith (D) offered no more than $5,000. After one day of trial, the case settled for $20,000. The trial judge then sanctioned Smith (D) $1,000 for refusing to settle in a timely fashion. Smith (D) appealed.

ISSUE: May a court sanction a party for refusing to settle?

HOLDING AND DECISION: (Van Graafeiland, J.) No. A court may not sanction a party for refusing to settle. Although the law favors the voluntary settlement of civil suits, judges may not effect settlements through coercion. While judges have the power to bring the parties together to discuss settlement, judges may not use such powers as a vehicle for clubbing a litigant into settlement. The ultimate decision as to whether a case shall be settled or tried rests in the parties, not the courts. Reversed.

EDITOR'S ANALYSIS: The extent to which judges involve themselves in settlements varies greatly, not only among the jurisdictions but among individual courts as well. Generally speaking, judges would rather see a case settled than be tried. The extent to which a judge will attempt to bring this about often depends on the judge himself.

NOTES:

[For more information on court-enforced alternatives, see Casenote Law Outline on Civil Procedure, Chapter 8, § I, Alternatives to Trial.]

CHAPTER 2
THE REWARDS AND COSTS OF LITIGATION
— OF REMEDIES AND RELATED MATTERS

QUICK REFERENCE RULES OF LAW

1. **Constitutional Standards for Proper Notice.** Procedural due process requires that parties whose rights are to be affected are entitled to be heard at a meaningful time, and in order that they may enjoy that right, they must be notified. (Fuentes v. Shevin)

    [For more information on constitutional standards for proper notice, see Casenote Law Outline on Civil Procedure, Chapter 2, § III, Jurisdiction and Valid Judgments.]

2. **Prejudgment Attachment.** An ex parte prejudgment attachment procedure is constitutional if it minimizes the risk of a wrongful taking. (Mitchell v. W.T. Grant)

    [For more information on prejudgment attachment, see Casenote Law Outline on Civil Procedure, Chapter 11, § III, Enforcement of Coercive Judgments.]

3. **Prejudgment Attachment.** Any substantial deprivation of property under state law requires that procedural protections be accorded the deprived party to avoid a due process challenge. (North Georgia Finishing v. Di-Chem, Inc.)

    [For more information on prejudgment attachment, see Casenote Law Outline on Civil Procedure, Chapter 11, § III, Enforcement of Coercive Judgments.]

4. **Prejudgment Attachment.** Prejudgment attachment of real estate without affording prior notice or the opportunity for a prior hearing to the individual whose property is subject to attachment does not satisfy due process requirements. (Connecticut v. Doehr)

    [For more information on prejudgment attachment, see Casenote Law Outline on Civil Procedure, Chapter 11, § III, Enforcement of Coercive Judgments.]

5. **Procedural Due Process.** In an action based on denial of procedural due process, only nominal damages may be awarded in the absence of actual injury. (Carey v. Piphus)

    [For more information on procedural due process, see Casenote Law Outline on Civil Procedure, Chapter 2, § III, Jurisdiction and Valid Judgments.]

6. **Injunctive Relief.** Injunctive relief is unavailable unless irreparable harm is otherwise likely to result and a plaintiff has no adequate remedy at law. (Smith v. Western Electric)

7. **Civil Rights Actions and Attorney Fees.** The plaintiff in a civil rights action may enter into a contingency-fee agreement with his attorney, even where such a fee exceeds subsequent court-awarded attorney fees. (Venegas v. Mitchell)

FUENTES v. SHEVIN
407 U.S. 67 (1972).

NATURE OF CASE: Constitutional challenge to Florida's prejudgment replevin procedure on due process grounds.

FACT SUMMARY: Fuentes (P) had her stove and stereo picked up by the sheriff prior to the adjudication of a suit filed by Firestone for nonpayment of the installment sales contract.

CONCISE RULE OF LAW: Procedural due process requires that parties whose rights are to be affected are entitled to be heard at a meaningful time, and in order that they may enjoy that right, they must be notified.

FACTS: Two prejudgment replevin statutes were attacked on due process grounds. Florida's statute permitted "[a]ny person whose goods or chattel are wrongfully detained by any other person . . . a writ of replevin to recover them." Florida did not require a convincing showing that the goods were wrongfully detained before seizure. A person merely filed a complaint and requested a writ of replevin alleging that the good had been wrongfully detained. A bond equal to twice the value of the property was filed, and the officer assigned picked up the chattels at the same time as he served the other party with the summons and complaint. After the property has been seized, the party eventually has a right to a hearing as the defendant in the suit which was filed, which plaintiff is required to pursue. While the Pennsylvania law was similar to Florida's in most respects, the party whose goods have been seized may never be granted a hearing. The writ of replevin was an independent action, and a lawsuit was not required. Therefore, to obtain a hearing, the party must himself initiate suit. Both statutes allowed the party whose property was seized to post a counterbond equal to twice the value of the property within three days of the replevin in order to retain possession of the property. If they did not, the property was transferred to the party who sought the writ. Fuentes (P), a Florida resident, had her stove and stereo picked up by the sheriff after she had fallen behind on her payments to Firestone Tire and Rubber Co. because of a dispute over repairs under her service policy. Firestone filed a complaint and requested that the property be seized. The complaint and summons were served simultaneously with the writ of replevin. Appellants attacking the Pennsylvania statute also fell behind in their payments and had their property repossessed. Finally, another Pennsylvania resident, Washington (P), had been divorced from a local deputy sheriff and was involved in a custody battle with him. He used the replevin process to have their child's clothing, furnishings, and toys picked up. Both statutes were upheld by their respective state courts. The U.S. Supreme Court combined the actions since they dealt with the same constitutional issues. The various plaintiffs in this action challenged the constitutionality of the prejudgment replevin statutes, claiming that they procedurally violated the Due Process Clause of the Fourteenth Amendment.

ISSUE: Are these state statutes constitutionally defective in that they fail to provide for a hearing at a meaningful time?

HOLDING AND DECISION: (Stewart, J.) Yes. Procedural due process requires that a party whose rights are being affected be given a meaningful opportunity to be heard, and in order that he may enjoy that right, he must be notified. The constitutional right to be heard is a basic aspect of the duty of government to follow a fair process of decision-making when it acts to deprive a person of his possessions. This right to be heard minimizes substantively unfair or mistaken deprivations of property, a danger that is especially great when the state seizes good simply upon the application of and for the benefit of a private party. Without due process of law, there would be no safeguards to protect a person's property from governmental interference. The right to speak out in one's own defense before an impartial arbitrator is a fundamental right which must be protected. If the right to notice and a hearing is to serve its full purpose, then it is clear that it must be granted at a time when the deprivation can still be prevented. While return of possession and damages can be granted at a later hearing, nothing can undo the fact that a person's property was arbitrarily taken from him without procedural due process of law. That the hearing required by due process is subject to waiver, and is not fixed in form, does not affect its root requirement that an individual be given an opportunity for a hearing before he is deprived of any significant property interest, except for extraordinary situations where some valid governmental interest is at stake that justifies postponing the hearing until after the event. The statute's requirements of requesting a writ, posting bond, and stating in a conclusory fashion that the property is wrongfully held merely tests the applicant's own belief in his rights. Since his private gain is at stake, the danger is all too great that his confidence in his cause will be misplaced. While possession may be reinstated by the posting of a counterbond, it is well settled that a temporary, nonfinal deprivation of property is nonetheless violative of the Due Process Clause of the Fourteenth Amendment. Moreover, the Due Process Clause encompasses both the possessory rights to property and situations where the title is in dispute. The Court distinguished Sniadach v. Family Financial Corporation, 395 U.S. 337, and Goldberg v. Kelly, 397 U.S. 254, which dealt with prejudgment garnishment statutes on the basis that the reasoning was similar and had nothing to do with the absolute necessities of life. These cases also required a hearing prior to a deprivation of rights, and, while emphasizing the special importance of wages and welfare benefits, they did not create a limited constitutional doctrine. Situations requiring a postponement of notice and hearing are truly unusual. They require an important governmental purpose, a special need for prompt action, and they must be initiated by and for the benefit of the government as opposed to a private individual (e.g., war effort, economic disaster, etc.). The contention that the parties waived their constitutional rights is also without merit since waiver requires clear and explicit language indicating exactly the rights to be waived. For the above-mentioned reasons, both Florida's and Pennsylvania's prejudgment replevin statutes violate the Due Process Clause of the Fourteenth Amendment.

DISSENT: (White, J.) The dissenters noted that state proceedings were in progress on this issue when the action was commenced, so

Continued on next page

7

jurisdiction should have been refused since there was an adequate remedy at law. There were conflicting interests here. There was the debtor who is in default and the creditor who desired either his money or the return of his property, the question being which party has a better right to possession prior to the hearing. The creditor wanted to prevent the further use and deterioration of his property, but the majority ignored his property rights totally. The creditor was in business to make money. His posting of the bond was a reasonable guarantee that frivolous claims would not be pursued. The current procedure protected the rights of both parties, and there appeared to be no compelling reason why possession should be retained by the debtor in default rather than by the creditor. Moreover, a counterbond was available to the debtor who honestly believed that the creditor was wrongfully attempting to repossess the property. Finally, it was very doubtful that the proposed hearing would in fact result in protections for the debtor substantially different from those the present law provided. An additional difficulty in the majority's reasoning was that all a creditor has to do in order to avoid the hearing requirement was to place an express waiver clause in the credit contract.

EDITOR'S ANALYSIS: In California, Michigan, and a large number of other states, the writ of replevin is now referred to as claim and delivery. In California, this action is contained in § 511.010, et seq. of the Code of Civil Procedure. A hearing is required for the granting of a writ of possession (comparable to the prior writ of replevin) under the guidelines set out in § 512.010. Exceptions are made for property feloniously taken, credit cards, and property acquired in the normal course of trade or business for commercial use. It must be alleged that the property is not necessary for the support of the defendant or his family and that there is a danger that the property will become unavailable to levy, its value will be substantially impaired, and it is necessary to protect the property (§ 512.020). At the hearing, the court will make its determination based on affidavits, pleadings, and other evidence on record. Upon showing a good cause, the court may admit additional evidence or continue the hearing until the new evidence can be obtained (§ 512.050). Finally, with regard to waiver of a hearing requirement, it appears that it is permissible if the parties are acting at arm's length and have equal bargaining power, D. H. Overmeyer Co. v. Frick Co., 405 U.S. 174 (1972); however, if the consumer has no option but to buy on credit, the parties are not equal in bargaining power and the clause is unconscionable, Kosches v. Nichols, 327 N.Y.S. 2d 968 (1971). This is but another example of consumer protection. The businessman can waive his constitutional rights, but the consumer cannot.

[For more information on constitutional standards for proper notice, see Casenote Law Outline on Civil Procedure, Chapter 2, § III, Jurisdiction and Valid Judgments.]

MITCHELL v. W.T GRANT CO.
416 U.S. 600 (1974).

NATURE OF CASE: Review of property attachment order.

FACT SUMMARY: Mitchell (D) attacked Louisiana's prejudgment attachment procedure, which permitted an ex parte sequestration order, as unconstitutional.

CONCISE RULE OF LAW: An ex parte prejudgment attachment procedure is constitutional if it minimizes the risk of a wrongful taking.

FACTS: Mitchell (D) purchased certain appliances from W.T. Grant Co. (P) on credit. Mitchell (D) went into default, and W.T. Grant (P) filed suit. W.T. Grant (P) obtained an ex parte sequestration order. Louisiana's attachment procedure mandated a verified, factual petition demonstrating the need for sequestration, the posting of a bond, and a hearing before a magistrate. Mitchell (D) challenged the procedure as unconstitutional. The Supreme Court accepted review.

ISSUE: Is an ex parte prejudgment attachment procedure constitutional if it minimizes the risk of a wrongful taking?

HOLDING AND DECISION: (White, J.) Yes. An ex parte prejudgment attachment procedure is constitutional if it minimizes the risk of a wrongful taking. Earlier decisions invalidating such procedures were not based on their ex parte natures but rather on the basis that the procedures did not adequately safeguard the rights of the parties in possession. Here, Louisiana's procedure required a verified, factual petition, a bond, and judicial oversight. This adequately protects a debtor's rights. Affirmed.

CONCURRENCE: (Powell, J.) Fuentes v. Shevin, 407 U.S. 67 (1972), appeared to prohibit ex parte attachment proceedings. The present case effectively overrules Fuentes and properly so.

EDITOR'S ANALYSIS: Fuentes v. Shevin did in fact appear to require an adversary hearing prior to attachment. This case appeared to represent the most extreme position of the Court in the line of debtors' rights cases which started with Sniadach v. Family Finance Corp., 395 U.S. 337 (1969). The present action retreated somewhat from the rule of Fuentes.

[For more information on prejudgment attachment, see Casenote Law Outline on Civil Procedure, Chapter 11, § III, Enforcement of Coercive Judgments.]

NOTES:

NORTH GEORGIA FINISHING, INC. v. DI-CHEM, INC.
419 U.S. 601 (1975).

NATURE OF CASE: Action to declare a prejudgment garnishment statute violative of the Due Process Clause of the Fourteenth Armndment.

FACT SUMMARY: Di-Chem (P) obtained a prejudgment writ of garnishment against North Georgia Finishing's (D) bank account.

CONCISE RULE OF LAW: Any substantial deprivation of property under state law requires that procedural protections be accorded the deprived party to avoid a due process challenge.

FACTS: Under Georgia law, plaintiffs may obtain a prejudgment writ of garnishment from a judicial officer or the court clerk. The writ may be served on a bank account of the debtor/defendant. The funds are held pending the outcome of the suit. The creditor must file a bond in twice the amount of the impounded funds. The debtor may secure a release by posting a counterbond. No prior notice or hearing is required. Di-Chem (P) filed suit against North Georgia Finishing (D) for the balance due on goods sold to it. After Di-Chem (P) filed an affidavit asserting that North Georgia (D) owed more than $51,000, the court clerk issued a summons of garnishment on North Georgia's (D) bank, freezing its bank account. North Georgia (D) then filed a motion to dissolve the writ, alleging that Georgia's prejudgment garnishment statute violated due process. The Georgia courts sustained the constitutionality of the statute. Sniadach v. Family Finance, 395 U.S. 337 (1969), was discounted as only applying to prejudgment garnishment of wages.

ISSUE: Is any prejudgment garnishment statute that does not offer procedural protections to the deprived party violative of due process?

HOLDING AND DECISION: (White, J.) Yes. Where the state undertakes to deprive one of the substantial use of his property, certain procedural protections must be accorded to avoid a due process challenge. Here, Georgia does not require a showing of merit, no notice is given, and no hearing is accorded. Neither the requirement of a double bond from the creditor nor the release of the funds upon the posting of a counterbond provides the needed procedural protection. The length of deprivation of the use of one's property is immaterial for due process considerations. Where the use of one's property is substantially impaired by application of state law, proper procedural safeguards must be accorded the deprived party to avoid unconstitutionality on due process grounds. The Georgia law contains no such safeguards and must fail. Reversed.

CONCURRENCE: (Powell, J.) The Court's opinion sweeps too broadly because procedural due process would be satisfied by the creditor's giving adequate security by bond and a requirement that he establish, before a neutral magistrate, a factual basis for the need for a garnishment. Due process would then require only a postgarnishment hearing.

CONCURRENCE: Fuentes v. Shevin should not have been decided by a 4-3 vote by a Court with two vacancies.

EDITOR'S ANALYSIS: This is the outermost extension for the position taken in Fuentes and Sniadach. A right to a hearing and to other procedural protections are necessary for any prejudgment attachment action. Unjustified attachments, e.g., where there is no question that any judgment will be collectible, are themselves actionable even if the plaintiff ultimately prevails. It is deemed an abuse of process. White Lightning Co. v. Wolfson, 66 Cal. Rptr. 697 (1968).

[For more information on prejudgment attachment, see Casenote Law Outline on Civil Procedure, Chapter 11, § III, Enforcement of Coercive Judgments.]

NOTES:

CONNECTICUT v. DOEHR
501 U.S. 1 (1991).

NATURE OF CASE: Appeal from reversal of a grant of summary judgment in favor of the plaintiff who had secured a prejudgment attachment under state law.

FACT SUMMARY: When DiGiovanni (D) had Doehr's (P) home attached in conjunction with a suit against Doehr (P) for assault and battery, Doehr (P) brought this action, claiming the Connecticut statute that allowed prejudgment attachment without prior notice or hearing was unconstitutional.

CONCISE RULE OF LAW: Prejudgment attachment of real estate without affording prior notice or the opportunity for a prior hearing to the individual whose property is subject to attachment does not satisfy due process requirements.

FACTS: In conjunction with a suit for assault and battery against Doehr (P), DiGiovanni (D) submitted an application for an attachment on Doehr's (P) home. The underlying suit did not involve Doehr's (P) real estate nor did DiGiovanni (D) have any preexisting interest in Doehr's (P) home. Doehr (P) received notice of the attachment only after the property had been attached. Rather than pursue any of his state remedies, Doehr (P) brought this action against DiGiovanni (D) in federal district court, claiming that the Connecticut (D) statute that allowed such prejudgment attachment without prior notice or hearing was unconstitutional under the Due Process Clause of the Fourteenth Amendment. The district court upheld the statute, granting summary judgment in favor of DiGiovanni (D). A divided panel of the court of appeals reversed. DiGiovanni appealed.

ISSUE: Does prejudgment attachment of real estate without affording prior notice or the opportunity for a prior hearing to the individual whose property is subject to attachment satisfy due process requirements?

HOLDING AND DECISION: (White, J.) No. Prejudgment attachment of real estate without affording prior notice or the opportunity for a prior hearing to the individual whose property is subject to attachment does not satisfy due process requirements. For a property owner like Doehr (P), attachment ordinarily clouds title, impairs the ability to sell or otherwise alienate the property, taints any credit rating, reduces the chance of obtaining a home equity loan or additional mortgage, and can even place an existing mortgage in technical default where there is an insecurity clause. Furthermore, the risk of erroneous deprivation that Connecticut (D) permits here is substantial. Finally, absent allegations that Doehr (P) was about to transfer or encumber his real estate, DiGiovanni's (D) interest in attaching the property does not justify burdening Doehr's (P) ownership rights in the absence a hearing to determine the likelihood of recovery. By failing to provide for a preattachment hearing without at least requiring a bond or a showing of some exigent circumstance, the provision clearly falls short of the demands of due process. The judgment of the court of appeals is affirmed.

CONCURRENCE: (Rehnquist, C.J.) The Connecticut attachment statute, as applied in this case, fails to satisfy the Due Process Clause of the Fourteenth Amendment. However, the Court should await concrete cases that present questions involving bonds and exigent circumstances before attempting to decide when and if the Due Process Clause of the Fourteenth Amendment requires them as prerequisites for a lawful attachment.

CONCURRENCE: (Scalia, J.) Since the manner of attachment here was not a recognized procedure at common law, its validity under the Due Process Clause should be determined by applying the test this Court set forth in Mathews v. Eldridge, 424 U.S. 319.

EDITOR'S ANALYSIS: A survey of state attachment provisions reveals that nearly every state requires either a preattachment hearing, a showing of some exigent circumstance, or both, before permitting an attachment to take place. As noted by the Court, disputes between debtors and creditors more readily lend themselves to accurate ex parte assessments of the merits. Tort action, like the assault and battery claim at issue here, do not. Although a majority of the Court did not reach the issue, Justices Marshall, Stevens, O'Connor, and White deemed it appropriate to consider whether due process also required a plaintiff to post a bond or other security in addition to requiring a hearing or showing of some exigency. They concluded that it did. It was this part of the opinion that the concurrers refrained from joining.

[For more information on prejudgment attachment, see Casenote Law Outline on Civil Procedure, Chapter 11, § III, Enforcement of Coercive Judgments.]

NOTES:

CAREY v. PIPHUS
435 U.S. 247 (1978).

NATURE OF CASE: Appeal of award of damages for civil violations.

FACT SUMMARY: Damages in excess of a nominal amount were awarded in absence of proof of injury.

CONCISE RULE OF LAW: In an action based on denial of procedural due process, only nominal damages may be awarded in the absence of actual injury.

FACTS: Piphus (P) was suspended from school for several days. He was reinstated but brought an action under 28 U.S.C. § 1983 anyway, contending he was denied procedural due process. The district court found no actual injury and dismissed. The court of appeals reversed, holding that Piphus (P) was entitled to injunctive relief and also that denial of procedural due process was compensable even in the absence of actual injury. The Supreme Court accepted renew of the latter portion of the appellate court's holding.

ISSUE: In an action based on denial of procedural due process, may damages in excess of a nominal amount be awarded in the absence of proof of injury?

HOLDING AND DECISION: (Powell, J.) No. In an action based on denial of procedural due process, only nominal damages may be awarded. The basic purpose of § 1983 is to compensate individuals for injuries caused by the deprivation of constitutional rights. The structure under which this is done borrows from tort law. Just as tort law requires injury for compensation to be merited, so does § 1983. It cannot be assumed that denial of procedural due process, in itself, is an injury. Many will suffer no distress when such denial leads to no injury, and in such cases compensation would be inappropriate. It is injury caused by deprivation, not the deprivation itself, that is compensable. Here, no evidence on the issue of injury was put forth, so actual damages would be inappropriate. Reversed.

EDITOR'S ANALYSIS: The decision was apparently rather purposefully limited in scope. The Court always limited its terms to procedural due process. Substantive due process was not mentioned. Also, the Court said in a footnote that punitive damages might be awarded in the absence of actual injury.

[For more information on procedural due process, see Casenote Law Outline on Civil Procedure, Chapter 2, § III, Jurisdiction and Valid Judgments.]

SMITH v. WESTERN ELECTRIC CO.
Mo. Ct. App., 643 S.W.2d 10 (1982).

NATURE OF CASE: Appeal from an order dismissing a petition for an injunction preventing an employer from allowing health hazards in the workplace.

FACT SUMMARY: After Western Electric (D) failed to provide a smoke-free workplace environment for Smith (P), who developed a severe adverse reaction to tobacco smoke, he sought an injunction to prevent his continued exposure to tobacco smoke in the workplace or any change in his pay or employment conditions because of his medical reaction to tobacco smoke.

CONCISE RULE OF LAW: Injunctive relief is unavailable unless irreparable harm is otherwise likely to result and a plaintiff has no adequate remedy at law.

FACTS: While Smith (P) was employed by Western Electric (D), he developed a severe adverse reaction to tobacco smoke. When Smith (P) complained about the tobacco smoke in the workplace, Western Electric (D) moved him to different work locations in the plant, but each location contained significant amounts of tobacco smoke. Western Electric (D) later developed a smoking policy but failed to improve the air in the workplace because it failed to make a reasonable effort to implement that policy. Smith (P) sought an injunction to prevent Western Electric (D) from further exposing him to a health hazard, thereby breaching its duty to provide a safe place in which to work. The court dismissed Smith's (P) petition for failure to state a claim upon which relief could be granted. Smith (P) appealed.

ISSUE: Is injunctive relief unavailable unless irreparable harm is otherwise likely to result and a plaintiff has no adequate remedy at law?

HOLDING AND DECISION: (Dowd, J.) Yes. Injunctive relief is unavailable unless irreparable harm is otherwise likely to result and a plaintiff has no adequate remedy at law. It is fair to characterize the deterioration of Smith's (P) health as irreparable and as a harm for which money damages cannot adequately compensate. This is particularly true where the harm has not yet resulted in full-blown disease or injury. Smith (P) should not be required to await the harm's fruition before he is entitled to seek an inadequate remedy. Moreover, the nature of Smith's (P) unsafe work environment represents a recurrent risk of harm that would necessitate a multiplicity of lawsuits. Injunction would be an appropriate remedy here. Because Smith (P) has stated a claim upon which relief can be granted, the trial court erred in dismissing the petition. Smith (P) should be allowed the opportunity to prove his allegations.

EDITOR'S ANALYSIS: The Occupational Safety and Health Act (OSHA) specifically states that it does not affect the common law regarding injuries, diseases, or death of employees arising out of employment. The Act also declares that it does not prevent a state court from asserting jurisdiction over an occupational safety or health issue for which no OSHA standard is in effect. The court found unpersuasive Western Electric's (D) argument that § 653(b)(4) of the Act refers only to the common law pertaining to workers' compensation.

VENEGAS v. MITCHELL
495 U.S. 82 (1990).

NATURE OF CASE: Appeal from a judgment allowing a contingency-fee agreement in a civil rights case to stand.

FACT SUMMARY: After Mitchell (D) won Venegas's (P) underlying civil rights suit, a dispute arose between the two as to whether Mitchell (D) was entitled to the 40% contingency fee negotiated in their contract.

CONCISE RULE OF LAW: The plaintiff in a civil rights action may enter into a contingency-fee agreement with his attorney, even where such a fee exceeds subsequent court-awarded attorney fees.

FACTS: In the underlying § 1983 action that Venegas (P) filed against the city of Long Beach, California, he signed a contingency-fee agreement with Mitchell (D), his attorney, for a fee of 40% of the gross amount of any recovery. Venegas (P) subsequently consented to the association of co-counsel who would share any contingent fee equally with Mitchell (D). After Venegas (P) obtained a judgment for $2.08 million, the court awarded him $117,000 in attorney's fees, with $75,000 attributable to the work done by Mitchell (D). After Mitchell (D) withdrew as counsel of record and Venegas (P) obtained different counsel for his appeal, Mitchell (D) asserted a $406,000 attorney's lien against the judgment proceeds representing his half of the 40% fee. The district court refused to disallow or reduce the fee, finding it reasonable. The court of appeals affirmed. Venegas (P) appealed.

ISSUE: May the plaintiff in a civil rights action enter into a contingency-fee agreement with his attorney even when such a fee exceeds subsequent court-awarded attorney fees?

HOLDING AND DECISION: (White, J.) Yes. The plaintiff in a civil rights action may enter into a contingency-fee agreement with his attorney, even when such a fee exceeds subsequent court-awarded attorney fees. The aim of the rule is to enable civil rights plaintiffs to employ reasonably competent lawyers without cost to themselves if they prevail. But there is nothing in § 1988 to regulate what plaintiffs may or may not promise to pay their attorneys if they lose or if they win. Depriving plaintiffs of the option of promising to pay more than the statutory fee if that is necessary to secure counsel of their choice would not further § 1988's general purpose of enabling plaintiffs in civil rights cases to secure competent counsel.

EDITOR'S ANALYSIS: A cause of action under § 1983 belongs to the injured individual, and, in at least some circumstances, that individual's voluntary waiver of a § 1983 cause of action may be valid. If § 1983 plaintiffs may waive their causes of action entirely, there is little reason to believe that they may not assign part of their recovery to an attorney if they believe that the contingency arrangement will increase their likelihood of recovery. A contrary decision would place § 1983 plaintiffs in the peculiar position of being freer to negotiate with their adversaries than with their own attorneys.

NOTES:

12

3

CHAPTER 3
DESCRIBING AND DEFINING THE DISPUTE

QUICK REFERENCE RULES OF LAW

1. **Pleading Requirements.** Facts must be alleged in the complaint upon which plaintiff's cause of action is based. (Gillispie v. Goodyear Service Stores)

   [For more information on pleading requirements, see Casenote Law Outline on Civil Procedure, Chapter 5, § III, Notice Pleading Requirements — The Complaint.]

2. **The Problem of Specificity.** A complaint need not be more specific if it is sufficient on its face to fairly notify the opposing party of the nature of the claim. (United States v. Board of Harbor Commission)

3. **Alternative Allegations.** A complaint may contain inconsistent allegations, even though the proof of one negates any fault on the basis of the other. (McCormick v. Kopmann)

   [For more information on alternative allegations, see Casenote Law Outline on Civil Procedure, Chapter 5, § V, Answers.]

4. **Rule 11 Sanctions.** Rule 11 establishes an affirmative duty to conduct an adequate prefiling investigation to substantiate the legal and factual claims presented. (Albright v. Upjohn Co.)

   [For more information on Rule 11 sanctions, see Casenote Law Outline on Civil Procedure, Chapter 5, § VI, Truthfulness in Pleading.]

5. **Legal Sufficiency of the Plaintiff's Claim.** In deciding whether a motion to dismiss was properly granted, the court is required to accept only well-pleaded facts as true without considering any new legal theory asserted by the plaintiff. (Mitchell v. Archibald and Kendall)

6. **Allegations of Fraud of Mistake.** A complaint alleging fraud must contain specific evidentiary factual allegations. (Ross v. A.H. Robins Co.)

   [For more information on allegations of fraud or mistake, see Casenote Law Outline on Civil Procedure, Chapter 5, § IV, Special Pleading Requirements.]

7. **Heightened Requirements for Specificity.** A higher standard of particularity of pleading will be required where a heightened concern for due process arises by reason of the drastic nature of the remedies sought. (Cash Energy, Inc. v. Weiner)

8. **Notice Pleading.** A plaintiff suing a municipality for a civil rights violation must state with factual detail the basis for the claim and why the municipality cannot successfully maintain an immunity defense. (Leatherman v. Tarrant County Narcotics)

   [For more information on notice pleading, see Casenote Law Outline on Civil Procedure, Chapter 5, § III, Notice Pleading Requirements — The Complaint.]

9. **Setting Aside Judgments.** Where a plaintiff will not be prejudiced and a meritorious defense is shown, a default should be set aside if it was the result of mere negligence. (Shephard Claims v. Will Darrah and Associates)

   [For more information on setting aside judgments, see Casenote Law Outline on Civil Procedure, Chapter 9, § VII, Extraordinary Post-judgment Relief in the Trial Court.]

10. **Admissions and Denials.** A denial based on lack of information will be deemed an admission if the facts relevant to the issue are within the denying party's knowledge and control. (David v. Crompton and Knowles)

   [For more information on admissions and denials, see Casenote Law Outline on Civil Procedure, Chapter 5, § V, Answers.]

11. **Pleading Requirements.** In an action to redress the deprivation of rights secured by the U.S. Constitution and law under 42 U.S.C. § 1983, the complaint need not allege the defendant's bad faith in order to state a claim for relief. (Gomez v. Toledo)

   [For more information on pleading requirements, see Casenote Law Outline on Civil Procedure, Chapter 5, § IV, Special Pleading Requirements.]

12. **Compulsory Counterclaims.** A party sued for violation of federal labor laws may not raise defamation as a compulsory counterclaim. (Wigglesworth v. Teamsters Local Union No. 592)

   [For more information on compulsory counterclaims, see Casenote Law Outline on Civil Procedure, Chapter 6, § I, Joinder of Claims.]

13. **Voluntary Dismissal.** A plaintiff has an absolute right to dismiss an action before the defendant files an answer or motion for summary judgment. (D.C. Electronics, Inc. v. Natron Corp.)

   [For more information on voluntary dismissal, see Casenote Law Outline on Civil Procedure, Chapter 8, § III, Rule 41 Voluntary and Involuntary Dismissals.]

14. **Permission to Amend Pleadings.** A court may deny a request to amend if the amendment will result in undue prejudice to the other party or has been unduly delayed. (David v. Crompton & Knowles Corp.)

   [For more information on permission to amend pleadings, see Casenote Law Outline on Civil Procedure, Chapter 5, § VII, Amendments to Pleadings.]

15. **Amendments Adding New Parties.** When a newly added defendant has been aware of litigation, the statute of limitations may not apply to him. (Swartz v. Gold Dust Casino, Inc.)

   [For more information on amendments adding new parties, see Casenote Law Outline on Civil Procedure, Chapter 5, § VII, Amendments to Pleadings.]

GILLISPIE v. GOODYEAR SERVICE STORES
N.C. Sup. Ct., 258 N.C. 487, 128 S.E.2d 762 (1963).

NATURE OF CASE: Appeal of a decision granting a demurrer in action to collect damages in a personal injury case.

FACT SUMMARY: Employees of Goodyear Service Stores (D) trespassed on Gillispie's (P) property, assaulted her, and caused her to be put in a public jail.

CONCISE RULE OF LAW: Facts must be alleged in the complaint upon which plaintiff's cause of action is based.

FACTS: Gillispie (P) alleged that she and each of the employees of the Goodyear Service Stores (D), as well as the store, were citizens and residents of North Carolina. The remaining allegations of the complaint and the prayer for relief were as follows: "4. On or about May 5, 1959 and May 6, 1959, the defendants, without cause or just excuse and maliciously, came upon and trespassed upon the premises occupied by the plaintiff as a residence, and by the use of harsh and threatening language and physical force directed against the plaintiff assaulted the plaintiff and placed her in great fear, and humiliated and embarrassed her by subjecting her to public scorn and ridicule, and caused her to be seized and exhibited to the public as a prisoner, and to be confined in a public jail, all to her great humiliation, embarrassment and harm. 5. By reason of the defendants' malicious and intentional assault against and humiliation of plaintiff, the plaintiff was and has been damaged and injured in the amount of $25,000. 6. The acts of the defendants as aforesaid were deliberate, malicious, and with the deliberate intention of harming the plaintiff, and the plaintiff is entitled to recover her actual damages as well as punitive damages from the defendants and each of them. THEREFORE, the plaintiff prays that she have and recover of the defendants the sum of $25,000 as damages and $10,000 in addition thereto as punitive damages, and that she have such other and further relief as may be just and proper." Goodyear Service Stores (D) demurred to the complaint on the grounds that the complaint did not state facts sufficient to constitute a cause of action and that there was a misjoinder of parties and causes of action. The court sustained the demurrer, and Gillispie (P) appealed the decision.

ISSUE: Can pleadings which contain only conclusions of law state a proper cause of action?

HOLDING AND DECISION: (Bobbitt, J.) No. A complaint must contain a plain and concise statement of the facts constituting a cause of action. Facts must be set out in the complaint that constitute a cause of action and not merely state the conclusions of the pleader. The requirement is that a complaint must allege the material, essential, and ultimate facts upon which plaintiff's right of action is based. When the complaint is challenged by a demurrer, only the facts alleged and not the pleader's conclusions are deemed admitted in determining if the complaint states a cause of action. Gillispie (P) alleged in a single sentence that Goodyear Service Stores (D), "without cause or just excuse and maliciously" trespassed upon premises occupied by her as a residence, assaulted her, and caused her to be seized and confined as a prisoner. The

complaint stated no facts upon which these legal conclusions could be predicated. Gillispie's (P) allegations do not disclose what occurred, where it occurred, who did what, the relationships between defendants and plaintiff, or of defendants inter se, or any other factual data that might identify the occasion or describe the circumstances of the alleged wrongful conduct of Goodyear Service Stores (D). There was no factual basis to which the court could apply the law. When considered in the light most favorable to Gillispie (P), the complaint fails to state a cause of action. Demurrer affirmed.

EDITOR'S ANALYSIS: It is often difficult to distinguish between evidentiary facts, ultimate facts, and conclusions of law. Only ultimate facts can properly be included in pleadings. One test used to determine which is which is when no other facts or conclusions can be drawn from a fact, then it is a legal conclusion. If the next logical deduction that can be draw from a fact is a legal conclusion, then it is an ultimate fact. If the next logical deduction from the pleaded fact is another fact, then it is an evidentiary fact. Because it is so difficult to determine the fine line between the ultimate facts, conclusions of law, and evidentiary material, some states are using notice pleading as the federal courts do. Notice pleading only requires that enough facts be pleaded to put the opposing party on notice of the charges against him. In states that still require that only ultimate facts be pleaded, complaints must be carefully drawn. If it appears that there is a basis for a valid cause of action but the pleadings are not properly drawn, courts are quite liberal in allowing the complaint to be amended.

[For more information on pleading requirements, see Casenote Law Outline on Civil Procedure, Chapter 5, § III, Notice Pleading Requirements — The Complaint.]

NOTES:

UNITED STATES v. BOARD OF HARBOR COMMISSIONERS
73 F.R.D. 460 (D. Del. 1977).

NATURE OF CASE: Motion under Fed. R. Civ. P. Rule 12(e) by defendants for a more definite statement of the charges filed against them.

FACT SUMMARY: After the SICO Company (D) and North American Smelting Company (D) were charged with discharging oil into navigable waters of the United States (P), both companies moved for a more definite statement of the government's (P) complaint on the ground that it was vague and ambiguous.

CONCISE RULE OF LAW: A complaint need not be more specific if it is sufficient on its face to fairly notify the opposing party of the nature of the claim.

FACTS: After the United States (P) filed a complaint against the SICO Company (SICO) (D) and North American Smelting Company (NASCO) (D), both companies filed a Rule 12(e) motion for a more definite statement on the ground that the complaint filed against them was so vague and ambiguous that they were unable to frame a responsive pleading. The complaint alleged that both companies own and operate onshore facilities from which oil was discharged into the Delaware River in violation of the Federal Water Pollution Control Act. SICO (D) and NASCO (D) sought to have the government (P) specify which company was responsible for the alleged discharge of oil, the amount of oil discharged and the removal costs incurred, and the actions that were alleged to have caused the discharge.

ISSUE: Need a complaint be more specific if it is sufficient on its face to fairly notify the opposing party of the nature of the claim?

HOLDING AND DECISION: (Latchum, C.J.) No. A complaint need not be more specific if it is sufficient on its face to fairly notify the opposing party of the nature of the claim. In this case, the complaint on its face can be fairly read to charge SICO (D) and NASCO (D) with owning or operating on-shore facilities that discharged oil into the Delaware River, or that each of them took actions causing such oil to be discharged. This allegation, together with the other averments in the complaint, fairly notifies SICO (D) and NASCO (D) of the nature of the claim against them. Accordingly, their motions for a more definite statement will be denied.

EDITOR'S ANALYSIS: SICO's (D) and NASCO's (D) motion for a more definite statement was really an effort to flesh out the Government's (D) case. As such, it was a misuse of Rule 12(e). The evidentiary information they sought was more properly the subject of discovery under Rules 26 through 36. According to 2A Moore's Federal Practice ¶ 12.18(1) at 2389 (2d ed. 1975), a motion for a more definite statement under Rule 12(e) is ordinarily restricted to situations where a pleading suffers from "unintelligibility rather than the want of detail."

NOTES:

McCORMICK v. KOPMANN
23 Ill. App. 2d 189, 161 N.E.2d 720 (1959).

NATURE OF CASE: Appeal of denial of motion for directed verdict.

FACT SUMMARY: McCormick (P) brought this action against Kopmann (D) for causing an accident in which her husband was killed. She also sued Huls (D) for violating a state law by serving the decedent alcohol. Kopmann (D) moved for a directed verdict.

CONCISE RULE OF LAW: A complaint may contain inconsistent allegations, even though the proof of one negates any fault on the basis of the other.

FACTS: McCormick's (P) husband was killed when his automobile collided with Kopmann's (D) truck. McCormick (P) brought this wrongful death action against Kopmann (D), alleging that he drove over the center line of the road and thereby caused the accident. In a separate allegation in the same complaint, McCormick (P) alleged that another defendant, Huls (D), violated the Dram Shop Act by serving the decedent alcohol after he was intoxicated and that this caused the accident. Kopmann (D) moved for a directed verdict on the ground that the decedent's intoxication constituted contributory negligence and precluded relief as against Kopmann (D). The motion was denied, and Kopmann (D) appealed.

ISSUE: May a complaint contain inconsistent allegations even though the proof of one negates any fault on the basis of another?

HOLDING AND DECISION: (Reynolds, J.) Yes. Sound policy weighs in favor of alternative pleading so that controversies may be sealed and complete justice may be accomplished in a single action. While in Count I, McCormick (P) alleged that the decedent was free from any contributory negligence and in Count IV alleged that he was intoxicated while driving, nothing indicates that McCormick (P) knew in advance of trial which of the averments was true. Thus, McCormick (P) had the right to adduce all proof she had under both counts. Furthermore, the allegations which are inconsistent with those against Kopmann (D) are not binding admissions on the part of McCormick (P). This would force a plaintiff into an election of theories for recovery, and that is not the aim of the pleading laws. A complaint, therefore, may contain inconsistent allegations even though the proof of one negates any fault on the basis of the other. Affirmed.

EDITOR'S ANALYSIS: Inconsistent pleading is nearly a universally permitted procedure in pleading a case. Since the trial is supposed to be a fact-determining event, it would not be logical to require a plaintiff to choose which set of facts is "true" before trial when different possibilities exist.

[For more information on alternative allegations, see Casenote Law Outline on Civil Procedure, Chapter 5, § V, Answers.]

NOTES:

ALBRIGHT v. UPJOHN COMPANY
788 F.2d 1217 (6th Cir. 1986).

NATURE OF CASE: Appeal from denial of sanctions.

FACT SUMMARY: Albright (P) contended her attorneys made reasonable inquiry into the facts of the case prior to filing suit and thus were not subject to sanctions under Fed. R. Civ. P. 11.

CONCISE RULE OF LAW: Rule 11 establishes an affirmative duty to conduct an adequate prefiling investigation to substantiate the legal and factual claims presented.

FACTS: Albright (P) sued in federal court, contending she suffered yellowed teeth due to her ingestion of certain prescription drugs. She could not establish the manufacturer of each such drug taken, yet she sued those she knew and those who may have been involved. Upjohn (D) successfully moved for summary judgment and sought sanctions under Rule 11, contending an adequate prefiling investigation would have prevented its involvement. The district court denied the sanctions, and Upjohn (D) appealed.

ISSUE: Does Rule 11 establish an affirmative duty to conduct an adequate prefiling investigation?

HOLDING AND DECISION: (Peck, J.) Yes. Rule 11 imposes an affirmative duty to conduct an adequate prefiling investigation. In this case, medical records available to Albright (P) listed the subject drugs, allowing for discovery for the manufacturers. Any remaining drugs were not documented; thus, no other manufacturers should have been sued. This failure to adequately investigate violated Rule 11 and sanctions should have been awarded. Reversed.

DISSENT: (Guy, J.) The trial judge is in the best position to ascertain if sanctions are appropriate. In this matter, this court should have remanded to the trial court for a determination of sanctions.

EDITOR'S ANALYSIS: Rule 11 was amended in 1983 to encourage courts to impose sanctions for its violation. No longer will a good-faith effort at prefiling investigation be sufficient. The new standard is one of reasonableness under the circumstances.

[For more information on Rule 11 sanctions, see Casenote Law Outline on Civil Procedure, Chapter 5, § VI, Truthfulness in Pleading.]

MITCHELL v. ARCHIBALD & KENDALL, INC.
573 F.2d 429 (2d Cir. 1978).

NATURE OF CASE: Appeal from dismissal of a complaint in a negligence action seeking damages for personal injury.

FACT SUMMARY: After Mitchell (P) was shot in the face while parked on the street waiting to unload a truckload of A & K's (D) products, he filed this action to recover damages for his injuries, but the complaint was dismissed.

CONCISE RULE OF LAW: In deciding whether a motion to dismiss was properly granted, the court is required to accept only well-pleaded facts as true without considering any new legal theory asserted by the plaintiff.

FACTS: Mitchell (P) drove a truckload of Archibald & Kendall's (D) products from New Jersey to its Chicago warehouse. When Mitchell (P) arrived, a truck was already in the dock area being loaded. Since there was room for only one truck at a time, A & K's (D) employees directed Mitchell (P) to remain in his truck and to park it on the street immediately opposite A & K's (D) warehouse and adjacent to its driveway until they could unload it. Although A & K's (D) employees had knowledge of repeated occasions of various criminal acts on and about A & K's (D) premises, they did not warn Mitchell (P) of any such danger. While he was waiting on the street, he was shot in the face with a shotgun during a robbery attempt, suffering permanent injuries to his face. The district court dismissed the complaint as legally insufficient. Rather than amend the complaint, Mitchell (P) appealed the dismissal.

ISSUE: In deciding whether a motion to dismiss was properly granted, is the court required to accept only well-pleaded facts as true without considering any new legal theory asserted by the plaintiff?

HOLDING AND DECISION: (Pell, J.) Yes. In deciding whether a motion to dismiss was properly granted, the court is required to accept only well-pleaded facts as true without considering any new legal theory asserted by the plaintiff. In dismissing the cause, the district court judge was in effect ruling that the complaint as drafted was legally insufficient. At that time, Mitchell (P) had the absolute right to file an amended complaint embodying his new theory that a jury could find that the street area was a part of A & K's (D) premises. By appealing instead, Mitchell (P) elected to stand on his original complaint, thereby relinquishing the legal theory he now asserts. In any event, it appears that surrounding streets and sidewalks are beyond the meaning of the term "premises." Furthermore, under the applicable Illinois law, a possessor of land is subject to liability to business invitees "while they are upon the land." Here, Mitchell (P) was parked upon a public thoroughfare. Thus, A & K (D) owed no duty to Mitchell (P), and the complaint was properly dismissed. Affirmed.

DISSENT: (Fairchild, C.J.) I agree with the general proposition that no duty is owed to protect against criminal acts of third persons on a public street. However, that proposition does not fit the facts of this case. Mitchell (P) followed A & K's (D) instructions to park on the street when A & K (D) knew or should have known that Mitchell (P) would be in danger of criminal attack. This affirmative conduct by A & K (D) greatly increased the risk of harm to Mitchell (P), thus creating a duty to warn him of the danger or to direct him to a place of safety until the delivery could be made.

EDITOR'S ANALYSIS: Where pleadings raise a contested issue of material fact, a Rule 12(b)(6) motion to dismiss must be denied. In reviewing the grant of a motion to dismiss a complaint for failure to state a claim, it is elementary that all material facts well pleaded in the complaint must be taken as true. However, the court is not required to accept legal conclusions that may be alleged or that may be drawn from the pleaded facts. The court of appeals determined that the Illinois courts would have applied the Restatement (Second) of Torts § 344 in determining the existence of a duty to protect against criminal acts of third persons on a public street.

NOTES:

ROSS v. A.H. ROBINS COMPANY
607 F.2d 545 (2d Cir. 1979).

NATURE OF CASE: Appeal of dismissal of action for damages for violation of federal securities laws.

FACT SUMMARY: A.H. Robins Co. (D) contended that a class-action suit against it, alleging fraud, required specific factual pleading.

CONCISE RULE OF LAW: A complaint alleging fraud must contain specific evidentiary factual allegations.

FACTS: Ross (P), a shareholder of A.H. Robins Co. (D), filed a class-action suit on behalf of other shareholders, alleging fraud against Robins (D) and various corporate officials in that they knew of or recklessly disregarded information concerning problems with the Dalkon Shield, particularly information contained in an unpublished 1972 report. Also alleged were "other things" which put the corporation on notice of the problems. The district court granted Robins' (D) motion to dismiss without leave to amend, and Ross (P) appealed.

ISSUE: Must a complaint alleging fraud contain specific evidentiary factual allegations?

HOLDING AND DECISION: (Mishler, J.) Yes. A complaint alleging fraud must contain specific evidentiary factual allegations. Under Fed. R. Civ. P. 9(b), the rules regarding complaints alleging fraud are given special treatment. Rather than adhere to the usual rule that complaints need only allege ultimate facts, Rule 9(b) requires detailed evidentiary pleading. This is predicated on the notion that fraud allegations accuse a defendant of serious moral turpitude, and a defendant is entitled to know specifically that of which he is accused. Here, no allegation was made as to why Robins (D) officials should have known of the alleged 1972 report or what the "other things" that should have put them on notice of Dalkon Shield problems might have been. This did not satisfy Rule 9(b)'s requirements. Nonetheless, this court believes that Ross (P) should be given an opportunity to amend. Affirmed in part; reversed in part.

EDITOR'S ANALYSIS: An argument can be made that Rule 9(b) is superfluous. The specific facts upon which a fraud action are predicated can always be ascertained via discovery. The rebuttal to this argument would appear to be that a defendant should not have to submit to discovery on a meritless fraud claim.

[For more information on allegations of fraud or mistake, see Casenote Law Outline on Civil Procedure, Chapter 5, § IV, Special Pleading Requirements.]

NOTES:

CASH ENERGY, INC. v. WEINER
768 F. Supp. 892 (D. Mass. 1991).

NATURE OF CASE: Action to recover cleanup costs required under federal law for the pollution of real property.

FACT SUMMARY: When Cash Energy, Inc. (P) filed a complaint against Weiner (D) to recover cleanup costs imposed under CERCLA, Weiner (D) contended that the complaint rested on bald assertion, failing utterly to state or outline the facts beneath the allegations.

CONCISE RULE OF LAW: A higher standard of particularity of pleading will be required where a heightened concern for due process arises by reason of the drastic nature of the remedies sought.

FACTS: Over a number of years, Weiner (D) engaged in the storage and/or transfer of chemical solvents on a site adjacent to property owned and developed by Cash Energy (P). As a result of Weiner's (D) activities, Cash Energy (P) sought to recover cleanup costs imposed under the Comprehensive Environmental Response, Compensation, and Liability Act. 42 U.S.C. § 9607 (CERCLA). The complaint named not only the corporation, but four corporate officers. Weiner (D) asserted that Cash Energy's (P) complaint rested heavily on bald assertion, failing utterly to state or outline the facts beneath the allegations. In response to this criticism, Cash Energy (P) pointed to the modest pleading requirements of the Federal Rules.

ISSUE: Will a higher standard of particularity of pleading be required where a heightened concern for due process arises by reason of the drastic nature of the remedies sought?

HOLDING AND DECISION: (Keeton, J.) Yes. A higher standard of particularity of pleading will be required where a heightened concern for due process arises by reason of the drastic nature of the remedies sought. A tension exists between the short and plain statement of the facts prescribed in Rule 8(a) and Rule 9(b)'s exception for allegations of fraud and mistake, requiring more than statements of mere conclusion. CERCLA involves many of the circumstances that have led courts to invoke higher standards of specificity in other contexts. The cost of establishing that a claim lacks merit is more likely to be subject to reasonable controls if some standard of specificity of pleading is enforced. Thus, the claims against the individual defendants will be dismissed unless Cash Energy (P) files an amended complaint that pleads at least an outline or summary of the factual basis for the claims rather than mere conclusions.

EDITOR'S ANALYSIS: Over time, the exception for fraud has been extended to a number of analogous areas involving statutory causes of action, such as civil rights and RICO actions. There, the original concern about opportunities for abuse inherent in the freedom to plead conclusions rather than facts applies with like force. The trend toward the requirement of higher standards of particularity has accelerated in recent years due to the rising cost of litigation and the caseload crisis in the federal courts.

LEATHERMAN v. TARRANT COUNTY NARCOTICS INTELLIGENCE AND COORDINATION UNIT
113 S. Ct. 1160 (1993).

NATURE OF CASE: Review of order dismissing civil rights action.

FACT SUMMARY: A court of appeals held that a plaintiff suing a municipality for a civil rights violation was subject to a heightened pleading standard.

CONCISE RULE OF LAW: A plaintiff suing a municipality for a civil rights violation must state with factual detail the basis for the claim and why the municipality cannot successfully maintain an immunity defense.

FACTS: Police raided two homes for suspected narcotics activities. Subsequent to the raids, the occupants (P) filed civil rights actions under 42 U.S.C. § 1983 against certain local officials (D), a county (D), and two municipal corporations (D) with respect to the municipal corporations, the district court held that the occupants (P) were subject to a heightened pleading standard, which they had failed to meet. The court granted the municipalities' (D) Fed. R. Civ. P. 12(b)(6) motions to dismiss, and the Fifth Circuit affirmed. The Supreme Court granted review.

ISSUE: Is a plaintiff suing a municipality for a civil rights violation subject to a heightened pleading standard?

HOLDING AND DECISION: (Rehnquist, C.J.) No. A plaintiff suing a municipality for a civil rights violation is not subject to a heightened pleading standard. This Court has held that municipalities may not be liable for their officials' actions on a respondeat superior theory but may be liable when the city's policies have independently caused the alleged official misconduct. This imposes a higher proof standard on a plaintiff. However, it does not follow from this that the plaintiff should be subject to a higher pleading standard. Per Fed. R. Civ. P. 8(a)(2), pleading in federal courts is subject only to the notice standard, meaning that a pleading is adequate if it contains a short and plain statement of the claim showing that the pleader is entitled to relief. Extensive pleading of evidentiary facts is unnecessary. Fed. R. Civ. P. 9(b) creates a couple of exceptions to this rule, but neither involves civil rights actions against municipalities. Consequently, a heightened pleading standard will not be imposed here. Reversed.

EDITOR'S ANALYSIS: Pleading requirements come in two basic forms, code pleading and notice pleading. Code pleading requires extensive pleading of evidentiary facts. Notice pleading requires only that ultimate facts be pleaded. Code pleading has largely fallen out of favor. Even those states that are technically code-pleading jurisdictions do not strictly enforce their own requirements.

[For more information on notice pleading, see Casenote Law Outline on Civil Procedure, Chapter 5, § III, Notice Pleading Requirements — The Complaint.]

SHEPARD CLAIMS SERVICE, INC.
v. WILLIAM DARRAH & ASSOCIATES
796 F.2d 190 (6th Cir. 1986).

NATURE OF CASE: Appeal of denial of motion to set aside a default.

FACT SUMMARY: Negligence on the part of William Darrah & Associates' (D) counsel resulted in a default being entered.

CONCISE RULE OF LAW: Where a plaintiff will not be prejudiced and a meritorious defense is shown, a default should be set aside if it was the result of mere negligence.

FACTS: Shepard Claims Service, Inc. (P) sued William Darrah & Associates (D) for breach of contract. Counsel for Darrah (D) obtained an extension of time in which to answer. Due to secretarial error, the date on which an answer was to be due was misstated in a confirming letter. Darrah's (D) counsel did not review the letter before it was mailed. When the date indicated on the letter passed, Shepard (P) took a default. Darrah (D) moved to set it aside. The district court found that setting aside the default would not prejudice Shepard (P) and that Darrah (D) could present a meritorious defense. The court nonetheless denied the motion, citing the negligence of Darrah's (D) counsel. Darrah (D) filed an interlocutory appeal.

ISSUE: Where a plaintiff will not be prejudiced and a meritorious defense is shown, should a default be set aside if it was the result of mere negligence?

HOLDING AND DECISION: (Lively, C.J.) Yes. Where a plaintiff will not be prejudiced and a meritorious defense is shown, a default should be set aside if it was the result of mere negligence. Under Fed. R. Civ. P. 55, a default entry may be set aside for "good cause." Cases decided under the rule have formulated three questions to be answered in deciding on such a motion: (1) whether the plaintiff will be prejudiced; (2) whether the defendant has a meritorious defense; and (3) whether culpable conduct of the defendant led to the default. Culpable conduct has been considered to be something worse than mere negligence. A willful disregard for the rules of civil procedure has generally been required for conduct to be considered culpable. Therefore, if the first two questions are answered in favor of the defendant, and the defendant is guilty only of negligence, it is an abuse of discretion not to set aside a default entry. Such was the case here. Reversed.

EDITOR'S ANALYSIS: Entries of default are governed by Fed. R. Civ. P. 55(c). Setting aside default judgments is governed by Fed. R. Civ. P. 60(b). The terms for setting aside default judgments are more stringent than for a mere entry of default. This is due to the judicial policy favoring the finality of judgments.

[For more information on setting aside judgments, see Casenote Law Outline on Civil Procedure, Chapter 9, § VII, Extraordinary Post-judgment Relief in the Trial Court.]

DAVID v. CROMPTON & KNOWLES CORP.
58 F.R.D. 444 (E.D. Pa. 1973).

NATURE OF CASE: Motion to amend answer in an action based on personal injury.

FACT SUMMARY: Crompton & Knowles (D) denied manufacturing a certain machine on lack of information, although the facts relevant to the issue of its connection to the machine were within its knowledge and control.

CONCISE RULE OF LAW: A denial based on lack of information will be deemed an admission if the facts relevant to the issue are within the denying party's knowledge and control.

FACTS: David (P) was injured on a machine manufactured by Hunter, predecessor to Crompton & Knowles Corp. (D). David (P) filed suit in federal court seeking damages. As to the allegation that Crompton (D) manufactured the machine, Crompton (D) denied on lack of information. Crompton (D) later moved to amend its answer to deny the allegation. This was based on the realization that the contract purchasing Hunter's assets disclaimed assumption of liabilities. The court first addressed the issue of whether the denial on lack of information should be considered an admission or denial.

ISSUE: Will a denial based on lack of information be deemed an admission if the facts relevant to the issue are within the denying party's knowledge and control?

HOLDING AND DECISION: (Huyett, J.) Yes. A denial based on lack of information will be an admission if the facts relevant to the issue are within the denying party's knowledge and control. Normally, a denial on lack of information will be deemed the same as a denial. However, such an averment will be deemed an admission when the matter is obviously one of which the defendant has knowledge. When the information relevant to this is within the defendant's control, such a case exists. Here, the relevant information was the denial of successor liability in the contract. This was obviously within the control of Crompton (D), and its denial on lack of information was therefore invalid. [The casebook excerpt did not state the court's ruling on the motion.]

EDITOR'S ANALYSIS: Some states permit defendants to generally deny all allegations of a plaintiff's complaint. This is not the case in federal court, under the Fed. R. Civ. P. There, each paragraph must be separately denied, admitted, or denied on lack of information. A bad-faith denial can lead to subsequent sanctions.

[For more information on admissions and denials, see Casenote Law Outline on Civil Procedure, Chapter 5, § V, Answers.]

GOMEZ v. TOLEDO
446 U.S. 635 (1980).

NATURE OF CASE: Appeal from dismissal for failure to allege bad faith.

FACT SUMMARY: Gomez (P) brought this action against Toledo (D), Superintendent of the Police in Puerto Rico, for discharging him after he had reported the falsification of evidence by colleagues, but Gomez' (P) complaint did not allege that Toledo (D) had acted in bad faith.

CONCISE RULE OF LAW: In an action to redress the deprivation of rights secured by the U.S. Constitution and law under 42 U.S.C. § 1983, the complaint need not allege the defendant's bad faith in order to state a claim for relief.

FACTS: Gomez (P) was an agent of the Puerto Rican police. In 1975, he submitted a sworn statement to his superior that certain coagents has falsified evidence with respect to a criminal investigation. He later testified in the trial arising out of that investigation as a defense witness and swore there that the coagents had falsified the evidence in question. Thereafter, criminal charges were brought against Gomez (P) for wiretapping the other agents' telephones, but the charges were dismissed upon a finding of no probable cause to believe the allegations to be true. In the meantime, Gomez (P) had been transferred out of the investigative branches and into Police Headquarters and then to the Police Academy. Gomez (P) was reinstated by court order and granted back pay but sought damages for the violation of his procedural due process rights under 42 U.S.C. § 1983. His complaint did not allege bad faith on the part of Toledo (D), who contended that his qualified immunity required such an allegation.

ISSUE: In an action to redress the deprivation of rights secured by the U.S. Constitution and law under 42 U.S.C. § 1983, must the complaint allege the defendant's bad faith in order to state a claim for relief?

HOLDING AND DECISION: (Marshall, J.) No. The purpose of § 1983 is to provide a damages remedy against an offending party who has deprived a plaintiff of constitutional guarantees and guarantees of federal law. Though a defendant has a qualified immunity as a public official if he acted in good faith, no allegation of bad faith is required in a complaint that alleges a deprivation in violation of the law. The immunity of a defendant is a defense which he must plead, not the plaintiff. Nothing in the legislative history of § 1983 suggests that a bad-faith allegation is required in a complaint of this type. In an action to redress the deprivation of rights secured by the U.S. Constitution and law under 42 U.S.C. § 1983, the complaint need not allege the defendant's bad faith in order to state a claim for relief. Reversed.

EDITOR'S ANALYSIS: If a right secured by the U.S. Constitution or law is taken away from a plaintiff, it is not easy to envision any state of mind on the part of the offender other than bad faith, unless the "right" is abrogated legally. In any case, it is up to the defendant to show that he acted in good faith or that the plaintiff did not have a right secured by federal law.

[For more information on pleading requirements, see Casenote Law Outline on Civil Procedure, Chapter 5, § IV, Special Pleading Requirements.]

NOTES:

WIGGLESWORTH v. TEAMSTERS LOCAL UNION NO. 592
68 F.R.D. 609 (E.D. Va. 1975).

NATURE OF CASE: Motion to dismiss counterclaim in action based on violation of federal labor laws.

FACT SUMMARY: Certain officials of the Teamsters Local Union No. 592 (D), when sued for violation of labor laws by Wigglesworth (P), counterclaimed for defamation.

CONCISE RULE OF LAW: A party sued for violation of federal labor laws may not raise defamation as a compulsory counterclaim.

FACTS: Wigglesworth (P) sued the Teamsters Local Union No. 592 (D) and various officials thereof for violations of federal labor laws. At the same time, he publicly accused the various officials of being associated with organized crime. The various individual defendants counterclaimed for defamation. Wigglesworth (P) moved to dismiss for lack of subject matter jurisdiction.

ISSUE: May a party sued for violation of federal labor laws raise defamation as a compulsory counterclaim?

HOLDING AND DECISION: (Warriner, J.) No. A party sued for violation of federal labor laws may not raise defamation as a compulsory counterclaim. Fed. R. Civ. P. 13 makes a counterclaim compulsory if it arises out of the transaction or occurrence forming the basis of the complaint. In this manner, a counterclaim not having a basis for federal subject matter jurisdiction may nonetheless be adjudicated in federal court. Whether a counterclaim arises out of the same transaction depends mainly upon their logical relationship. Here, the two separate events complained of are quite distinct, being separated both by time and distance. One was in reaction to the other. In no sense can they be considered the same transaction, and therefore the counterclaim was not compulsory. As there is no independent basis for federal jurisdiction in the counterclaim, it must be dismissed. Motion granted.

EDITOR'S ANALYSIS: Under the Fed. R. Civ. P., counterclaims come under two basic types. The first is the compulsory counterclaim, which must be brought at the time of answer or is waived. The second type is the permissive counterclaim. It need not be brought at the time of answer. Unlike the compulsory counterclaim, it must always have independent federal subject matter jurisdiction.

[For more information on compulsory counterclaims, see Casenote Law Outline on Civil Procedure, Chapter 6, § I, Joinder of Claims.]

NOTES:

D.C. ELECTRONICS, INC. v. NARTRON CORP.
511 F.2d 294 (6th Cir. 1975).

NATURE OF CASE: Appeal of order vacating a voluntary dismissal.

FACT SUMMARY: D.C. Electronics (P) dismissed an antitrust action before Nartron Corp. (D) had filed an answer or motion for summary judgment.

CONCISE RULE OF LAW: A plaintiff has an absolute right to dismiss an action before the defendant files an answer or motion for summary judgment.

FACTS: D.C. Electronics, Inc. (P) filed an antitrust action against Nartron Corp. (D). A TRO was issued, which was soon thereafter dissolved. After several months of procedural maneuvers, D.C. (P) filed a notice of voluntary dismissal. Nartron (D) had filed neither an answer nor a motion for summary judgment. The district court entered an order vacating the dismissal, holding that the action had proceeded too far to permit a dismissal without court approval. D.C. (P) appealed.

ISSUE: Does a plaintiff have an absolute right to dismiss an action before the defendant files an answer or motion for summary judgment?

HOLDING AND DECISION: (Peck, J.) Yes. A plaintiff has an absolute right to dismiss an action before the defendant files an answer or motion for summary judgment. Fed. R. Civ. P. 41(a)(1)(i) permits a plaintiff to voluntarily dismiss an action before a responsive pleading has been filed. There is no exception made under the rule. Whether or not there have been papers or motions exchanged prior to the filing of an answer or motion for summary judgment does not appear to make any difference. The language of the rule is clear, and the district court had no discretion to vacate such a dismissal. Reversed.

EDITOR'S ANALYSIS: The Fed. R. Civ. P. provide three avenues for dismissing an action. Rule 41(a)(2) provides for a motion to dismiss by a plaintiff. Rule 41(a)(1)(ii) permits a stipulated dismissal. The third avenue is the method at issue here. Unlike the latter avenue for dismissal, the prior ones may come at any time during the pendency of a litigation.

[For more information on voluntary dismissal, see Casenote Law Outline on Civil Procedure, Chapter 8, § III, Rule 41 Voluntary and Involuntary Dismissals.]

NOTES:

DAVID v. CROMPTON & KNOWLES CORP.
58 F.R.D. 444 (E.D. Pa., 1973).

NATURE OF CASE: Request for leave to amend in a products liability action.

FACT SUMMARY: Claiming that it had only recently discovered new information about its liability, Crompton & Knowles Corp. (D) sought to amend its answer to a products liability complaint filed by David (P) to deny that it designed, manufactured, or sold the shredding machine that injured David (P).

CONCISE RULE OF LAW: A court may deny a request to amend if the amendment will result in undue prejudice to the other party or has been unduly delayed.

FACTS: David (P) was injured by a shredding machine. The machine was allegedly designed, manufactured, and sold by Crompton (D) to Crown Products Corporation. In its answer to David's (P) complaint, Crompton (D) averred that it was without sufficient knowledge or information to admit or deny the allegation and demanded proof. The court decided that Crompton's (D) denial on grounds of lack of knowledge of David's (P) allegation that it designed, manufactured and sold the machine that injured David (P) was ineffective and constituted an admission. Crompton (D) then sought to amend its answer to David's (P) complaint to deny that it had designed, manufactured, or sold the machine in question.

ISSUE: May a court deny a request to amend if the amendment will result in undue prejudice to the other party or has been unduly delayed?

HOLDING & DECISION: (Huyett, J.) Yes. A court may deny a request to amend if the amendment will result in undue prejudice to the other party or has been unduly delayed. Fed. R. Civ. P. 15(a) provides that leave to amend an answer should be freely given when justice requires. The purpose of a permissive attitude toward an amendment is to encourage decision of the case on the merits by allowing parties to present the real issues of the case. Crompton (D) bases its proferred denial upon information it claims to have discovered in 1972. Crompton (D) now alleges that the machine was designed, manufactured, and sold by James Hunter Corp. prior to Crompton's (D) purchase of Hunter, and that it did not assume liabilities for the negligent design, manufacture, or sale of machines by Hunter prior to the purchase of Hunter's assets in 1961. However, Crompton (D) knew the basic facts surrounding the manufacture and delivery of the machine no later than October 1, 1971, and possibly much earlier, when it filed answers to David's (P) interrogatories. The proferred reason for this delay, i.e., Crompton's (D) recent discovery that it was not liable for liabilities of Hunter, cannot be considered good cause. The effect of the delay could be highly prejudicial to David (P). The two-year statute of limitations has expired and David (P) is now barred from instituting this action against another party. To allow amendment would be to prejudice David (P), who is without fault, and leave him without a possible remedy for very serious injuries. Therefore, Crompton's (D) motion to amend is denied.

EDITOR'S ANALYSIS: In James v. McCloskey & Co., 40 F.R.D. 486 (E.D. Pa., 1966), cited by the court in the above case, the district court allowed a defendant to amend its answer to deny ownership of a building belonging to its wholly-owned subsidiary. The effect of the amendment was to deny recovery from one defendant since the statute of limitations had run. The action had been filed just nine days before the expiration of the statute and the answer was not filed until after the statute had run. The court in Jacobs allowed this defendant to amend because the plaintiff, unlike David (P), did not suffer any prejudice.

[For more information on permission to amend pleadings, see Casenote Law Outline on Civil Procedure, Chapter 5, § VII, Amendments to Pleadings.]

NOTES:

SWARTZ v. GOLD DUST CASINO, INC.
91 F.R.D. 543 (D. Nev. 1981).

NATURE OF CASE: Motion for summary judgment in action for damages for personal injury.

FACT SUMMARY: Cavanaugh (D), added as a defendant after the statute of limitations had run, had been aware of the action prior to his addition.

CONCISE RULE OF LAW: When a newly added defendant has been aware of litigation, the statute of limitations may not apply to him.

FACTS: Swartz (P) slipped and fell down a stairway. She sued Gold Dust Casino, Inc. (D), lessee of the premises where the fall occurred. The complaint alleged negligent maintenance. Upon discovering a basis for an allegation of defective construction, Swartz (P) amended the complaint to add Cavanaugh (D), a partner in the partnership owning the building. Cavanaugh (D) was also president of Gold Dust Casino, Inc. (D). Cavanaugh's (D) addition was after the statute of limitations had run. Cavanaugh (D) moved for summary judgment.

ISSUE: When a newly added defendant has been aware of a litigation, will the statute of limitations necessarily apply to him?

HOLDING AND DECISION: (Reed, J.) No. When a newly added defendant has been aware of a litigation, the statute of limitations may not apply to him. Under Fed. R. Civ. P. 15, an amendment adding a new defendant will relate back to the original filing date if the new defendant's potential liability arises out of the same transaction as that of which the complaint is originally made, the new defendant was aware of the original litigation before the limitations period ran, and the new defendant knew or should have known that he was a proper defendant. When these conditions are met, the statute of limitations will not bar the addition of a new defendant. As to the second condition, formal notice is not necessary. Real notice of any kind will suffice. Here, Cavanaugh (D), as president of Gold Dust Casino (D), certainly had notice of the suit. The other conditions appearing to be met, the addition of Cavanaugh (D) relates back, and the statute of limitations is inapplicable. Motion denied.

EDITOR'S ANALYSIS: Many jurisdictions permit plaintiffs to add fictitious-name defendants, commonly referred to as "Does." Technically, this is not authorized under the Federal Rules. However, the rules regarding the addition of new defendants are functionally similar.

[For more information on amendments adding new parties, see Casenote Law Outline on Civil Procedure, Chapter 5, § VII, Amendments to Pleadings.]

NOTES:

CHAPTER 4
ESTABLISHING THE STRUCTURE AND SIZE OF THE DISPUTE

QUICK REFERENCE RULES OF LAW

1. **The Capacity to Sue.** As a partial subrogor, a "real party in interest" under Fed. R. Civ. P. 17 can bring suit against a defendant without joining the subrogee, and a motion for joinder by the defendant, although appropriate, will not be granted for the purpose of destroying diversity jurisdiction and requiring dismissal of the subrogor's action. (Virginia Electric & Power Co. v. Westinghouse Electric Corp.)

   [For more information on the capacity to sue, see Casenote Law Outline on Civil Procedure, Chapter 4, § VII, Federal Venue.]

2. **The Form of Pleading.** Plaintiffs in a gender discrimination action under Title VII of the Civil Rights Act may not proceed anonymously. (Southern Methodist University Ass'n of Women Law Students v. Wynne & Jaffe)

   [For more information on the form of pleading, see Casenote Law Outline on Civil Procedure, Chapter 5, § V, Answers.]

3. **Rules of Joinder.** The fact that certain claims and parties relevant thereto span a lengthy period of time will not, in itself, prevent joinder. (Kedra v. City of Philadelphia)

   [For more information on rules of joinder, see Casenote Law Outline on Civil Procedure, Chapter 6, § I, Joinder of Claims.]

4. **Permissive Joinder.** A party may not join as a defendant a party who has not had an effect upon him. (Cohen v. District of Columbia National Bank)

   [For more information on permissive joinder, see Casenote Law Outline on Civil Procedure, Chapter 6, § II, Joinder of Parties.]

5. **Compulsory Joinder.** If a contract imposes joint and several liability on its co-obligors, complete relief can be granted in a suit when only one of the co-obligors has been joined as a defendant. (Janney Montgomery Scott, Inc. v. Shepard Niles, Inc.)

   [For more information on compulsory joinder, see Casenote Law Outline on Civil Procedure, Chapter 6, § I, Joinder of Claims.]

6. **Impleader.** Under Fed. R. Civ. P. 14, impleader is proper only if the third-party defendant is or may be liable to the third-party plaintiff for all or part of the plaintiff's claims against the third-party plaintiff. (Clark v. Associates Commerical Corp.)

   [For more information on impleader, see Casenote Law Outline on Civil Procedure, Chapter 6, § III, Joinder of Additional Parties.]

7. **Statutory Interpleader.** Insurance companies can invoke the federal interpleader before claims against them have been reduced to judgment. A party to a multiparty litigation can only interplead the claimants seeking the funds of that party. (State Farm Fire & Casualty Co. v. Tashire)

   [For more information on statutory interpleader, see Casenote Law Outline on Civil Procedure, Chapter 6, § IV, Additional Procedural Devices for Joinder of Parties.]

8. **Intervenors as of Right.** A party may intervene in an action under Fed. R. Civ. P. 24(a)(2) if he has an interest upon which the disposition of that action will have a significant legal effect. (Natural Resources Defense Council, Inc. v. U.S. Nuclear Regulatory Committee)

[For more information on intervenors as of right, see Casenote Law Outline on Civil Procedure, Chapter 6, § V, Supplemental Jurisdiction in Aid of Liberal Joinder in the Federal Courts.]

9. **Intervention as of Right.** An economic interest in an outcome of a litigation is not sufficient to permit intervention as of right. (New Orleans Public Service, Inc. v. United Gas Pipe Line Co.)

[For more information on intervention as of right, see Casenote Law Outline on Civil Procedure, Chapter 6, § V, Supplemental Jurisdiction in Aid of Liberal Joinder in the Federal Courts.]

10. **Class Actions.** There must be adequate representation of the members of a class action or the judgment is not binding on the parties not adequately represented. (Hansberry v. Lee)

[For more information on class actions, see Casenote Law Outline on Civil Procedure, Chapter 6, § IV, Additional Procedural Devices for Joinder of Parties.]

11. **Class Actions.** The prerequisites of a class action are that (1) the class is so numerous that joinder of all members is impracticable; (2) there are questions of law or fact common to the class; (3) the claims or defenses of the representative parties are typical of the claims or defenses of the class; and (4) the representative parties will fairly and adequately protect the interests of the class. (Holland v. Steele)

[For more information on class actions, see Casenote Law Outline on Civil Procedure, Chapter 6, § IV, Additional Procedural Devices for Joinder of Parties.]

12. **Class Certification.** When appropriate, a class may be certified for resolution of a relevant issue. (Jenkins v. Raymark Industries, Inc.)

[For more information on class certification, see Casenote Law Outline on Civil Procedure, Chapter 6, § IV, Additional Procedural Devices for Joinder of Parties.]

13. **Class Certification.** Fed. R. Civ. P. 23(c)(2) requires that, in any class action, individual notice of the pendency of such action must be given to all class members who can be identified through reasonable efforts, and the cost of such notice must be borne by the prospective class representative (i.e., plaintiff). (Eisen v. Carlisle and Jacquelin)

[For more information on notice to class members, see Casenote Law Outline on Civil Procedure, Chapter 6, § IV, Additional Procedural Devices for Joinder of Parties.]

VIRGINIA ELECTRIC & POWER CO. v.
WESTINGHOUSE ELECTRIC CORP.
485 F.2d 78 (4th Cir. 1973).

NATURE OF CASE: Interlocutory appeal from denial of a motion to dismiss.

FACT SUMMARY: By agreement, Insurance Company of North America was subrogated to the rights of its insured, Virginia Electric (P), so Westinghouse (D) claimed it was the "real party in interest" that had to file the action.

CONCISE RULE OF LAW: As a partial subrogor, a "real party in interest" under Fed. R. Civ. P. 17 can bring suit against a defendant without joining the subrogee, and a motion for joinder by the defendant, although appropriate, will not be granted for the purpose of destroying diversity jurisdiction and requiring dismissal of the subrogor's action.

FACTS: When one of the power generating stations built by Westinghouse (D) and Storie and Webster (D) failed, Virginia Electric (P) made a settlement agreement with its insurer, Insurance Company of North America (INA), that resulted in INA's paying $1.95 million of the damage, leaving Virginia Electric (P) with an unreimbursed loss of $150,000. Furthermore, INA was to furnish counsel, prosecute the claims for the uninsured loss remaining, have exclusive control over the suit, and be subrogated to the rights of Virginia Electric (P). Westinghouse (D) claimed that INA was the "real party in interest," that it, therefore, had to bring the action, and that it could not maintain diversify jurisdiction so that the action should be dismissed. It also argued that INA was an indispensable person that could not be made a party, as that would destroy diversity jurisdiction, so a dismissal was called for. Motion for dismissal was denied, and an interlocutory appeal was granted.

ISSUE: Is a partial subrogor a "real party in interest" so that he may bring an action in his own name without joining the subrogee?

HOLDING AND DECISION: (Craven, J.) Yes. Because a partial subrogor is a "real party in interest" under Fed. R. Civ. P. 17, he may bring an action in his own name without joining the subrogee, and an otherwise appropriate motion for joinder of the subrogee, by the defendant, will not be granted for the purpose of destroying diversity jurisdiction and requiring dismissal of the subrogor's suit. Rule 17, which now functions primarily to protect defendants against a multiplicity of suits, allows an action to be brought by anyone who possesses the right to enforce the claim and who has a significant interest in the litigation, which covers both subrogor and subrogee. Here, the subrogor, Virginia Electric (P), still has an unreimbursed loss and a significant interest in the litigation, and INA is clearly precluded from subjecting Westinghouse (D) to further suits. Thus, Virginia Electric (P) can maintain the present suit. INA, as partial subrogee, is a person to be joined, if feasible, under Rule 19. It is not feasible to join INA and destroy diversity jurisdiction, but since INA is not an indispensable party, that is not fatal to this action. Denial of motion affirmed.

EDITOR'S ANALYSIS: Knowing of the prejudices involved when a big insurance company sues in its own name, insurers developed ways of avoiding having to do so. One was to "loan" the insured the money he would recover under his policy in return for an agreement to sue in his own name and repay the loan only from proceeds from the suit.

[For more information on the capacity to sue, see Casenote Law Outline on Civil Procedure, Chapter 4, § VII, Federal Venue.]

NOTES:

SOUTHERN METHODIST UNIVERSITY ASSOCIATION OF WOMEN LAW STUDENTS v. WYNNE AND JAFFE

599 F.2d 707 (6th Cir. 1979).

NATURE OF CASE: Appeal of pretrial order in gender discrimination action.

FACT SUMMARY: Various plaintiffs in a gender discrimination action under Title VII of the Civil Rights Act wished to proceed anonymously.

CONCISE RULE OF LAW: Plaintiffs in a gender discrimination action under Title VII of the Civil Rights Act may not proceed anonymously.

FACTS: Various individuals and entities brought an action under Title VII of the 1964 Civil Rights Act against various Dallas-area law firms for alleged gender bias. Several individual plaintiffs sued anonymously. Several defendants moved to compel disclosure of their true names. The trial court ordered disclosure, and an interlocutory appeal was taken.

ISSUE: May plaintiffs in a gender discrimination action under Title VII of the Civil Rights Act proceed anonymously?

HOLDING AND DECISION: (Ainsworth, J.) No. Plaintiffs in a gender-based discrimination action under Title VII of the Civil Rights Act may not proceed anonymously. Fed. R. Civ. P. 10(a) provides that an action shall contain the names of the parties. There is no specific exception to this in Title VII. Courts have carved out an exception to this rule in certain types of cases involving particularly private matters, such as abortion. However, a gender discrimination action does not fall within such a category, particularly one against a private party under Title VII. Since no particularly private matter is involved in such an action, the usual rule of Fed. R. Civ. P. 10(a) must be followed. Affirmed.

EDITOR'S ANALYSIS: Parties are names anonymously or fictitiously for a variety of reasons. Rarely will plaintiffs be granted anonymity for reasons of privacy, as the court stated herein. Fictitiously named defendants usually are anonymous due to lack of knowledge on the part of a plaintiff as to their true identities.

[For more information on the form of pleading, see Casenote Law Outline on Civil Procedure, Chapter 5, § V, Answers.]

KEDRA v. CITY OF PHILADELPHIA

454 F. Supp. 652 (E.D. Pa. 1978).

NATURE OF CASE: Motion to dismiss for improper joinder in civil rights action.

FACT SUMMARY: Kedra (P), suing for civil rights violations, joined parties and claims spanning a lengthy period of time.

CONCISE RULE OF LAW: The fact that certain claims and parties relevant thereto span a lengthy period of time will not, in itself, prevent joinder.

FACTS: Kedra (P) and her children filed a civil rights action against the City of Philadelphia (D), stemming from an alleged series of incidents constituting police brutality. The incidents involved various individuals over a 15-month period. Several defendants moved to dismiss, contending that joinder had been improper due to the expansive length of time involved.

ISSUE: Will the fact that certain claims and parties relevant thereto span a lengthy period of time in itself prevent joinder?

HOLDING AND DECISION: (Luongo, J.) No. The fact that certain claims and parties thereto span a lengthy period of time will not in itself prevent joinder. The joinder provisions of the Federal Rules are very liberal. The impulse is toward entertaining the broadest possible scope of action consistent with fairness to the parties. As long as a claim or party is "reasonably related" to the main claim, joinder will be appropriate. Here, even though the various acts of which complaint is made span a considerable period of time, they are part of an alleged pattern. Consequently, sufficient relationship for joinder exists. Motion denied.

EDITOR'S ANALYSIS: Joinder rules often interact with jurisdictional mandates. State-law claims are often joined to the claim brought in federal court, even though they could not originally have been brought there. This is known as "pendant jurisdiction."

[For more information on rules of joinder, see Casenote Law Outline on Civil Procedure, Chapter 6, § I, Joinder of Claims.]

COHEN v. DISTRICT OF COLUMBIA NATIONAL BANK
59 F.R.D. 84 (D.D.C. 1972).

NATURE OF CASE: Motion to join new parties in a usury/antitrust action.

FACT SUMMARY: In a usury/antitrust action, Cohen (P) sought to join defendants with whom he had not had contact.

CONCISE RULE OF LAW: A party may not join as a defendant a party who has not had an effect upon him.

FACTS: Cohen (P), contending that certain loan practices of banks from whom he had borrowed constituted usury and antitrust law violations, brought suit. He then moved to join as defendants all banks in the District of Columbia, which had the allegedly improper practices, even though he had never borrowed money from these institutions.

ISSUE: May a party join as a defendant a party who has not had an effect upon him?

HOLDING AND DECISION: (Gasch, J.) No. A party may not join as a defendant a party who has not had an effect on him. It is elementary that plaintiffs may not join a defendant for the purpose of asserting a claim which is not the claim of a named plaintiff. A plaintiff must have a right to relief against a defendant before that defendant may be joined. Here, Cohen (P) has never borrowed from any bank he wished to join as a defendant, and consequently he has no right to relief against them. Motion denied.

EDITOR'S ANALYSIS: Permissive joinder is dealt with in Fed. R. Civ. P. 20. The Rule permits joinder of all parties involved in a transaction or series of transactions. Although the Rule is liberal, as the present case illustrates, it has its limits.

[For more information on permissive joinder, see Casenote Law Outline on Civil Procedure, Chapter 6, § II, Joinder of Parties.]

NOTES:

JANNEY MONTGOMERY SCOTT, INC. v. SHEPARD NILES, INC.
11 F.3d 399 (3d Cir. 1993).

NATURE OF CASE: Appeal from grant of motion for judgment on the pleadings in a breach of contract action.

FACT SUMMARY: Shepard Niles (D) moved to dismiss for failure to join Underwood, its parent and co-obligor to the contract Janney Montgomery Scott, Inc. (P) sued on, on the ground that Underwood was both necessary and indispensable under Rule 19.

CONCISE RULE OF LAW: If a contract imposes joint and several liability on its co-obligors, complete relief can be granted in a suit when only one of the co-obligors has been joined as a defendant.

FACTS: Janney (P), an investment banking corporation, entered into an investment banking agreement with Underwood, a closely held corporation. Janney (P) agreed to serve as an advisor to Underwood and its subsidiaries, including Niles (D), and to assist them in obtaining private placement financing to refinance Niles' (D) debt obligations. Later, when Janney's (P) efforts had yet to show results, Underwood negotiated with Unibank to provide private placement financing that Niles (D) needed. Janney (P) did not introduce Unibank to Underwood, but Janney (P) alleged that it provided substantial advice and support to Underwood and Niles (D) throughout the negotiations. Janney (P) contended that under its agreement with Underwood, this advice and support entitled it to a contingent fee which it sought, unsuccessfully, to recover from Niles (D). Janney (P) filed a breach of contract action against Underwood in state court. Janney (P) then filed a breach of contract action against Niles (D) in federal district court. Niles (D) moved for judgment on the pleadings based on Janney's (P) failure to join Underwood as an indispensable party. The district court granted Niles' (D) motion and Janney (P) appealed.

ISSUE: Can complete relief be granted in a suit when only one of two co-obligors to a contract has been joined as a defendant?

HOLDING AND DECISION: (Hutchinson, J.) Yes. If a contract imposes joint and several liability on its co-obligors, complete relief can be granted in a suit when only one of the co-obligors has been joined as a defendant. Fed. R. Civ. P. 19 determines when joinder of a party is compulsory. A court must first determine whether a party should be joined if "feasible" under Rule 19(a). If the party should be joined but joinder is not feasible because it would destroy diversity, the court must then determine whether the absent party is "indispensable" under Rule 19(b). If the party is indispensable, the action cannot go forward. Analysis of whether joinder is "feasible," i.e., which parties are "necessary"under Rule 19(a), is a multi-step process. Under Rule 19(a), the court must inquire whether complete relief can be given to the parties to the action in the absence of the unjoined party. Rule 19(a)(1) inquires whether complete relief can be granted to the persons who are already parties to the action. Here, because there is a strong trend in favor of the principle that co-obligors on a contract are jointly and severally liable for its performance and the agreement between Niles (D) and Underwood as co-obligors can be construed to be joint and several liability, Underwood is not a necessary party under Rule 19 (a)(1). Though the district court did not hold Underwood to be a necessary party under Rule 19(a)(1), it did conclude that Underwood's joinder was compulsory under Rule 19(a)(2)(i) and 19(a)(2)(ii). Rule 19(a)(2)(i) requires a court to decide whether determination of the right of present parties would impair an absent party's ability to protect its interest in the subject matter of the litigation. Here, the district court held that Underwood was a necessary party because any decision in the federal action would be a persuasive precedent against Underwood in the ongoing state action. On the contrary, however, Underwood, a co-obligor, is not a party whose joinder Rule 19(a)(2)(i) requires because continuation of the federal litigation in Underwood's absence will not create a precedent that might persuade another court to rule against Underwood on principles of stare decisis or some other unidentified basis not encompassed by the rules of collateral estoppel or issue preclusion. The district court erred in holding that the mere possibility that its decision in the present action would be a "persuasive precedent" in any subsequent state action against Underwood could impair Underwood's interest under Rule 19(a)(2)(i). Therefore, Underwood is not an absent party whose joinder is compulsory, if feasible, under Rule 19(a)(2)(i). Rule 19(a)(2)(ii) asks whether continuation of this action in the absence of Underwood would expose Niles (D) to the substantial risk of incurring double or inconsistent obligations by reason of the claimed interest. The district court answered in the affirmative because Niles (D) could be found liable under the agreement in the federal action while Underwood may be found liable in the state court action that Janney (P) has filed against it. The possibility that Niles (D) may bear the whole loss if it is found liable is not the equivalent of double or inconsistent liability. It is instead the common result of joint and several liability and should not be equated with prejudice. Inherent in the concept of joint and several liability is the right of a plaintiff to satisfy its whole judgment by execution against any one of multiple defendants who are liable to him, thereby forcing the debtor who has paid to protect itself by an action for contribution against the other joint obligors. Niles (D) is free to implead Underwood, using Fed. R. Civ. P. 14, to assert its claim for contribution or indemnity upon principles of restitution if it is ultimately found liable to Janney (P). The continuation of this case in the absence of Underwood does not subject Niles (D) to double or inconsistent liabilities. Therefore, Underwood is not a necessary party under Rule 19(a)(2)(ii). To summarize, Underwood's joinder is not necessary under Rule 19(a)(1) because the district court can give complete relief to Janney (P) and Niles (D) in this action. It is thus unnecessary to decide whether the district court abused its discretion when it decided that Underwood was an indispensable party under Rule 19(b). Reversed.

EDITOR'S ANALYSIS: Note that Niles (D), not Underwood, filed the Rule 12(c) motion for judgment on the pleadings for failure to join Underwood as an indispensable party. This is because Underwood, as an absent party, did not have status to object to its nonjoinder, and

Continued on next page

34

therefore, must rely on Niles (D), as the defendant, to protect its interests. Alternatively, Underwood might have utilized one of two devices to join the suit and achieve the same result — intervention or interpleader.

[For more information on compulsory joinder, see Casenote Law Outline on Civil Procedure, Chapter 6, § I, Joinder of Claims.]

NOTES:

CLARK v. ASSOCIATES COMMERCIAL CORP.
149 F.R.D. 629 (D. of Kan., 1993).

NATURE OF CASE: Motion to dismiss a third-party complaint in an action in tort and contract for damages to person and property.

FACT SUMMARY: After Clark (P) sued Associates Commercial Corp. (D) for damages to his person and property when Associates' (D) employee repossessed Clark's (P) tractor, Associates (D) brought a third-party complaint seeking indemnity against the employee and two assistants who had effected the repossession.

CONCISE RULE OF LAW: Under Fed. R. Civ. P. 14, impleader is proper only if the third-party defendant is or may be liable to the third-party plaintiff for all or part of the plaintiff's claims against the third-party plaintiff.

FACTS: Clark (P) brought an action against Associates (D) for damages to his person and property when Associates's (D) agents repossessed by force a tractor that was collateral for a loan that Associates (D) had made to Clark (P). Clark (P) alleged causes of action in tort and contract (by negative implication in the security agreement prohibiting the secured party from proceeding contrary to a plaintiff's rights under the Uniform Commercial Code (U.C.C.)). Associates (D) then filed a third-party complaint seeking indemnity from its agents who had effected the repossession. Associates (D) alleged that it hired Howard, one of the third-party defendants, and Howard, without Associates's (D) knowledge, hired two other persons to help with the repossession. Howard and the other third-party defendants then moved to dismiss Associates's (D) third-party complaint and Clark (P) moved to strike the third-party complaint, or in the alternative, for a separate trial of the issues it raised.

ISSUE: Under Fed. R. Civ. P. 14, is impleader proper only if the third-party defendant is or may be liable to the third-party plaintiff for all or part of the plaintiff's claims against the third-party plaintiff?

HOLDING AND DECISION: (Belot, J.) Yes. Under Fed. R. Civ. P. 14, impleader is proper only if the third-party defendant is or may be liable to the third-party plaintiff for all or part of the plaintiff's claims against the third-party plaintiff. Here, the third-party defendants, Howard et al., allege that Associates' (D) claim is based on "implied indemnity," which is no longer recognized in Kansas. They note that under the Kansas comparative fault statute, each defendant is liable only in proportion to his relative fault. Because impleader is proper only if the party has a right to relief under the governing substantive law, the third-party defendants contend that Associates (D) has no valid claim for indemnity against them. However, the basis for Associates' (D) indemnity claim against the third-party defendants is an agency theory, whereby Associates (D) seeks to hold its alleged agents liable for any amounts that Associates (D) is found liable to Clark (P). The State of Kansas continues to recognize the right of an employer to seek indemnity against his employees for liability resulting from the employees' tortious acts. Thus, Associates (D) has properly impleaded the third-party defendants. Clark (P) also opposes

Associates's (D) third-party complaint, arguing that his claims against Associates (D) are based upon duties imposed under the U.C.C. and by contract, and thus, third-party defendants have "no duty" under the contract between Clark (P) and Associates (D). But, a proper third-party complaint does not depend upon the existence of a duty on the parts of the third-party defendants toward the plaintiff. Also, a third-party defendant need not be necessarily liable over to the third-party plaintiff in the event the third-party plaintiff is found liable toward plaintiff. Although Rule 14 does not allow a defendant to assert an independent claim for relief from a liability that does not arise out of the plaintiff's claim against the defendant, Rule 14(a) expressly allows impleader of a person who is or may be liable to the third-party plaintiff for all or part of the plaintiff's claim against the third-party plaintiff. The third-party claim need not be based on the same theory as the main claim, and impleader is proper even though Howard's liability is not automatically established once Associates' (D) liability to Clark (P) has been determined. Therefore, Associates (D) has stated a valid claim for indemnity against the third-party defendants. Motion denied.

EDITOR'S ANALYSIS: The impleader suit is rooted historically in a common law practice called "vouching to warranty." Under the common law, if a person holding title to land came under attack regarding the validity of the title, he could "vouch in" his grantor because the grantor had warranted the title. The grantor then might or might not take part in the action, but would be bound by the outcome of the action if he was later sued by the grantee. Vouching warranty is rarely used today because two lawsuits must necessarily take place. Like vouching in warranty, impleader is used to resolve like questions of fact and law, but accomplishes it in one lawsuit without delay or inconsistent results.

[For more information on impleader, see Casenote Law Outline on Civil Procedure, Chapter 6, § III, Joinder of Additional Parties.]

NOTES:

STATE FARM FIRE & CAS. CO. v. TASHIRE
386 U.S. 523 (1967).

NATURE OF CASE: Action in the nature of an interpleader in a tort action.

FACT SUMMARY: State Farm (P) insured three individuals involved in a collision involving a Greyhound bus and attempted to interplead all claimants.

CONCISE RULE OF LAW: Insurance companies can invoke the federal interpleader before claims against them have been reduced to judgment. A party to a multiparty litigation can only interplead the claimants seeking the funds of that party.

FACTS: In September 1964, a Greyhound bus collided with a pickup truck in northern California. Two of the passengers aboard the bus were killed; 33 others were injured, as were the bus driver and the driver of the truck and its passenger. Four of the injured passengers filed suit in California state courts seeking damages in excess of $1 million. Greyhound, the bus driver, the driver of the truck, and the owner of the truck, who was the passenger in the truck, were named as defendants. Before these cases could come to trial, State Farm (P) brought this action in the nature of interpleader in the U.S. District Court for the District of Oregon. State Farm (P) had in force an insurance policy with respect to the driver of the truck providing for bodily injury liability up to $10,000 per person and $20,000 per occurrence. State Farm (P) asserted that claims already filed against it far exceeded its maximum amount of liability under the policy. It paid the $20,000 into the court and asked that the court require all claimants to establish their claims against the driver of the truck in this single proceeding and in no other. State Farm (P) named Greyhound, the bus driver, the driver of the truck, the owner of the truck, and each of the prospective claimants as defendants. Tashire (D) moved to have this action dismissed and, in the alternative, for a change of venue to the Northern District of California. The court refused to dismiss the action and granted the injunction that State Farm (P) had wanted, which provided that all suits against the driver of the pickup truck, State Farm (P), Greyhound, and the bus driver be prosecuted in the interpleader proceeding. On interlocutory appeal, the Ninth Circuit Court of Appeals reversed the district court's decision. They ruled that an insurance company may not invoke the federal interpleader until the claims against it have been reduced to judgment. The case was then appealed to the Supreme Court.

ISSUE: Can insurance companies invoke the federal interpleader before the claims against them have been reduced to judgment?

HOLDING AND DECISION: (Fortas, J.) Yes. The Supreme Court ruled that the 1948 revision of the Judicial Code made clear that insurance companies do not have to wait until claims against them have been reduced to judgment before making use of the federal interpleader. Even though State Farm (P) had properly invoked the federal interpleader, it was not entitled to an injunction enjoining prosecution of suits against it outside the confines of the interpleader proceeding and also extending the same protection to its insured, the alleged tortfeasor. Greyhound (D) was even less entitled to have

the order expanded to require all actions to be brought against it and its driver to be brought in the interpleader proceeding. State Farm's (P) interest in this case is protected when the court restrains claimants from seeking to enforce against the insurance company any judgment obtained against its insured, except in the interpleader proceeding itself. State Farm (P) shouldn't be allowed to determine where dozens of tort plaintiffs must bring their claims. The interpleader was not made to force all the litigants in multiparty litigation to bring their actions in a particular court. Interpleader is to control the allocation of a fund among successful tort plaintiffs and not to control the underlying litigation against alleged tortfeasors. The decision of the court of appeals was reversed, and the district court was to modify the injunction prohibiting the bringing of all other actions connected with the accident in any court except the interpleader proceedings. The injunction should only restrain claimants from seeking to enforce against the insurance company any judgment obtained against its insured, except in the interpleader proceeding itself.

EDITOR'S ANALYSIS: This case points up the general nature of federal interpleader. Generally, the interpleader device allows a party to join all adverse claimants asserting several mutually exclusive claims (regarding the same property or debt) against him and require them to litigate to determine their own interests. Note that there are two types of federal interpleader. Rule 22 interpleader, limited by normal federal jurisdiction (e.g., federal question greater than $10,000, diversity of citizenship) venue and procedure requirements is available to any so qualified parties who may be exposed to multiple liability if not permitted to interplead. 28 U.S.C. § 1335 interpleader (statutory) is more liberal as to jurisdiction than most federal rules and requires: (1) diversity of citizenship; (2) greater than only $500 be involved; and (3) payment into the court of bond. Perhaps the greatest advantage of § 1335 interpleader, however, is "nationwide service of process."

[For more information on statutory interpleader, see Casenote Law Outline on Civil Procedure, Chapter 6, § IV, Additional Procedural Devices for Joinder of Parties.]

NOTES:

NATURAL RESOURCES DEFENSE COUNCIL, INC. v. UNITED STATES NUCLEAR REGULATORY COMMISSION
578 F. 2d 1341 (10th Cir. 1978).

NATURE OF CASE: Appeal of denial of motion to intervene.

FACT SUMMARY: The American Mining Congress (AMC) and Kerr-McGee (KM) appealed the denial of their motion to intervene in an action brought by the Natural Resources Defense Council (NRDC) (P) against the Nuclear Regulatory Commission (NRC) (D) seeking a declaration that state-granted nuclear power operation licenses are subject to the requirement of filing an environmental impact statement and seeking an injunction of the grant of one such license by the New Mexico Environmental Improvement Agency (NMEIA).

CONCISE RULE OF LAW: A party may intervene in an action under Fed. R. Civ. P. 24(a)(2) if he has an interest upon which the disposition of that action will have a significant legal effect.

FACTS: The NRC (D) was permitted by federal law to give the several states the power to grant licenses to operate nuclear power facilities. The NRC (D) was also empowered to grant such licenses subject to a requirement that such "major federal action" be preceded by the preparation of an environmental impact statement. The NRC (D) entered into an agreement with NMEIA permitting it to issue a license, which it did, to United Nuclear without preparing an impact statement. NRDC (P) brought this action, seeking a declaration that state-granted licenses are the product of "major federal action" and subject to the statement requirement and seeking an injunction against the issuance of the license. United Nuclear intervened without objection. KM, a potential recipient of an NMEIA license, and MAC, a public interest group, sought to intervene, but their motions were denied. Both appealed.

ISSUE: May a party intervene in an action under Fed. R. Civ. P. 24(a)(2) if he has an interest upon which the disposition of that action will have a significant legal effect?

HOLDING AND DECISION: (Doyle, J.) Yes. Fed. R. Civ. P. 24(a) gives a party the right to intervene when he has a sufficiently protectable interest related to the property or transaction which is the subject of the action and the disposition will "as a practical matter, impair or impede his ability to protect that interest." The argument that the effect upon the movant's right must be a res judicata effect is unpersuasive. The effect must "as a practical matter" impair or impede the ability to protect the right. A party may thus intervene in an action under Fed. R. Civ. P. 24(a)(2) if he has an interest upon which the disposition of that action will have a significant legal effect. It need not be a strictly legal effect. KM and MAC each have rights, not protected by other parties to the litigation, which will be thus effected, and they must be allowed to intervene. Reversed and remanded.

EDITOR'S ANALYSIS: Fed. R. Civ. P. 24(a) covers the intervention of right, while Rule 24(b) sets forth criteria for permissive intervention. Intervention is permissive if there is a common question of law or fact or if a statute gives a conditional right to intervene. In either case, an intervenor has the same status in the litigation as an original party, but he cannot raise any new issues. Ancillary jurisdiction attaches over the intervenor.

[For more information on intervenors as of right, see Casenote Law Outline on Civil Procedure, Chapter 6, § V, Supplemental Jurisdiction in Aid of Liberal Joinder in the Federal Courts.]

NOTES:

NEW ORLEANS PUBLIC SERVICE, INC. v. UNITED GAS PIPE LINE COMPANY
732 F.2d 452 (5th Cir. 1984).

NATURE OF CASE: Appeal of order denying plaintiff intervention in a breach of contract action.

FACT SUMMARY: Officials of the City of New Orleans sought to intervene in a contract dispute between the city's electricity supplier and its fuel supplier due to the city's economic interest in the outcome.

CONCISE RULE OF LAW: An economic interest in an outcome of a litigation is not sufficient to permit intervention as of right.

FACTS: New Orleans Public Service, Inc. (P) supplied electricity to the City of New Orleans. It brought a breach of contract action against the supplier of fuel used to operate its electrical generators, United Gas Pipe Line Company (D). Officials of the city moved to intervene as party plaintiffs, contending an economic interest in the success of the litigation. The district court denied intervention both permissively and as of right. The Fifth Circuit affirmed as to the denial as of right but reversed as to permissive intervention. The Fifth Circuit granted a rehearing en banc.

ISSUE: Is an economic interest in an outcome of a litigation sufficient to permit intervention as of right?

HOLDING AND DECISION: (Garwood, J.) No. An economic interest in an outcome of a litigation is not sufficient to permit intervention as of right. Fed. R. Civ. P. 24(a)(2), which governs intervention, and the cases thereunder make it clear that intervention as of right requires an interest in the litigation which is not only direct and substantial but legally protectable as well. A mere economic interest in the litigation will not suffice. A definable, protectable legal interest must be involved. Here, while the city has an economic interest in minimizing costs to New Orleans Public Service, Inc. (P), the litigation involves a breach of a contract to which the city is not a party. Therefore, the city does not have a protectable legal interest. [The court went on to reverse the panel decision as to permissive intervention, reinstating the district court's holding.]

DISSENT: (Williams, J.) The city and its citizens will be profoundly affected by the outcome of this litigation. Since no showing of prejudice to either litigant in the event of intervention has been made, permissive intervention should have been granted.

EDITOR'S ANALYSIS: The standard of review for a grant or denial of permissive intervention is one of abuse of discretion. The majority found the appellate panel to have overreached in its reversal of the district court. Finding the city's interests to be adequately represented by New Orleans Public Service (P), the court held that the district court legitimately denied permissive intervention.

[For more information on intervention as of right, see Casenote Law Outline on Civil Procedure, Chapter 6, § V, Supplemental Jurisdiction in Aid of Liberal Joinder in the Federal Courts.]

NOTES:

HANSBERRY v. LEE
311 U.S. 32 (1940).

NATURE OF CASE: A class action to enforce a racially restrictive covenant.

FACT SUMMARY: Lee (P) sought to enjoin a sale of land to Hansberry (D) on the grounds that the sale violated a racially restrictive covenant.

CONCISE RULE OF LAW: There must be adequate representation of the members of a class action or the judgment is not binding on the parties not adequately represented.

FACTS: Hansberry (D), a black, purchased land from a party who had signed a restrictive covenant forbidding the sale of the land to blacks. Lee (P), one of the parties who signed the covenant, sought to have the sale enjoined because it breached the covenant, contending that the validity of the covenant was established in a prior case in which one of the parties was a class of landowners involved with the covenant. To be valid, 95% of the landowners had to sign the covenant, and the trial court in the prior case held that 95% of the landowners had signed the covenant. That case was appealed, and the Illinois Supreme Court upheld the decision, even though it found that 95% of the landowners had not signed the covenant, but it held that since it was a class action, all members of the class would be bound by the decision of the court. Hansberry (D) claimed that he and the party selling him the house were not bound by the res judicata effect of the prior decision, as they were not parties to the litigation. The lower court held that the decision of the Illinois Supreme Court would have to be challenged directly in order that it be set aside or reversed. Otherwise, its decision was still binding. The case was appealed to the U.S. Supreme Court.

ISSUE: For a judgment in a class action to be binding, must all of the members of the class be adequately represented by parties with similar interests?

HOLDING AND DECISION: (Stone, J.) Yes. It is not necessary that all members of a class be present as parties to the litigation to be bound by the judgment if they are adequately represented by parties who are present. In regular cases, to be bound by the judgment the party must receive notice and an opportunity to be heard. If due process isn't afforded the individual, then the judgment is not binding. The class action is an exception to the general rule. Because of the numbers involved in class actions, it is enough if the party is adequately represented by a member of the class with a similar interest. Hansberry (D) was not adequately represented by the class of landowners. Their interests were not similar enough to even be considered members of the same class. Lee (P) and the landowners were trying to restrict blacks from buying any of the land, and Hansberry (D) was a black man attempting to purchase land. When there is such a conflicting interest between members of a class, there is most likely not adequate representation of one of the members of the class. There must be a similarity of interest before there can even be a class. Since there was no similarity of interests between Lee (P) and Hansberry (D), Hansberry (D) could not be considered a member of the class, and so the prior judgment was not binding on Hansberry (D). Hansberry (D) was not afforded due process because of the lack of adequate representation. Reversed.

EDITOR'S ANALYSIS: Rule 23(c)(3) requires that the court describe those whom the court finds to be members of the class. The court is to note those to whom notice was provided and also those who had not requested exclusion. These members are considered members of the class and are bound by the decision of the court whether it is in their favor or not. The federal rules allow a member of the class to request exclusion from the class, and that party will not be bound by the decision of the court. Since a party must receive notice of the class action before he can request exclusion from the class, the court must determine if a party received sufficient notice of the action or if sufficient effort was made to notify him of the action. The rules state if the court finds that the party did have sufficient notice and was considered a member of the class, he is bound by the decision.

[For more information on class actions, see Casenote Law Outline on Civil Procedure, Chapter 6, § IV, Additional Procedural Devices for Joinder of Parties.]

NOTES:

HOLLAND v. STEELE
92 F.R.D. 58 (N.D. Ga. 1981).

NATURE OF CASE: Motion for class certification.

FACT SUMMARY: Holland (P) was a member of a class composed of Dade County jail inmates, who alleged that Steele (D) denied them counsel in violation of their rights guaranteed under the Sixth and Fourteenth Amendments of the U.S. Constitution.

CONCISE RULE OF LAW: The prerequisites of a class action are that (1) the class is so numerous that joinder of all members is impracticable; (2) there are questions of law or fact common to the class; (3) the claims or defenses of the representative parties are typical of the claims or defenses of the class; and (4) the representative parties will fairly and adequately protect the interests of the class.

FACTS: Holland (P), an inmate at the Dade County Jail in Georgia, alleged that he and about 40 other inmates and detainees housed at the jail were denied access to counsel in violation of their Sixth and Fourteenth Amendment rights. Holland (P) filed a motion to have the class certified as "all persons who are and will be detained in the Dade County Jail in Trenton, Georgia," alleging that the proposed class had the requisite numerosity, common questions of law, typicality, and adequate representation necessary for certification.

ISSUE: Do the prerequisites of a class action exist where (1) the class is so numerous that joinder of all members is impracticable; (2) there are questions of law or fact common to the class; (3) the claims or defenses of the representative parties are typical of the claims or defenses of the class; and (4) the representative parties will fairly and adequately protect the interests of the class?

HOLDING AND DECISION: (Murphy, J.) Yes. The prerequisites of a class action are that (1) the class is so numerous that joinder of all members is impracticable; (2) there are questions of law or fact common to the class; (3) the claims or defenses of the representative parties are typical of the claims or defenses of the class; and (4) the representative parties will fairly and adequately protect the interests of the class. To satisfy the numerosity requirement, there must be a reasonable estimate or some evidence of the number of purported class members. At least 40 inmates and detainees will be housed in the jail in the next 12 months. Smaller classes, such as the class here, are less objectionable where plaintiff seeks injunctive relief on behalf of future class members as well as past and present members. Here, Holland (P) sought counsel for himself, present inmates, and future inmates. Therefore, the numerosity requirement was satisfied. Here, there are common factual questions relating to Steele's (D) acts, omissions, and policies of denying access to counsel to the inmates. Also, the class members had common legal questions of whether Steele's (D) practices violated the members' constitutional rights. Therefore, the requirement of common questions of law or fact was satisfied. Holland (P), the representative party, was a detainee at the jail who was denied access to counsel. Holland's (P) claims were typical of the class of inmates denied access to counsel at the jail since Steele's (D) policy allegedly applied across the board to all inmates under his supervision. Two factors were critical to determine whether an individual was an adequate representative: the representative must have common interests with the unnamed members, and it must appear that the representative would vigorously prosecute the interests of the class through qualified counsel. Holland's (P) interests were in no way antagonistic to the interests of other potential class members. Also, Holland (P) was represented by counsel who had wide experience in conducting civil rights class-action litigation. It is clear that Holland (P) met all the burdens of class certification.

EDITOR'S ANALYSIS: In an analogous case, a plaintiff sued on behalf of a class of Mexican-Americans employed by the defendant phone company who claimed discrimination on the basis of national origin with respect to compensation, terms, and conditions of employment and hiring. The Supreme Court held that the plaintiff failed to meet the "typicality" requirement necessary for class certification. The plaintiff failed the "across the board" rule applied in the principal case because the plaintiff's allegations were limited to promotion, while the other class members alleged a much wider range of discriminatory claims. General Telephone Company of Southwest v. Falcon, 457 U.S. 147 (1982).

[For more information on class actions, see Casenote Law Outline on Civil Procedure, Chapter 6, § IV, Additional Procedural Devices for Joinder of Parties.]

NOTES:

JENKINS v. RAYMARK INDUSTRIES, INC.
782 F.2d 468 (5th Cir. 1986).

NATURE OF CASE: Appeal of order certifying a class in a mass tort litigation.

FACT SUMMARY: In an asbestos litigation, a class of plaintiffs was certified for resolution of the question of a "state-of-the-art" defense.

CONCISE RULE OF LAW: When appropriate, a class may be certified for resolution of a relevant Issue.

FACTS: Approximately 900 asbestos-related claims were pending in the East District of Texas in 1985. Ten plaintiffs moved to certify the plaintiffs therein on the issue of the defense of "state of the art." This defense was raised in every case. The court found this issue to be relevant to all plaintiffs, that the named plaintiffs would adequately represent the other plaintiffs, and that the claims of the named plaintiffs were typical of all plaintiffs. The court certified the class, and various defendants appealed.

ISSUE: May a class be certified for resolution of a relevant issue?

HOLDING AND DECISION: (Reavley, J.) Yes. A class may be certified for resolution of a relevant issue when appropriate. If the conditions prescribed in Fed. R. Civ. P. 23 are met, a class may be certified as to all issues in an action or as to any issue or issues. Here, the district court found the requisite elements of commonality, numerosity, typicality, and representativeness as they related to the "state-of-the-art" defense. While class actions have largely been disfavored in mass tort cases because of differences in individual plaintiffs, when a court finds the dictates of Rule 23 to have been met, class certification is appropriate. This was the case here. Affirmed.

EDITOR'S ANALYSIS: Class-action suits are most commonly used in civil rights cases, particularly when a law or practice is challenged on its face. This is because the analysis in such an instance is largely theoretical. Mass tort actions are much more fact-oriented. For this reason, class actions are less commonly found in such instances.

[For more information on class certification, see Casenote Law Outline on Civil Procedure, Chapter 6, § IV, Additional Procedural Devices for Joinder of Parties.]

NOTES:

EISEN v. CARLISLE & JACQUELIN
417 U.S. 156 (1974).

NATURE OF CASE: Class action for damages from antitrust violations.

FACT SUMMARY: After the remand of this antitrust class action, the federal district court permitted Eisen (P) to proceed (1) with notice only to certain members of his class and (2) costs of notice to be assumed by Carlisle & Jacquelin (D).

CONCISE RULE OF LAW: Fed. R. Civ. P. 23(c)(2) requires that, in any class action, individual notice of the pendency of such action must be given to all class members who can be identified through reasonable efforts, and the cost of such notice must be borne by the prospective class representative (i.e., plaintiff).

FACTS: In May 1960, Eisen (P) commenced this antitrust action against Carlisle & Jacquelin (D), alleging that they had monopolized "odd-lot" trading on the New York Stock Exchange to the detriment of all odd-lot traders on the Exchange. The first action (Eisen I) was dismissed by the district court as unmanageable as a class action. After reversal of this dismissal by the court of appeals (Eisen II), the case was remanded to the district court. Thereupon, the district court permitted Eisen (P) to proceed as a class representative of the odd-lot traders. Concern over the manageability of this class action, however, prompted the district court to substantially modify the ordinary notice practices set forth in Fed. R. Civ. P. 23. First, since some 6 million potential class members were involved, the court permitted Eisen (P) to implement a four-step notice scheme rather than send individual notice to each: (1) individual notice to exchange members; (2) individual notice to the 2,000 odd-lot traders who had 10 or more transactions in the violation period; (3) individual notice to 5,000 other randomly selected class members; and (4) publication notice to all the rest. Second, after holding a hearing to determine that Eisen (P) was likely to prevail, the court ordered Carlisle & Jacquelin (D) to bear 90% of the $21,720 cost of notice — in light of the fact that Eisen (P) only stood to collect $70 on his claim. In Eisen III, the court of appeals reversed, and, after certification, this opinion from the Supreme Court followed.

ISSUE: Does Fed. R. Civ. P. 23(c)(2) permit a class representative to proceed in a class action without (1) giving notice to all identifiable members of the class and (2) bearing the whole cost of such notice?

HOLDING AND DECISION: (Powell, J.) No. Fed. R. Civ. P. 23(c)(2) requires that, in any class action, individual notice of the pendency of such action must be given to all class members who can be identified through reasonable efforts, and the cost of such notice must be borne by the prospective class representative (i.e., plaintiff). This Court has long observed that notice and an opportunity to be heard are fundamental requisites of the constitutional guarantee of procedural due process. As a result, Fed. R. Civ. P. 23 expressly mandates that each prospective class-action member be advised of the pendency of the action, his choice to exclude himself therefrom, and the fact that he will be bound by any class judgment he does not so exclude himself from. These requirements

are not discretionary; they are mandatory. The scheme adopted by the district court here violates almost every one of them, as, despite Eisen's (P) claims to the contrary, it is well settled that publication notice is not Fed. R. Civ. P. 23 notice. Finally, there is nothing in the history of either Fed. R. Civ. P. 23 or the Constitution which would sanction a pretrial determination of the merits of a case such as the district court undertook here in order to assign the costs of notice. Such costs must fall, at least initially, upon the plaintiff in a class action. The district court was properly reversed.

CONCURRENCE AND DISSENT: (Douglas, J.) The Court's decision today is correct as far as it goes, but an alternative method of dealing with the problems here should be stressed. Fed. R. Civ. P. 23(c)(4) provides that "a class may be divided into subclasses and each subclass treated as a class." There is no reason here why Eisen (P) could not limit his notice requirements by simply defining a smaller subclass and proceeding as its representative.

EDITOR'S ANALYSIS: Some writers believe that Eisen, with its notice and cost of notice rulings, practically eliminated the federal class action as an effective tool for redress of individually small but collectively great consumer claims. The Court did leave some liberal standards, however. For example, the Court in Eisen did not, as it might have, put a definite ceiling on the maximum possible number of potential class-action members — as it could well have under the heading of "unmanageability." Similarly, the Court did not require "actual notice" to all potential class members, only "reasonable efforts" to do so. Note further that the Court did not rule out the approach proposed by Justice Douglas. (Indeed, in a section of the decision not reported in the casebook, the Court affirmatively sanctioned it.) One of the greatest limitations placed on potential class representatives by Eisen, however, is only implicit. It stems from the basic mathematical fact of life that consumers representing smaller subclasses will necessarily have a smaller aggregate claim to begin with. This will, of course, necessarily mean that the class representatives will have less leverage in settlement negotiations.

[For more information on notice to class members, see Casenote Law Outline on Civil Procedure, Chapter 6, § IV, Additional Procedural Devices for Joinder of Parties.]

NOTES:

NOTES

CHAPTER 5
OBTAINING INFORMATION FOR TRIAL

QUICK REFERENCE RULES OF LAW

1. **Pretrial Discovery.** The pretrial discovery process should be self-executing and have minimum judicial intervention. (In re Convergent Technologies Securities Litigation)

   [For more information on pretrial discovery, see Casenote Law Outline on Civil Procedure, Chapter 7, § III, Outline of the Scope of Discovery Under the Federal Rules.]

2. **Limitations on Discovery.** Information on a defendant's net worth may not be discovered until a verdict awarding punitive damages is made. (Davis v. Ross)

   [For more information on limitations on discovery, see Casenote Law Outline on Civil Procedure, Chapter 7, § III, Outline of the Scope of Discovery Under the Federal Rules.]

3. **Requests to Produce Documents.** If difficulty in locating records is the fault of the party requested to produce, production will not be excused. (Kozlowski v. Sears, Roebuck & Co.)

   [For more information on requests to produce documents, see Casenote Law Outline on Civil Procedure, Chapter 7, § IV, Specific Discovery Devices.]

4. **Attorney Work Product Privilege.** Material obtained by counsel in preparation for litigation is the work product of the lawyer, and while such material is not protected by the attorney-client privilege, it is not discoverable on mere demand without a showing of necessity or justification. (Hickman v. Taylor)

   [For more information on the attorney work product privilege, see Casenote Law Outline on Civil Procedure, Chapter 7, § III, Outline of the Scope of Discovery Under the Federal Rules.]

5. **Attorney-client Privilege.** The attorney-client privilege may be applied to communications between all corporate employees and corporate counsel. (Upjohn Co. v. United States)

   [For more information on the attorney-client privilege, see Casenote Law Outline on Civil Procedure, Chapter 7, § III, Outline of the Scope of Discovery Under the Federal Rules.]

6. **Exceptions to Discovery.** The facts known and opinions held by nontestifying experts who are retained or specially employed in anticipation of litigation or preparation for trial are subject to discovery only in exceptional circumstances. (In re Shell Oil Refinery)

   [For more information on exceptions to discovery, see Casenote Law Outline on Civil Procedure, Chapter 7, § III, Outline of the Scope of Discovery Under the Federal Rules.]

7. **Limits on Discovery.** An order requiring all interviews of adverse witnesses outside the presence of the adverse attorneys to be transcribed and made available to the court is a deprivation of the right to effective counsel and the right to explore the witnesses' relevant knowledge and memory. (International Business Machines Corp. v. Edelstein)

   [For more information on limits on discovery, see Casenote Law Outline on Civil Procedure, Chapter 7, § III, Outline of the Scope of Discovery Under the Federal Rules.]

8. **Discovery under the Federal Rules.** A defendant must disclose the identity of all potential witnesses, documents, and tangible evidence that are relevant to the disputed facts as framed by the pleadings. (Scheetz v. Bridgestone/Firestone, Inc.)

[For more information on discovery under the Federal Rules, see Casenote Law Outline on Civil Procedure, Chapter 7, § III, Outline of the Scope of Discovery Under the Federal Rules.]

9. **Abuse of Discovery.** A grossly negligent failure to obey an order compelling discovery is sufficient to justify the severest disciplinary measures available under Fed. R. Civ. P. 37. (Cine Forty-Second St. Theatre Corp. v. Allied Artists Pictures Corp.)

   [For more information on the abuse of discovery, see Casenote Law Outline on Civil Procedure, Chapter 7, § VI, Discovery: Abuse and Sanctions: Federal Rules 26(f)-(g) and 37.]

IN RE CONVERGENT TECHNOLOGIES SECURITIES LITIGATION
108 F.R.D. 328 (N.D. Cal. 1985).

NATURE OF CASE: Motion to compel responses to interrogations in civil securities litigation.

FACT SUMMARY: Unable to agree on the propriety of certain interrogatories, the litigants sought judicial oversight and relief.

CONCISE RULE OF LAW: The pretrial discovery process should be self-executing and have minimum judicial intervention.

FACTS: In a large securities litigation, over 1,000 contention interrogatories were served upon the plaintiff. The dispute as to their propriety became bitter, and a motion to compel was filed.

ISSUE: Should the pretrial discovery process be self-executing and have minimum judicial intervention?

HOLDING AND DECISION: (Brazil, M.) Yes. The pretrial discovery process should be self-executing and have minimum judicial intervention. It has always been the spirit of civil discovery that parties are to cooperate as fully as possible in exchanging discovery. The judicial system is completely incapable of refereeing more than a minuscule number of such disputes. The 1983 amendments to Fed. R. Civ. P. 26 make it clear that discovery should only be served when it is reasonably calculated to lead to the discovery of evidence both admissible and sufficiently significant to justify the burdens on both the serving and responding parties. This requires analysis and cooperation on the parts of all parties involved, which should make judicial oversight unnecessary. [The court went on to hold most of the interrogatories to be premature and denied the motion in the greater part.]

EDITOR'S ANALYSIS: The scope of discovery has always been broad. The 1983 amendments to the Fed. R. Civ. P. tightened the scope a bit. Besides being calculated to lead to admissible evidence, discovery had to lead to useful evidence as well. Despite the changes, discovery remains, as a policy matter, expansively construed.

[For more information on pretrial discovery, see Casenote Law Outline on Civil Procedure, Chapter 7, § III, Outline of the Scope of Discovery Under the Federal Rules.]

DAVIS v. ROSS
107 F.R.D. 326 (S.D.N.Y. 1985).

NATURE OF CASE: Motion to compel responses to discovery in action for damages for libel.

FACT SUMMARY: Davis (P), who sued Ross (D) for libel, sought information on Ross' (D) net worth.

CONCISE RULE OF LAW: Information on a defendant's net worth may not be discovered until a verdict awarding punitive damages is made.

FACTS: Davis (P) sued Ross (D) for libel, seeking compensatory and punitive damages. Davis (P) propounded discovery, seeking information on Ross' (D) net worth. Ross (D) refused to divulge such information, and Davis (P) moved to compel.

ISSUE: May information on a defendant's net worth be discovered during pretrial discovery?

HOLDING AND DECISION: (Carter, J.) No. Information on a defendant's net worth may not be discovered until a verdict awarding punitive damages is made. When punitive damages are alleged, a defendant's net worth is relevant as to the appropriate damage amount. However, the law recognizes the confidential nature of a person's finances. This, plus the relative ease of alleging punitives, has led to the rule that information regarding a defendant's net worth may not be forcibly disclosed until a jury has decided that punitives would in fact be awarded. Here, the action has not reached this stage, so disclosure cannot be compelled. Motion denied.

EDITOR'S ANALYSIS: The rule stated by the court here is fairly common among the jurisdictions. Some states, such as New York here, have evolved it through common law. Others, such as California, have codified it.

[For more information on limitations on discovery, see Casenote Law Outline on Civil Procedure, Chapter 7, § III, Outline of the Scope of Discovery Under the Federal Rules.]

KOZLOWSKI v. SEARS, ROEBUCK & CO.
73 F.R.D. 73 (D. Mass. 1976).

NATURE OF CASE: Motion to set aside default entry.

FACT SUMMARY: Sears (D) refused to produce records because it claimed it was impossible to locate them.

CONCISE RULE OF LAW: If difficulty in locating records is the fault of the party requested to produce, production will not be excused.

FACTS: Kozlowski (P) was burned when a pair of pajamas purchased from Sears, Roebuck & Co. (D) caught fire. Kozlowski (P) demanded production of all reports of similar occurrences. Sears (D) refused. A court ordered production. Sears (D) did not comply. Upon motion, Sears' (D) default was entered. Sears (D) moved to set aside the default, contending that Sears' (D) complaint indexing system was by name, not occurrence, making compliance impossibly burdensome.

ISSUE: If difficulty in locating records is the fault of the party requested to produce, will production be excused?

HOLDING AND DECISION: (Julian, J.) No. If difficulty in locating records is the fault of the party requested to produce, production will not be excused. Under Fed. R. Civ. P. 34, the party from whom discovery is sought has the burden of showing some sufficient reason why discovery should not be allowed once it has been shown that the items sought are within the scope of discovery. While burdensomeness may be a reason, it will not be so considered if it is the responding party's own actions or inaction that created the burden. Here, Sears (D) employed an indexing system making compliance difficult. The indexing system was created and controlled by Sears (D). This being so, no good excuse for not mandating discovery exists. Motion denied.

EDITOR'S ANALYSIS: Sears (D) offered to open its records warehouse doors to let Kozlowski's (P) attorney search for the records. The court held this insufficient, considering it a thinly disguised attempt to shift the burden of the request onto Kozlowski (P).

[For more information on requests to produce documents, see Casenote Law Outline on Civil Procedure, Chapter 7, § IV, Specific Discovery Devices.]

NOTES:

HICKMAN v. TAYLOR
329 U.S. 495 (1974).

NATURE OF CASE: Action for damages for wrongful death.

FACT SUMMARY: Five crew members drowned when a tug sank. In anticipation of litigation, the attorney for Taylor (D), the tug owner, interviewed the survivors. Hickman (P), as representative of one of the deceased, brought this action and tried by means of discovery to obtain copies of the statements Taylor's (D) attorney obtained from the survivors.

CONCISE RULE OF LAW: Material obtained by counsel in preparation for litigation is the work product of the lawyer, and while such material is not protected by the attorney-client privilege, it is not discoverable on mere demand without a showing of necessity or justification.

FACTS: Five of nine crew members drowned when their tug sank. A public hearing was held at which the four survivors were examined. Their testimony was recorded and was made available to all interested parties. A short time later, the attorney for Taylor (D), the tug owner, interviewed the survivors in preparation for possible litigation. He also interviewed other persons believed to have information on the accident. Ultimately, claims were brought by representatives of all five of the deceased. Four were settled. Hickman (P), the fifth claimant, brought this action. He filed interrogatories asking for any statements taken from crew members as well as any oral or written statements, records, reports, or other memoranda made concerning any matter relative to the towing operation, the tug's sinking, the salvaging and repair of the tug, and the death of the deceased. Taylor (D) refused to summarize or set forth the material on the ground that it was protected by the attorney-client privilege.

ISSUE: Does a party seeking to discover material obtained by an adverse party's counsel in preparation for possible litigation have a burden to show a justification for such production?

HOLDING AND DECISION: (Murphy, J.) Yes. The deposition-discovery rules are to be accorded a broad and liberal treatment since mutual knowledge of all the relevant facts gathered by both parties is essential to proper litigation. But discovery does have ultimate and necessary boundaries. Limitations arise upon a showing of bad faith or harassment or when the inquiry seeks material which is irrelevant or privileged. In this case, the material sought by Hickman (P) is not protected by the attorney-client privilege. However, such material as that sought here does constitute the work product of the lawyer. The general policy against invading the privacy of an attorney in performing his various duties is so well recognized and so essential to the orderly working of our legal system that the party seeking work product material has a burden to show reasons to justify such production. Interviews, statements, memoranda, correspondence, briefs, mental impressions, etc., obtained in the course of preparation for possible or anticipated litigation fall within the work product. Such material is not free from discovery in all cases. Where relevant and nonprivileged facts remain hidden in an attorney's file and where production of

those facts is essential to the preparation of one's case, discovery may be had. But there must be a showing of necessity and justification. In this case, Hickman (P) sought discovery of oral and written statements of witnesses whose identities were well known and whose availability to Hickman (P) appeared unimpaired. Here, no attempt was made to show why it was necessary that Taylor's (D) attorney produce the material. No reasons were given to justify this invasion of the attorney's privacy. Hickman's (P) counsel admitted that he wanted the statements only to help him prepare for trial. That is insufficient to warrant an exception to the policy of protecting the privacy of an attorney's professional activities.

EDITOR'S ANALYSIS: The Hickman decision left open a number of questions as to the scope of the work product doctrine and the showing needed to discover work product material. In 1970, Fed. R. Civ. P. 26(b)(3) was added to deal with the discovery of work product. It provides that documents and tangible things which were prepared in anticipation of litigation or for trial are discoverable only upon a showing that the party seeking such materials has substantial need of them and that he is unable without undue hardship to obtain the substantial equivalent of the materials by other means. The rule states that mental impressions, conclusions, opinions, or legal theories of an attorney or other representative of a party are to be protected against disclosure.

[For more information on the attorney work product privilege, see Casenote Law Outline on Civil Procedure, Chapter 7, § III, Outline of the Scope of Discovery Under the Federal Rules.]

NOTES:

UPJOHN CO. v. UNITED STATES
449 U.S. 383 (1981).

NATURE OF CASE: Appeal from order to produce documents.

FACT SUMMARY: Upjohn (D) contended that certain questionnaires prepared as part of an internal company investigation were protected from disclosure by the attorney-client privilege.

CONCISE RULE OF LAW: The attorney-client privilege may be applied to communications between all corporate employees and corporate counsel.

FACTS: In January 1976, independent accountants conducting an audit of one of Upjohn's (D) foreign subsidiaries discovered that the subsidiary made payments to, or for the benefit of, foreign government officials in order to secure government business. The accountants so informed Thomas, Upjohn's (D) general counsel, who subsequently undertook an internal investigation of these activities. As part of this investigation, Upjohn's (D) attorneys prepared a questionnaire, which was sent to all foreign general and area managers, regarding the alleged payments. On March 26, 1976, Upjohn (D) voluntarily submitted a preliminary report to the Securities and Exchange Commission disclosing certain questionable payments. After a copy of the report was sent to the Internal Revenue Service, the Service issued a summons demanding production of all files relative to the investigation. Upjohn (D) declined to produce the documents specified in the summons on the grounds that they were protected from disclosure by the attorney-client privilege and constituted the work product of attorneys prepared in anticipation of litigation. After the Government (P) filed a petition seeking enforcement of the summons, the court of appeals held that only senior management personnel were protected by the privilege. Upjohn (D) appealed, contending that the privilege applied to all corporate personnel who answered the questionnaire.

ISSUE: May the attorney-client privilege be applied to communications between all corporate employees and corporate counsel?

HOLDING AND DECISION: (Rehnquist, J.) Yes. The attorney-client privilege may be applied to communications between all corporate employees and corporate counsel. The privilege exists to protect not only the giving of professional advice to those who can act on it but also the giving of information to the lawyer to enable him to give sound and informed advice. Middle- and lower-level employees can, by actions within the scope of their employment, embroil the corporation in serious legal difficulties, and it is only natural that these employees would have the relevant information needed by corporate counsel if he is adequately to advise the client with respect to such actual or potential difficulties. The control group test adopted by the court of appeals frustrates the very purpose of the privilege by discouraging the communication of relevant information by employees of the client to attorneys seeking to render legal advice to the client corporation. Here, because the privilege does not protect the disclosure of the underlying facts by those who communicated with the attorney, the Government (P) was free to

question the employees who communicated with Thomas as a means of conducting discovery. Reversed.

CONCURRENCE: (Burger, C.J.) As a general rule, a communication is privileged at least when, as here, an employee or former employee speaks at the direction of the management with an attorney regarding conduct or proposed conduct within the scope of employment.

EDITOR'S ANALYSIS: As the Court notes in its opinion, the attorney-client privilege is the oldest of the privileges for confidential communications known to the common law. Its purpose is to encourage full and frank communication between attorneys and their clients and to thereby promote broader public interests in the observance of law and administration of justice.

[For more information on the attorney-client privilege, see Casenote Law Outline on Civil Procedure, Chapter 7, § III, Outline of the Scope of Discovery Under the Federal Rules.]

NOTES:

IN RE SHELL OIL REFINERY
132 F.R.D. 437 (E.D. La. 1990).

NATURE OF CASE: Motion for reconsideration of the court's ruling on plaintiffs' request for discovery of defendant's experts.

FACT SUMMARY: During pretrial discovery, the court denied discovery motions by which the Plaintiffs' Legal Committee (P) sought the results of tests conducted by Shell (D) after an explosion at its refinery and leave of court to depose Shell's (D) in-house experts, even though Shell (D) did not intend to use them at trial.

CONCISE RULE OF LAW: The facts known and opinions held by nontestifying experts who are retained or specially employed in anticipation of litigation or preparation for trial are subject to discovery only in exceptional circumstances.

FACTS: After an explosion at a Shell Oil Refinery (D), several suits ultimately certified as a class action were filed. In preparation for the litigation, Shell (D) conducted certain tests. Its legal department and outside counsel requested that two of Shell's (D) in-house experts, present at the tests, prepare preliminary reports and help the investigation team defend the lawsuits. The Plaintiffs' Legal Committee (PLC) (P) sought the results of Shell's (D) tests and also sought to depose the two in-house experts. Shell (D) stated that it did not intend to call its in-house experts at trial or to use their preliminary reports. On these facts, the court ruled against the PLC's (P) motions for expert discovery. The PLC (P) filed a motion for reconsideration.

ISSUE: Are the facts known and opinions held by nontestifying experts who are retained or specially employed in anticipation of litigation or preparation for trial subject to discovery only in exceptional circumstances?

HOLDING AND DECISION: (Mentz, J.) Yes. The facts known and opinions held by nontestifying experts who are retained or specially employed in anticipation of litigation or preparation for trial are subject to discovery only in exceptional circumstances. Although Shell's (D) in-house experts might have studied the cause of the explosion regardless of litigation, their usual duties did not include litigation assistance. Thus, they were retained or specially employed by Shell (D) in preparation for trial. The PLC (P) had access to the materials tested by Shell (D) and can conduct its own expert tests. The parties could also discover the basis for each other's expert's conclusions during the period set aside for expert discovery. Thus, the PLC (P) has failed to show exceptional circumstances.

EDITOR'S ANALYSIS: Neither Fed. R. Civ. P. 26(b)(4)(A), which the court applied here, nor the Advisory Committee Notes explain when a general employee may become retained or specially employed. If their work was in anticipation of litigation, then discovery must be analyzed under the work product doctrine of Rule 26(b)(3). The exceptional circumstances requirement has been interpreted by the courts to mean an inability to obtain equivalent information from other sources.

[For more information on exceptions to discovery, see Casenote Law Outline on Civil Procedure, Chapter 7, § III, Outline of the Scope of Discovery Under the Federal Rules.]

NOTES:

INTERNATIONAL BUSINESS MACHINES CORP. v. EDELSTEIN
526 F.2d 37 (2d Cir. 1975).

NATURE OF CASE: Petition for writ of mandamus for relief from discovery procedure order.

FACT SUMMARY: IBM (P) sought relief from the trial judge's order that all of IBM's (P) interviews with adverse witnesses conducted outside of the presence of the adverse attorneys be transcribed and made available to the court.

CONCISE RULE OF LAW: An order requiring all interviews of adverse witnesses outside the presence of the adverse attorneys to be transcribed and made available to the court is a deprivation of the right to effective counsel and the right to explore the witnesses' relevant knowledge and memory.

FACTS: Trial Judge Edelstein (D) ordered IBM (P) to transcribe and produce for the court all interviews that IBM (P) conducted with adverse witnesses outside the presence of the adverse attorneys pursuant to certain pending litigation before Edelstein (D). In view of the hardship to IBM (P) and its attorneys, IBM (P) petitioned for a writ of mandamus preventing the enforcement of this order as a deprivation of its right to effective counsel and right of discovery.

ISSUE: Is an order requiring all interviews of adverse witnesses outside the presence of the adverse attorneys to be transcribed and made available to the court a deprivation of the right to effective counsel or the right to explore the witnesses' relevant knowledge and memory?

HOLDING AND DECISION: (Per curiam) Yes. The restrictions imposed upon the interviewing of witnesses exceeded the authority of Edelstein (D). Counsel for all parties have a right to interview an adverse party's witnesses outside of the adverse party's attorney's presence, so long as the witness is willing. This right permits the attorneys to explore what knowledge any of the witnesses have and the extent of their memory of it. An order requiring all interviews of adverse witnesses outside the presence of the adverse attorneys to be transcribed and made available to the court is a deprivation of the right to effective counsel and the right to explore the witnesses' relevant knowledge and memory. Petition for writ of mandamus granted.

EDITOR'S ANALYSIS: This "right" to interview witnesses applies to willing witnesses. An unwilling witness may be compelled through other means of discovery to give up information in his possession also. These are laden with safeguards against overextensive questioning or irrelevant inquiry. In most cases, opposing counsel or the attorney for the witness appears or participates.

[For more information on limits on discovery, see Casenote Law Outline on Civil Procedure, Chapter 7, § III, Outline of the Scope of Discovery Under the Federal Rules.]

NOTES:

SCHEETZ v. BRIDGESTONE/FIRESTONE, INC.
152 F.R.D. 628 (D. Mont. 1993).

NATURE OF CASE: Request for review of a magistrate judge's denial of plaintiff's motion to compel disclosure in a product liability action.

FACT SUMMARY: When a magistrate judge denied Scheetz's (P) motion to compel in connection with his product liability action against Bridgestone/Firestone (D), Scheetz (P) sought review of that denial in the district court.

CONCISE RULE OF LAW: A defendant must disclose the identity of all potential witnesses, documents, and tangible evidence that are relevant to the disputed facts as framed by the pleadings.

FACTS: Scheetz (P) alleged that he was injured as a result of the defective design of the RH5 degrees rim, designed, manufactured, and marketed by Bridgestone/Firestone's (D) predecessor in interest, Firestone Tire & Rubber Company (D). Because Risjord, the attorney representing Scheetz (P), had represented numerous other plaintiffs in the prosecution of actions against Firestone (D) and its successor, Bridgestone/Firestone (D) contended it should not have to produce the requested information since Risjord had previously deposed the witnesses and reviewed and selected copies of the documents. The magistrate judge denied Scheetz's (P) motion to compel. Scheetz (P) then sought review of the magistrate's denial in the district court.

ISSUE: Must a defendant disclose the identity of all potential witnesses, documents, and tangible evidence that are relevant to the disputed facts as framed by the pleadings?

HOLDING AND DECISION: (Hatfield, C.J.) Yes. A defendant must disclose the identity of all potential witnesses, documents, and tangible evidence that are relevant to the disputed facts as framed by the pleadings. Mandatory discovery disclosure encourages cost-effective discovery through voluntary exchange of information and through the use of cooperative discovery devices. The fact that Scheetz (P) was represented by counsel who had participated in innumerable cases involving the RH5 degrees assembly is irrelevant to a determination as to the sufficiency of Bridgestone/Firestone's (D) disclosure statement. Bridgestone/Firestone (D) shall not be allowed to effectively defeat the goal of Montana's comprehensive Civil Justice Expense and Delay Reduction Plan through merely declaring that counsel for the adverse party is aware of the information falling within the purview of the rule. Thus, Bridgestone/Firestone (D) is ordered to file, within twenty days, a supplemental prediscovery disclosure statement that satisfies the rule.

EDITOR'S ANALYSIS: The Plan adopted by the District of Montana was implemented in response to the mandate of the Civil Justice Reform Act of 1990 (28 U.S.C. §§ 471 et seq.). Portions of Rule 200-5, applied here by the court, derive from Fed. R. Civ. P. 26. However, Rule 200-5 requires a broader disclosure than that mandated by the Federal Rules of Civil Procedure.

[For more information on discovery under the Federal Rules, see Casenote Law Outline on Civil Procedure, Chapter 7, § III, Outline of the Scope of Discovery Under the Federal Rules.]

NOTES:

CINE 42ND ST. THEATRE CORP. v. ALLIED ARTISTS
606 F.2d 1062 (2d Cir. 1979).

NATURE OF CASE: Action seeking damages and injunctive relief for anticompetitive practices.

FACT SUMMARY: The Magistrate concluded that Cine (P) had engaged in repeated and willful noncompliance with the court's orders regarding answering Allied's (D) interrogatories on the issue of damages, with the result that she precluded it from introducing evidence on that issue.

CONCISE RULE OF LAW: A grossly negligent failure to obey an order compelling discovery is sufficient to justify the severest disciplinary measures available under Fed. R. Civ. P. 37.

FACTS: Cine (P) brought an action charging Allied (D) and others operating competing movie theaters with engaging in a conspiracy with motion picture distributors to cut off its access to first-run, quality films. It sought treble damages under the antitrust laws and injunctive relief. Allied (D) proposed interrogatories on the issue of damages, which Cine (P) repeatedly failed to answer adequately or on time, although given several extensions. Finally, the Magistrate held that Cine (P) acted willfully in not complying with the court's orders concerning discovery as to the issue of damages and precluded Cine (P) from introducing evidence on that issue. This effectively amounted to a dismissal of the damage claim, leaving only the claim for injunctive relief. The district judge, to whom the order was submitted for approval, felt Cine (P) had been grossly negligent and no more and that this was insufficient to impose the severest sanctions of Fed. R. Civ. P. 37. Being unsure of the law, however, he certified an interlocutory appeal on his own motion.

ISSUE: Is gross negligence in failing to obey discovery orders sufficient to justify the severest disciplinary measures available under Fed. R. Civ. P. 37?

HOLDING AND DECISION: (Kaufman, C.J.) Yes. A grossly negligent failure to obey an order compelling discovery is sufficient to justify the severest disciplinary measures available under Fed. R. Civ. P. 37. Negligent, no less than intentional, wrongs are fit subjects for general deterrence. Gross professional incompetence no less than deliberate tactical intransigence may be responsible for the interminable delays and costs which plague modern complex lawsuits. In fact, Cine (P) has, by its gross negligence, frozen this litigation in the discovery phase for nearly four years. There is simply no reason to avoid imposing harsh sanctions in such a situation. Reversed.

CONCURRENCE: (Oakes, J.) An unknowing client should not pay for the sins of his counsel.

EDITOR'S ANALYSIS: Under Fed. R. Civ. P. 37, a party who willfully disobeys a court order pertaining to discovery can be held in contempt and imprisoned or fined. On the other hand, the court may strike or dismiss any or all of that party's claim or defense, preclude the introduction of evidence in support of such, or hold certain facts to be established.

[For more information on the abuse of discovery, see Casenote Law Outline on Civil Procedure, Chapter 7, § VI, Discovery: Abuse and Sanctions: Federal Rules 26(f)-(g) and 37.]

NOTES:

6

CHAPTER 6
ADJUDICATION BEFORE TRIAL: SUMMARY JUDGMENT

QUICK REFERENCE RULES OF LAW

1. **Summary Judgment.** In an action based on conspiracy, summary judgment may not be granted unless a defendant can show that no evidence thereof exists. (Adickes v. S.H. Kress & Co)

   [For more information on summary judgment, see Casenote Law Outline on Civil Procedure, Chapter 8, § IV, Summary Judgments.]

2. **Summary Judgment.** Summary judgment must be entered against a party who fails to make a showing sufficient to establish the existence of an element essential to his case and on which he bears the burden of proof at trial. (Celotex Corp. v. Catrett)

   [For more information on summary judgment, see Casenote Law Outline on Civil Procedure, Chapter 8, § IV, Summary Judgments.]

3. **Credibility of the Parties and Summary Judgment.** Where credibility of the parties is crucial, summary judgment is improper and a trial indispensable. (Arnstein v. Porter)

   [For more information on credibility of the parties and summary judgment, see Casenote Law Outline on Civil Procedure, Chapter 8, § IV, Summary Judgments.]

4. **Significant Summary Judgment Issues.** Summary judgment is appropriate in a defamation action when all individuals supposedly receiving the defamatory statements deny such receipt. (Dyer v. MacDougall)

   [For more information on significant summary judgment issues, see Casenote Law Outline on Civil Procedure, Chapter 8, § IV, Summary Judgments.]

ADICKES v. S.H. KRESS & CO.
398 U.S. 144 (1970).

NATURE OF CASE: Appeal of summary judgment denying damages for civil rights violation.

FACT SUMMARY: In a civil rights action in which a conspiracy between the police and a grocery store was alleged, summary judgment was granted when Adickes (P) could not produce evidence to support a conspiracy.

CONCISE RULE OF LAW: In an action based on conspiracy, summary judgment may not be granted unless a defendant can show that no evidence thereof exists.

FACTS: Adickes (P) was refused service at a restaurant owned by S.H. Kress & Co. (D) and arrested for loitering. She then brought an action seeking damages under § 1983, alleging a conspiracy between Kress (D) and the police. Under the circumstances of the case, a conspiracy could have existed only if police had been present at the store before the arrest. When Adickes (P) could not show that police had earlier been present, Kress (D) moved for summary judgment. This was granted and affirmed on appeal. Adickes (P) appealed to the Supreme Court.

ISSUE: In an action based on conspiracy, may summary judgment be granted if a defendant has not shown that no evidence thereof exists?

HOLDING AND DECISION: (Harlan, J.) No. In an action based on conspiracy, summary judgment may not be granted unless a defendant can show that no evidence thereof exists. In a motion for summary judgment, the burden is on the moving party to affirmatively show that a triable issue exists as to the material fact or facts. The fact that the burden would be on the other party on the same fact at trial is of no matter. Here, while at trial, Adickes (P) would have to prove the presence of police earlier in the day; at the summary judgment level, the burden was on Kress (D) to prove they were not. This it did not do. Reversed.

EDITOR'S ANALYSIS: The present case's rule was modified by the Court 16 years later in Celotex Corp. v. Catrett, 477 U.S. 317 (1986). The Court there liberalized the burden on a moving party, holding that such a party, on an issue the opposing party has the ultimate burden of proving, could prevail on the basis that the nonmoving party could not produce evidence on the issue. This has made summary judgment a much easier procedure to obtain in federal courts than in most state courts, as most states' procedural rules are similar to that announced in the present action.

[For more information on summary judgment, see Casenote Law Outline on Civil Procedure, Chapter 8, § IV, Summary Judgments.]

CELOTEX CORP. v. CATRETT
477 U.S. 317 (1986).

NATURE OF CASE: Appeal from reversal of grant of summary judgment.

FACT SUMMARY: The court of appeals reversed summary judgment in favor of Celotex (D) on the basis that Celotex (D) had not offered sufficient evidence rebutting Catrett's (P) allegations.

CONCISE RULE OF LAW: Summary judgment must be entered against a party who fails to make a showing sufficient to establish the existence of an element essential to his case and on which he bears the burden of proof at trial.

FACTS: Catrett's (P) husband died, and she sued several asbestos manufacturers, claiming the death resulted from exposure to their products. Celotex (D), one of the manufacturers, moved for summary judgment on the basis that no evidence existed that the decedent had been exposed to Celotex's (D) products. The district court granted the motion, and the court of appeals reversed, holding that Celotex (D) had not offered sufficient evidence to rebut Catrett's (P) allegations. The Supreme Court granted certiorari.

ISSUE: Must summary judgment be entered against a party who fails to meet his burden of proof on any essential element of the cause of action?

HOLDING AND DECISION: (Rehnquist, J.) Yes. Summary judgment must be entered against a party who fails to make a showing sufficient to establish the existence of an element essential to his case and on which he has the burden of proof. Catrett (P) had the burden of showing that Celotex (D) had some level of culpability in order to go forward on her claim. She thus bore the burden of proof on this issue. Her failure to meet this burden and thus establish a genuine issue of material fact justified entry of summary judgment. Reversed and remanded.

CONCURRENCE: (White, J.) A moving defendant need not support his motion with sufficient rebuttal evidence in all cases.

EDITOR'S ANALYSIS: Summary judgment is a radical judicial tool which completely disposes of a case or issue prior to trial. The basis for the motion is the absence of a genuine issue of material fact. When such occurs, the only questions remaining are legal questions which are determined by the court. Because the result of a successful motion is the end of a case, the court exercises great restraint in granting them.

[For more information on summary judgment, see Casenote Law Outline on Civil Procedure, Chapter 8, § IV, Summary Judgments.]

ARNSTEIN v. PORTER
154 F.2d 464 (2d Cir. 1946).

NATURE OF CASE: Appeal from summary judgment in an action for infringement of copyright.

FACT SUMMARY: Arnstein (P) appealed summary judgment for Porter (D), who, Arnstein (P) alleged, had stolen tunes for several popular songs Porter (D) had written.

CONCISE RULE OF LAW: Where credibility of the parties is crucial, summary judgment is improper and a trial indispensable.

FACTS: Arnstein (P), a songwriter, alleged that Porter (D), a songwriter, infringed copyrights to several of Arnstein's (P) songs. Specifically, Porter's (D) "Begin the Beguine" was allegedly plagiarized from Arnstein's (P) "The Lord Is My Shepherd" and "A Mother's Prayer," the latter of which sold over 1 million copies. Also, Porter's (D) "Night and Day" was allegedly taken from Arnstein's (P) "I Love You Madly," while "Don't Fence Me In" came from "A Modern Messiah." While not all of Arnstein's (P) songs had been published, copies had been distributed to bands and radio stations. Arnstein (P) claimed that Porter (D) had "stooges" watching him and stealing from him, even though many of the songs had been publicly sung. Porter (D) categorically denied every allegation and was granted summary judgment on grounds of vexatiousness and that Arnstein (P) previously had brought five similar and unsuccessful suits against others. Arnstein (P) appealed on grounds that there were triable issues of fact and that he was denied a jury trial.

ISSUE: Where credibility of the parties is crucial, is summary judgment improper and a trial indispensable?

HOLDING AND DECISION: (Frank, C.J.) Yes. Where credibility of the parties is crucial, summary judgment is improper and a trial indispensable. If there is the slightest doubt to the facts, a trial is necessary. In copyright infringement cases, there are two separate elements: (1) that defendant has copied from plaintiff's work and (2), if proved, the copying went so far as to be an improper appropriation. If there is evidence of similarities and access, the court must determine if there was copying. Here, enough similarities in the songs existed so that a jury could infer that no coincidence was involved. Arnstein's (P) songs being public provides the opportunity for access. Thus, a jury should hear each side of the story. A witness' demeanor at trial is an important aid to the jury in settling the matter. While it is not denied that Arnstein's (P) allegations are "fantastic," the decision must be reversed and remanded.

DISSENT: (Clark, J.) It is error to deny a trial when there is a genuine issue as to material facts but just as erroneous to deny summary judgment when there is no such issue. There was none here.

EDITOR'S ANALYSIS: At trial, Arnstein (P) failed to win his sixth action for copyright infringement, 158 F.2d 795 (C.A. 2d 1947). Note that while a copyright infringement case involves two elements, had one element — access — not been shown in the pleadings, then clearly summary judgment could have been granted. In that case, with no access, no copying could have occurred.

[For more information on credibility of the parties and summary judgment, see Casenote Law Outline on Civil Procedure, Chapter 8, § IV, Summary Judgments.]

NOTES:

DYER v. MacDOUGALL
201 F.2d 265 (2d Cir. 1952).

NATURE OF CASE: Appeal of summary judgment partially dismissing an action based on defamation.

FACT SUMMARY: Summary judgment in a defamation action was granted in favor of MacDougall (D) when he produced evidence that everyone to whom the alleged defamation was published denied receiving such statements.

CONCISE RULE OF LAW: Summary judgment is appropriate in a defamation action when all individuals supposedly receiving the defamatory statements deny such receipt.

FACTS: Dyer (P) brought an action based on slander, alleging four separate acts of same. MacDougall (D) moved for summary adjudication as to three of the counts. As evidence thereof, he submitted declarations and deposition testimony from each individual to whom the allegedly slanderous statements were made denying receipt of same. The trial court granted summary adjudication as to two counts, and Dyer (P) appealed.

ISSUE: Is summary judgment appropriate in a defamation action when all individuals supposedly receiving the defamatory statements deny such receipt?

HOLDING AND DECISION: (Hand, J.) Yes. Summary judgment is appropriate in a defamation action when all individuals supposedly receiving the defamatory statements deny such receipt. On a purely theoretical level, it is possible that each such witness, giving uncontroverted testimony at trial, might appear so incredible to a jury that all their testimony would be disbelieved by a jury, who would then render a judgment contrary to the substance of their testimony. However, it would seem that any court would grant a directed verdict based on the evidence before the trial court, and this court would have no problem affirming same. Consequently, summary adjudication, which is designed to obviate unnecessary trials, would be appropriate in such a situation. Affirmed.

CONCURRENCE: (Frank, J.) The opinion's reference to a directed verdict and the appeal thereof was unnecessary. Under the facts here, summary adjudication would be proper even in the absence of such considerations.

EDITOR'S ANALYSIS: This case is difficult to reconcile with Arnstein v. Porter, 154 F.2d 464 (2d Cir. 1946). This case seemed to stand for the proposition that if there was any doubt whatsoever, summary judgment was inappropriate. The present action involved some theoretical doubt, but summary adjudication was affirmed anyway. The Supreme Court's more recent decision in Celotex v. Catrett, 477 U.S. 317 (1986), would seem to have buried the Arnstein rule completely.

[For more information on significant summary judgment issues, see Casenote Law Outline on Civil Procedure, Chapter 8, § IV, Summary Judgments.]

NOTES

7

CHAPTER 7
JUDICIAL SUPERVISION OF PRETRIAL AND PROMOTION OF SETTLEMENT

QUICK REFERENCE RULES OF LAW

1. **Pretrial Conferences.** A district court may order litigants — even those represented by counsel — to appear in person at a pretrial conference to discuss the posture and settlement of their case. (G. Heileman Brewing Co., Inc. v. Joseph Oat Corp.)

   [For more information on pretrial conferences, see Casenote Law Outline on Civil Procedure, Chapter 8, § II, Pre-trial Conferences and Pre-trial Orders.]

2. **Pre-trial Orders.** A court may not impose sanctions for a party's refusal to participate in a summary jury trial. (Strandell v. Jackson County, Illinois)

   [For more information on pre-trial orders, see Casenote Law Outline on Civil Procedure, Chapter 8, § II, Pre-trial Conferences and Pre-trial Orders.]

3. **Taxation of Costs.** Attorney fees incurred by a plaintiff subsequent to an offer of settlement will not be paid when the plaintiff recovers less than the offer. (Marek v. Chesny)

   [For more information on taxation of costs, see Casenote Law Outline on Civil Procedure, Chapter 11, § II, Self-enforcing Judgments Distinguished From Coercive Judgments.]

4. **Pretrial Conferences.** A court may not issue an automatic fine against a party for settling after a court-imposed deadline. (Newton v. A.C. & S., Inc.)

   [For more information on pretrial conferences, see Casenote Law Outline on Civil Procedure, Chapter 8, § II, Pre-trial Conferences and Pre-trial Orders.]

G. HEILEMAN BREWING CO. v. JOSEPH OAT CORP.
871 F.2d 648 (7th Cir. 1989).

NATURE OF CASE: Appeal from order imposing sanctions for failure to comply with a court order in a case involving a $4 million claim.

FACT SUMMARY: A district court sanctioned Joseph Oat Corp. (D) for failing to comply with a court order that a corporate representative with full settlement authority attend a settlement conference.

CONCISE RULE OF LAW: A district court may order litigants — even those represented by counsel — to appear in person at a pretrial conference to discuss the posture and settlement of their case.

FACTS: G. Heileman Brewing Co. (P) sued Joseph Oat Corp. (D) for $4 million in a case involving complex legal and factual issues. As trial approached, the court ordered each side to send a "corporate representative with authority to settle" to a pretrial conference. Oat (D), which had already indicated that it did not intend to pay anything, sent an attorney to represent as much to the court. The court, upon learning that the attorney had no money to offer, imposed monetary sanctions for failing to obey its order. Oat (D) appealed, contending that the court did not have the authority to order represented litigants to appear and, even if it did, it would be unreasonable to expect the president of Oat (D) to leave his business to participate in the conference.

ISSUE: May a district court order represented litigants to appear in person at a pretrial conference?

HOLDING AND DECISION: (Kanne, J.) Yes. A district court may order represented litigants to appear in person at a pretrial conference. Rule 16 of the Fed. R. Civ. P. enables a court to compel attendance of attorneys of record and pro se litigants at a pretrial conference; it does not empower a court to compel a represented party's attendance. However, Rule 16 is not the sole source of a court's powers in these matters. The Supreme Court has long recognized that district courts have broad inherent supervisory powers over the parties appearing before them. Rule 1 of the Fed. R. Civ. P. provides that the Rules exist to promote speedy and orderly litigation. They shape certain aspects of a court's inherent powers, yet allow the court to exercise that power where discretion is available. Part of a court's inherent powers is the ability to compel attendance at a settlement conference. In this case, the imposition of monetary sanctions was an appropriate vehicle for enforcing this authority. The stakes were so high and involved such substantial trial time and expenses that the burden of sending a corporate representative did not outweigh the benefits to be gained from a settlement conference. Affirmed.

DISSENT: (Posner, J.) A court cannot coerce settlement. Oat (D) had made it clear it would not settle. It was therefore a pointless exercise for the court to have ordered Oat (D) to attend. It was therefore an abuse of discretion to sanction Oat (D).

DISSENT: (Coffey, J.) Rule 16 mandates unambiguously that only unrepresented parties and attorneys may be ordered to attend pretrial conferences.

DISSENT: (Easterbrook, J.) A court should not be able to impose upon a party its will as to what sort of agent it must send to a conference. To demand "full settlement authority" in many cases would mean demanding attendance of a quorum of the board of directors, clearly an unreasonable demand.

DISSENT: (Ripple, J.) The majority's decision strains the relationship between the judiciary and Congress and was not contemplated by the Rules Enabling Act.

EDITOR'S ANALYSIS: "Q: How does a federal judge change a light bulb? A: He holds it in place and the universe revolves around him." All who have practiced in federal court are quite familiar with the highhandedness of many federal judges who seem to think that their dockets are the only things that matter. Unfortunately for those appearing before them, the law often supports this attitude, as this case shows.

———————————

[For more information on pretrial conferences, see Casenote Law Outline on Civil Procedure, Chapter 8, § II, Pre-trial Conferences and Pre-trial Orders.]

NOTES:

STRANDELL v. JACKSON COUNTY
838 F.2d 884 (7th Cir. 1987).

NATURE OF CASE: Appeal of contempt citation.

FACT SUMMARY: When counsel for Strandell (P) refused to participate in a court-ordered summary jury trial under Fed. R. Civ. P. 16, he was held in contempt.

CONCISE RULE OF LAW: A court may not impose sanctions for a party's refusal to participate in a summary jury trial.

FACTS: Strandell (P) sued Jackson County (D) for civil rights violations. The court, noting that the trial was expected to last six weeks and that its calendar was very congested, ordered the litigants to submit to a nonbinding summary jury trial. Counsel for Strandell (P) refused, contending that this would compel him to disclose materials protected by the work-product privilege. The court held counsel in contempt, and he appealed.

ISSUE: May a court impose sanctions for a party's refusal to participate in a summary jury trial?

HOLDING AND DECISION: (Ripple, J.) No. A court may not impose sanctions for a party's refusal to participate in a summary jury trial. Fed. R. Civ. P. 16 authorizes courts to use various pretrial settlement devices for the resolution of disputes. However, the rule was not designed as a means for clubbing the parties into an involuntary compromise. In this instance, counsel entertained the court's suggestion and declined for reasons which appear quite reasonable to this court. Therefore, the contempt citation was improper. Reversed.

EDITOR'S ANALYSIS: In this day of crowded court calendars, the use of summary jury trials has gained increasing favor. While the details may vary, it generally involves each side's summarizing its evidence to a jury. The jury then renders a verdict. In this manner, the parties can get a feel for how their respective cases might look to a fact finder.

[For more information on pretrial orders, see Casenote Law Outline on Civil Procedure, Chapter 8, § II, Pre-trial Conferences and Pre-trial Orders.]

NOTES:

MAREK v. CHESNY
473 U.S. 1 (1985).

NATURE OF CASE: Appeal of denial of award of attorney fees.

FACT SUMMARY: Chesny (P) refused a settlement offer in a § 1983 action and was awarded less in trial.

CONCISE RULE OF LAW: Attorney fees incurred by a plaintiff subsequent to an offer of settlement will not be paid when the plaintiff recovers less than the offer.

FACTS: Chesny (P) sued Marek (D) under 42 U.S.C. § 1983. Prior to trial, Marek (D) and the other defendants offered $100,000 to settle. Chesny (P) refused and was awarded $60,000 at trial. The court awarded Chesny (P) $32,000 in costs and fees incurred before the offer but refused to award costs and fees subsequent to the offer, per Fed. R. Civ. P. 68, which shifts to the plaintiff all costs incurred subsequent to an offer of judgment not exceeded by the ultimate recovery. The district court held that fees recoverable by a plaintiff in a § 1983 action were considered costs for purposes of Fed. R. Civ. P. 68. The Seventh Circuit disagreed and reversed. The Supreme Court granted certiorari.

ISSUE: Will attorney fees incurred by a plaintiff subsequent to an offer of settlement be paid when the plaintiff recovers less than the offer?

HOLDING AND DECISION: (Burger, C.J.) No. Attorney fees incurred by a plaintiff subsequent to an offer of settlement will not be paid when the plaintiff recovers less than the offer. Legislative history shows that when Fed. R. Civ. P. 68 was drafted, attorney fees were considered part of costs. When 42 U.S.C. § 1988 was enacted, enabling successful plaintiffs to recover costs and fees, Congress was aware that Fed. R. Civ. P. 68 included fees in its operation, and it could have exempted plaintiffs in § 1983 actions from the force of Fed. R. Civ. P. 68, but it did not do so. In the absence of this, the salutary effect of Fed. R. Civ. P. 68, the encouragement of settlements, should not be hindered. Reversed.

DISSENT: (Brennan, J.) The Court's reasoning is wholly inconsistent with the history and structure of the Federal Rules. Its application to the over 100 attorney fees statutes enacted by Congress will produce absurd variations in Rule 68's operation among the statutes. This is contrary to the purpose of the Federal Rules, which is a uniform procedure in federal courts.

EDITOR'S ANALYSIS: 42 U.S.C. § 1988 was enacted in 1976. As the Court states, it provides that prevailing plaintiffs in § 1983 actions will be awarded costs and fees. The purpose of the section was to ensure that civil rights plaintiffs obtained effective access to the judicial process.

[For more information on taxation of costs, see Case-note Law Outline on Civil Procedure, Chapter 11, § II, Self-enforcing Judgments Distinguished From Coercive Judgments.]

NEWTON v. A.C & S., INC.
918 F.2d 1121 (3rd Cir. 1990).

NATURE OF CASE: Appeal from fines issued for violation of court orders in consolidated asbestos injury cases.

FACT SUMMARY: A district court issued monetary sanctions against defendants in complex litigation who failed to settle prior to the deadline imposed by the court.

CONCISE RULE OF LAW: A court may not issue an automatic fine against a party for settling after a court-imposed deadline.

FACTS: Faced with a complex and massive asbestos litigation, a district court issued a pretrial order that parties, if they were to settle, could do so no later than two weeks prior to trial. This was so that the court could "stack" the cases efficiently, i.e., move the next case into the trial slot formerly occupied by the settled case. In one case, the court issued a $1,000 fine against parties who settled just prior to trial but after the court's deadline. In another case, each defendant who settled in a case during trial was fined $250. In both cases, the sanctioned parties appealed.

ISSUE: May a court issue an automatic fine against a party settling after a court-imposed deadline?

HOLDING AND DECISION: (Rusern, J.) No. A court may not issue an automatic fine against a party settling after a court-imposed deadline. Fed. R. Civ. P. 16 gives a district court broad powers to manage their calendars, including the ability to compel parties to engage in settlement proceedings. A court may enforce this right through sanctions. However, Rule 16 apparently limits the courts to using this power to compensate parties and the courts for their reasonable expenses. An automatic fine is more akin to contempt. When contempt is at issue, due process requires that a party is allowed a hearing for determination subject to appellate review as to whether the circumstances justify sanctions. One party may be more blameworthy, or entirely blameworthy. An automatic fine does not take this into account. Here, as the fines were automatic, they violated due process. Reversed.

EDITOR'S ANALYSIS: The present opinion hardly constitutes a significant restraint of a district court's power. A court may still levy fines for not engaging in settlement practices, per the opinion here. It simply must consider each party's case individually.

[For more information on pretrial conferences, see Casenote Law Outline on Civil Procedure, Chapter 8, § II, Pre-trial Conferences and Pre-trial Orders.]

8

CHAPTER 8
TRIAL

QUICK REFERENCE RULES OF LAW

1. **Mixed Issues of Law and Equity.** Only under the most imperative circumstances can the right to a jury trial of legal issues be lost through prior determination of equitable claims, and in view of the flexible procedures of the federal rules, the Supreme Court cannot anticipate such circumstances. (Beacon Theatres, Inc. v. Westover)

   [For more information on mixed issues of law and equity, see Casenote Law Outline on Civil Procedure, Chapter 9, § II, The Right to Jury Trial in Federal Court.]

2. **Right to a Jury Trial in Mixed Law and Equity Cases.** Where equitable and legal claims are joined, the legal claims are triable by a jury as a matter of right in federal courts under the Seventh Amendment. (Dairy Queen, Inc. v. Wood)

   [For more information on the right to a jury trial in mixed law and equity cases, see Casenote Law Outline on Civil Procedure, Chapter 9, § II, The Right to Jury Trial in Federal Court.]

3. **Right to a Jury Trial.** The right to a jury trial is available in a shareholder's derivative suit. (Ross v. Bernhard)

   [For more information on the right to a jury trial, see Casenote Law Outline on Civil Procedure, Chapter 9, § II, The Right to Jury Trial in Federal Court.]

4. **Right to a Jury Trial.** The Seventh Amendment of the Constitution applies to actions enforcing statutory rights and requires a jury trial on demand if the statute creates legal rights and remedies enforceable in an action for damages in the ordinary courts of law. (Curtis v. Loether)

   [For more information on the right to a jury trial, see Casenote Law Outline on Civil Procedure, Chapter 9, § II, The Right to Jury Trial in Federal Court.]

5. **Right to a Jury Trial.** In a civil suit under the Federal Clean Water Act, a defendant is entitled to a jury trial as to liability. (Tull v. United States)

   [For more information on the right to a jury trial in statutory cause of action, see Casenote Law Outline on Civil Procedure, Chapter 9, § II, The Right to Jury Trial in Federal Court.]

6. **Right to Jury Trial.** An employee who seeks relief in the form of back pay for a union's alleged breach of its duty of fair representation has a right to trial by jury. (Teamsters, Local No. 391 v. Terry)

   [For more information on right to jury trial, see Casenote Law Outline on Civil Procedure, Chapter 9, § II, The Right to Jury Trial in Federal Court.]

7. **Right to Jury Trial.** When sued by the trustee in bankruptcy to recover an allegedly fraudulent monetary transfer, a person who has not submitted a claim against a bankruptcy estate has a right to a jury trial. (Granfinanciera, S.A. v. Nordberg)

   [For more information on right to jury trial, see Casenote Law Outline on Civil Procedure, Chapter 9, § II, The Right to Jury Trial in Federal Court.]

8. **Directed Verdicts.** A directed verdict does not violate the Seventh Amendment. (Galloway v. United States)

8

CASENOTE LEGAL BRIEFS —CIVIL PROCEDURE

[For more information on directed verdicts, see Casenote Law Outline on Civil Procedure, Chapter 9, § V, Directed Verdicts.]

9. **Standards of Appellate Review.** An appellate court's function in reviewing a jury verdict is exhausted as soon as it determines that there is an evidentiary basis for the jury's verdict, and only when it finds a complete absence of probative facts to support a verdict may the court reverse it as clearly erroneous. (Lavender v. Kurn)

[For more information on standards of appellate review, see Casenote Law Outline on Civil Procedure, Chapter 10, § I, The Mechanics of Appeal.]

10. **Role of the Judge at Trial.** Whether or not a crucial piece of evidence is authentic is a jury issue. (Guenther v. Armstrong Rubber Co.)

[For more information on the role of the judge at trial, see Casenote Law Outline on Civil Procedure, Chapter 9, § IV, The Role of Judge and Jury Before and During Trial.]

11. **Motion for a New Trial.** A jury verdict is to stand unless seriously erroneous; mere disagreement with the verdict will not justify the granting of a new trial. (Keeler v. Hewitt)

[For more information on motion for a new trial, see Casenote Law Outline on Civil Procedure, Chapter 9, § VI, Post-verdict Motions.]

12. **Post-trial Motion Procedure.** A court of appeals may, after reversing a defendant's motion for judgment n.o.v., enter an order of dismissal. (Neely v. Martin K. Eby Const. Co.)

[For more information on post-trial motion procedure, see Casenote Law Outline on Civil Procedure, Chapter 9, § VI, Post-verdict Motions.]

13. **The Process of Additur.** Although the damages awarded by the jury may be deemed inadequate, the court has no power to increase them even though the defendant consents to such an increase. (Dimick v. Schiedt)

[For more information on the process of additur, see Casenote Law Outline on Civil Procedure, Chapter 9, § VI, Post-verdict Motions.]

14. **Motion for a New Trial.** A jury's answers to interrogatories will not be a basis for overturning a verdict if any means of reconciling them with the verdict exists. (Whitlock v. Jackson)

[For more information on motion for a new trial, see Casenote Law Outline on Civil Procedure, Chapter 9, § VI, Post-verdict Motions.]

15. **Motion for a New Trial.** Affidavits of jurors may not be used to impeach a verdict. (Sopp v. Smith)

[For more information on motion for a new trial, see Casenote Law Outline on Civil Procedure, Chapter 9, § VI, Post-verdict Motions.]

16. **Misconduct by Counsel or Jury.** Jurors may testify as to objective facts to impeach a verdict. (People v. Hutchison)

[For more information on misconduct by counsel or jury, see Casenote Law Outline on Civil Procedure, Chapter 9, § VI, Post-verdict Motions.]

BEACON THEATRES, INC. v. WESTOVER
359 U.S. 500 (1959).

NATURE OF CASE: Petition for writ of mandamus to require a district judge to reverse denial for jury trial in a declaratory relief action.

FACT SUMMARY: Beacon (D) threatened to bring an antitrust action against Fox (P) based on Fox's (P) contract granting it exclusive rights to show first-run movies. Fox (P) brought a declaratory relief action against Beacon (D). Beacon (D) counterclaimed, seeking treble damages and demanding a jury trial.

CONCISE RULE OF LAW: Only under the most imperative circumstances can the right to a jury trial of legal issues be lost through prior determination of equitable claims, and in view of the flexible procedures of the federal rules, the Supreme Court cannot anticipate such circumstances.

FACTS: According to its complaint, Fox (P) operated a movie theater in San Bernardino. Its contracts with movie distributors granted it the exclusive right to show first-run movies in the San Bernardino competitive area and provided for "clearance," a period of time during which no other theater could exhibit the same picture. Beacon (D) built a theater 11 miles away and notified Fox (P) that it considered Fox's (P) contracts to be in violation of the antitrust laws. Fox (P) alleged that this notification together with threats of lawsuits gave rise to duress and coercion and deprived Fox (P) of its right to negotiate for first-run contracts. Fox (P) prayed for a declaration that the clearances were not in violation of the antitrust laws and an injunction to prevent Beacon (D) from bringing an antitrust action against Fox (P). Beacon (D) filed a counterclaim, asserting that there was no substantial competition between the two theaters, and, hence, the clearances were unreasonable. It also alleged that a conspiracy existed between Fox (P) and its distributors to restrain trade and monopolize first-run movies in violation of the antitrust laws. Beacon (D) asked for treble damages. The district court found that Fox's (P) complaint for declaratory relief presented basically equitable issues. It directed that these issues be tried by the court without a jury before jury determination of the validity of Beacon's (D) charges of antitrust violations.

ISSUE: Where a complaint alleges circumstances which traditionally have justified equity to take jurisdiction, in light of the Declaratory Judgment Act and the Federal Rules of Civil Procedure, would a court be justified in denying defendant a trial by jury on all legal issues?

HOLDING AND DECISION: (Black, J.) No. In this case, the reasonableness of the clearances granted Fox (P) was an issue common to Fox's (P) action for declaratory relief and to Beacon's (D) counterclaim. Hence, the effect of the district court's action could be to limit Beacon's (D) opportunity to try before a jury every issue which has a bearing on its treble damage suit. The determination of the issues of the clearances by the judge might operate by way of res judicata or collateral estoppel so as to conclude both parties with respect to those issues at the subsequent trial of the treble damage claim. Since the right to trial by jury applies to treble damage suits under the antitrust laws, the antitrust issues were essentially jury questions. Assuming that Fox's (P) complaint supports a request for an injunction and further alleges the kind of harassment by a multiplicity of lawsuits which traditionally have justified equity to take jurisdiction, in light of the Declaratory Judgment Act and the Federal Rules of Civil Procedure, a court would not be justified in denying a defendant a jury trial on all the legal issues. Only under the most imperative circumstances can the right to a jury trial of legal issues be lost through prior determination of equitable claims. In view of the flexible procedures of the federal rules, the court cannot now anticipate such circumstances. Under the federal rules, the same court may try both legal and equitable claims in the same action. Hence, any defenses, equitable or legal, that Fox (P) may have to Beacon's (D) charges can be raised either in its declaratory relief suit or in its answer to Beacon's (D) counterclaim. Any permanent injunctive relief to which Fox (P) might be entitled could be given by the court after the jury renders its verdict. The judgment denying Beacon's (D) jury demand is reversed.

DISSENT: (Stewart, J.) The federal rules make possible the trial of legal and equitable claims in the same proceeding, but they expressly affirm the power of a trial judge to determine the order in which claims shall be heard. They did not expand the substantive law. In this case, Beacon's (D) counterclaim could not be held to have transformed Fox's (P) original complaint into an action at law.

EDITOR'S ANALYSIS: The right to a jury trial depends not so much on the form of the action as on the kind of relief sought. Hence, as long as the ultimate remedy is legal in nature, the right is recognized, even though the plaintiff has invoked an historically equitable procedural device, as demonstrated by this case. Here, the effect of the declaration of its rights sought by Fox (P) would be to defeat (or establish) Beacon's (D) claim for money damages. Hence, the issues must be tried before a jury.

[For more information on mixed issues of law and equity, see Casenote Law Outline on Civil Procedure, Chapter 9, § II, The Right to Jury Trial in Federal Court.]

NOTES:

DAIRY QUEEN, INC. v. WOOD
369 U.S. 469 (1962).

NATURE OF CASE: On writ of certiorari regarding denial of mandamus.

FACT SUMMARY: Wood (D), sued by Dairy Queen (P) for breach of contract in their trademark agreement, demanded a jury trial based on Dairy Queen's (P) having sought a money judgment as part of its complaint.

CONCISE RULE OF LAW: Where equitable and legal claims are joined, the legal claims are triable by a jury as a matter of right in federal courts under the Seventh Amendment.

FACTS: Dairy Queen (P) originally brought an action against Wood (D) in district court, alleging breach of contract based on Wood's (D) failure to make the required payments for the use of Dairy Queen's (P) trademark. The complaint sought injunctive relief to restrain further use of the trademark, an accounting to determine the amount of money owed to Dairy Queen (P) by Wood (D), and a judgment for that amount. Wood's (D) answer demanded, among other things, a jury trial. The district court struck down this demand. Wood (D) sought mandamus in the U.S. court of appeals to compel the district judge to vacate the order. The request was denied. Wood (D) argued that, insofar as the complaint requested a money judgment, he, Wood (D), was entitled to a jury trial since the action was one of law. Dairy Queen (P) argued that the money claim was "purely equitable" since it was cast in terms of an "accounting" rather than as an action for a "debt" or "damages" and that the legal claim was only "incidental" to the equitable issues.

ISSUE: Is the right to a trial by jury in federal court lost as to legal issues when the legal issues are incidental to the equitable issues?

HOLDING AND DECISION: (Black, J.) No. The holding of Scott v. Neeley (1891), that the right to jury trial of legal issues must be preserved, was not changed by the Federal Rules of Civil Procedure, but, on the contrary, Rule 38(a) expressly reaffirmed that constitutional principle. Even so, until the decision in Beacon Theatres, Inc. v. Westover, attempts were made to indirectly undercut that right by having federal courts — in cases involving both legal and equitable claims — decide the equitable claims first, with the result that the court determined any issue common to both legal and equitable claims, thereby depriving the party seeking trial by jury of that right. Beacon Theatres stated that where both legal and equitable issues are presented in a single case, "only under the most imperative circumstances" can the right to a jury trial of legal issues by lost through prior determination of equitable claims. There being no question in the instant case of imperative circumstances (or of a timely demand for jury trial), the sole question is whether this action contains legal issues. The request for a money judgment on the part of Dairy Queen (P), as well as an action for damages based upon a charge of trademark infringement, are unquestionably legal in nature. To accede to Dairy Queen's (P) rationale that its money claim was "purely equitable" since it was cast in terms of an "accounting" rather than as an action for "debt" or "damages" would be to make the constitutional right to trial by jury depend on the choice of words used in the pleadings. This complaint, insofar as it requests a money judgment, presents a legal claim, triable by a jury in federal court as a matter of right under the Seventh Amendment. Reversed.

EDITOR'S ANALYSIS: Stating that legal claims are not magically converted into equitable issues by the presentation to a court of equity, the Court, in Ross v. Bernhard (1970) — a stockholders' derivative suit — ruled that, where equitable and legal claims are joined in the same action, there is a right to a jury trial on the legal claims which must not be infringed upon, either by trying the legal issues as incidental to the equitable ones or by a court trial of a common issue existing between the claims. This principle has been reiterated by the court in many cases involving legal and equitable issues. Note that it is often said that the Seventh Amendment right to a jury trial depends not upon the form of the action but rather upon the true nature of the kind of relief sought (i.e., legal or equitable). Note, finally, that although Dairy Queen expressly disapproved of the practice of circumventing jury trials by first trying equitable issues, the Court has approved the use of bifurcated trials (i.e., one for legal issues, the other for equitable) where the interests are best served thereby (e.g., right to possession and right to damages hearings for leases).

[For more information on the right to a jury trial in mixed law and equity cases, see Casenote Law Outline on Civil Procedure, Chapter 9, § II, The Right to Jury Trial in Federal Court.]

NOTES:

ROSS v. BERNHARD
396 U.S. 531 (1970).

NATURE OF CASE: Shareholder's derivative suit for damages.

FACT SUMMARY: Ross (P) brought a derivative suit on behalf of Lehman Corporation for damages resulting from breaches of fiduciary duty and negligence by Lehman Brothers (D), who controlled the corporation.

CONCISE RULE OF LAW: The right to a jury trial is available in a shareholder's derivative suit.

FACTS: Lehman Brothers (D) were brokers for Lehman Corporation and controlled the corporation through an illegally large representation on the board of directors. Ross (P), a shareholder in the corporation, brought a derivative action for damages resulting from Lehman Brothers' (D) negligence and breach of fiduciary duties. Ross (P) demanded a jury trial on the issue of the claims made on behalf of the corporation.

ISSUE: Is the right to jury trial available in a shareholder's derivative suit?

HOLDING AND DECISION: (White, J.) Yes. The Seventh Amendment preserved the right to jury trials, not only in suits at common law but in all those dealing with legal rights. At common law, a corporation could sue and be sued, but a shareholder of the corporation could not bring the action on behalf of the corporation, such shareholder suit being recognized only in equity. The first case in which the issue of jury trials in derivative suits arose was in Fleitmann v. Welsbach Street Lighting, an antitrust action seeking treble damages. There, Justice Holmes noted that Fleitmann's only remedy was at law, and the defendant should not have been denied a jury trial because the plaintiff was unable to get the corporation to sue. Since, however, the decision there was based on antitrust statutes, it could not extend to this case. However, the Federal Rules of Civil Procedure and a Ninth Circuit case, Depinto v. Provident Life Ins. Co., indicate that jury trials are proper in derivative suits. Depinto applied the reasoning of previous cases, that when there are both legal and equitable claims, a jury trial should be granted on the legal issues. Thus, where the derivative suit deals with legal issues on behalf of the corporation, it would require a jury trial since equity is available only when no adequate remedy at law exists. Under the Federal Rules of Civil Procedure, there is only one action, the distinction between legal and equitable actions having merged. Thus, the court must first determine if the plaintiff can sue on behalf of the corporation, and, if so, a jury trial is required. The federal rules, by merging law and equity, did away with the necessity of having a corporation's claims presented only by the corporation's directors and not by one of its shareholders.

DISSENT: (Stewart, J.) The Seventh Amendment preserves jury trials only in those actions in which the right existed at common law. Since the federal rules only grant jury trials as required by the Seventh Amendment, the two taken together cannot extend jury trials to actions where there was no right at common law.

EDITOR'S ANALYSIS: The merger of law and equity, although providing easier forms of pleading, raises serious problems in regard to the extent to which defenses and rights recognized at law will be upheld or discarded when the action is equitable in nature. As the Ross case indicates, the question of the right to a jury trial depends more on the issue to be tried, rather than the general character of the entire action. In making this determination, however, a court is forced to ignore the merger of law and equity and first consider whether, in premerger custom, the issue is legal in nature. If so, and if the remedy is one available at law, then, if practical, the issue should be given to a jury. Yet, given the type of analysis required to determine if the issue is basically legal, a plaintiff can virtually dictate his choice for a jury by framing his complaint around legal issues. Other than cases like derivative suits, where a plaintiff has no real choice as to his status and the claims he must make, the merger of law and equity has apparently extended a right to jury trial in cases which essentially involve equitable claims.

[For more information on the right to a jury trial, see Casenote Law Outline on Civil Procedure, Chapter 9, § II, The Right to Jury Trial in Federal Court.]

NOTES:

CURTIS v. LOETHER
415 U.S. 189 (1974).

NATURE OF CASE: On writ of certiorari in action for injunctive relief and damages for violation of fair housing provisions.

FACT SUMMARY: The Loethers (D), whites, having been charged with racial discrimination in violation of the 1968 Civil Rights Act for failure to rent an apartment to Curtis (P), an African-American, sought a jury trial under the Seventh Amendment.

CONCISE RULE OF LAW: The Seventh Amendment of the Constitution applies to actions enforcing statutory rights and requires a jury trial on demand if the statute creates legal rights and remedies enforceable in an action for damages in the ordinary courts of law.

FACTS: Curtis (P), an African-American woman, brought an action under § 812 of the 1968 Civil Rights Act, claiming that the Loethers (D), whites, refused to rent an apartment to her because of her race, in violation of Title VIII of the fair housing provisions of the Act. Following the voluntary dissolution of a preliminary injunction, the case was tried on the issues of actual and punitive damages. The Loethers (D) made a timely request for a jury trial, which the district court denied, holding that a jury trial was authorized neither by Title VIII nor by the Seventh Amendment. The district court then found that the Loethers (D) had, in fact, racially discriminated against Curtis (P). No actual damage was found, but $250 in punitive damages was awarded. The court of appeals reversed on the issue of the right to jury trial, holding that it was guaranteed by the Seventh Amendment. Curtis (P) appealed, arguing that the Seventh Amendment is inapplicable to new causes of action created by congressional enactment.

ISSUE: Are jury trials required under the Seventh Amendment in actions enforcing statutory rights if the statute creates legal rights and remedies enforceable in an action for damages in the ordinary courts of law?

HOLDING AND DECISION: (Marshall, J.) Yes. Although from a review of the legislative history to Title VIII, the question of whether jury trials were intended can be susceptible to arguments for and against; it is clear that the Seventh Amendment entitles either party to demand a jury trial in an action for damages in the federal courts under § 812 of the 1968 Civil Rights Act. It has long been settled that the Seventh Amendment right to jury trials extends beyond the common law actions existing when the Amendment was framed. As Justice Story pointed out in Parsons v. Bedford, the Amendment may be construed to cover all suits, of whatever form, dealing with legal rights as distinct from equity and admiralty jurisdiction. The applicability of the constitutional right to a jury trial in actions enforcing statutory rights has been regarded as a matter too obvious to be doubted. To dispel any further doubt, the Court holds that the Seventh Amendment does apply to actions enforcing statutory rights and requires a jury trial upon demand, if the statute creates legal rights and remedies enforceable in an action for damages in the ordinary courts of law. Curtis (P) relied on NLRB v. Jones and Laughlin Steel, but those cases merely stand for the proposition that the Seventh Amendment is inapplicable to administrative proceedings since jury trials would be incompatible with the concept of administrative adjudication. Katchen v. Landry, also relied on by Curtis (P), was also inapplicable since it dealt with a bankruptcy proceeding, which is regarded as a matter of equity. However, the instant action was a damage action, sounding in tort and enforcing legal rights, and when Congress provided for the civil enforcement of statutory rights involving rights and remedies of the sort typically enforced in actions at law, a jury trial must be available. Affirmed.

EDITOR'S ANALYSIS: If a legal claim is joined with an equitable claim, the right to jury trial on the legal claim, including all issues common to both claims, remains intact, and the right cannot be abridged by characterizing the legal claim as "incidental to the equitable relief sought." The above case illustrates another instance in which the Seventh Amendment's guarantee of right to jury trial is applicable. Others include (1) declaratory actions presenting traditional common law issues; (2) actions for the recovery and possession of land; (3) proceedings in rem for the confiscation of goods on land; (4) stockholders' derivative actions for damages; and (5) civil rights actions to recover damages. Examples of cases in which the Seventh Amendment has been held applicable to statutory rights include (1) trademarks, (2) immigration cases, and (3) antitrust actions. Note, finally, that even if the preliminary injunction here had not been dissolved before trial, the fact that a damage action was involved here would make the Seventh Amendment applicable.

[For more information on the right to a jury trial, see Casenote Law Outline on Civil Procedure, Chapter 9, § II, The Right to Jury Trial in Federal Court.]

NOTES:

TULL v. UNITED STATES
481 U.S. 412 (1987).

NATURE OF CASE: Appeal of award of damages for violations of the Federal Clean Water Act.

FACT SUMMARY: Tull (D), charged with violations of the Federal Clean Water Act in a civil action, requested and was denied a jury trial.

CONCISE RULE OF LAW: In a civil suit under the Federal Clean Water Act, a defendant is entitled to a jury trial as to liability.

FACTS: Tull (D) was sued by the Government (P) for illegal waste dumping in violation of the Clean Water Act. Tull (D) requested, and was denied, a jury trial. The court refused and, after a bench trial, awarded $75,000 plus further fines unless expensive restoration efforts were undertaken. This was affirmed on appeal. The Supreme Court granted review.

ISSUE: In a civil suit under the Federal Clean Water Act, is a defendant entitled to a jury trial as to liability?

HOLDING AND DECISION: (Brennan, J.) Yes. In a civil suit under the Federal Clean Water Act, a defendant is entitled to a jury trial as to liability. Under the Seventh Amendment, a right to a jury trial is guaranteed for suits at common law. In actions based on statute, courts often indulge in searches for antiquated causes of action, seeking a common law analog to the statutory cause of action, to decide whether a right to jury trial exists. However, this emphasis is misplaced. It is the remedy sought, not the cause of action, that dictates whether a statutory action comes within the ambit of the Seventh Amendment. Here, damages were sought. Historically, damages were the remedy for suits at common law. This being so, Tull (D) was entitled to a jury trial. [The Court held that this right extended only to liability, not damages.] Reversed.

CONCURRENCE AND DISSENT: (Scalia, J.) A right to a jury trial on liability by necessity involves a right to jury trial as to damages.

EDITOR'S ANALYSIS: The test rejected by the Court has been called the "historical test." As described by the Court, it involved reaching back into early common law causes of action to see if the statutory action has an analog. The test approved is also historically based but relates to remedy, not right of action.

[For more information on the right to a jury trial in statutory cause of action, see Casenote Law Outline on Civil Procedure, Chapter 9, § II, The Right to Jury Trial in Federal Court.]

NOTES:

TEAMSTERS LOCAL NO. 391 v. TERRY
494 U.S. 558 (1990).

NATURE OF CASE: Appeal from denial of a defendant's motion to strike a jury demand in an action for breach of a union's duty of fair representation.

FACT SUMMARY: Terry (P) and other truck drivers (P) covered by a collective-bargaining agreement between the Union (D) and their employer brought this action against the Union (D) for allegedly breaching its duty of fair representation, seeking compensatory damages and requesting a jury trial.

CONCISE RULE OF LAW: An employee who seeks relief in the form of back pay for a union's alleged breach of its duty of fair representation has a right to trial by jury.

FACTS: Terry (P) and others who were truck drivers for McLean Trucking (D) were covered by a collective-bargaining agreement between McLean (D) and the Teamsters Union (D). When the Union (D) refused to refer a grievance to the grievance committee, Terry (P) and the other truck drivers (P) filed an action in the district court, seeking, among other things, compensatory damages for lost wages and health benefits. They alleged that McLean (D) had breached the collective-bargaining agreement in violation of § 301 of the Labor Management Relations Act and that the Union (D) had violated its duty of fair representation. McLean (D) was voluntarily dropped from the suit after filing for bankruptcy. Terry (P) and the others (P) requested a jury trial. The Union (D) moved to strike the jury demand. The district court denied the motion, and the court of appeals affirmed. This appeal followed.

ISSUE: Does an employee who seeks relief in the form of back pay for a union's alleged breach of its duty of fair representation have a right to trial by jury?

HOLDING AND DECISION: (Marshall, J.) Yes. An employee who seeks relief in the form of back pay for a union's alleged breach of its duty of fair representation has a right to trial by jury. This action against the Union (D) encompasses both equitable and legal issues. Congress specifically characterized back pay under Title VII as a form of equitable relief but made no similar pronouncement regarding the duty of fair representation. Back pay sought from an employer under Title VII would generally be restitutionary in nature, in contrast to the damages sought here. Moreover, the fact that Title VII's back pay provision may have been modeled on a provision in the NLRA concerning remedies for unfair labor practices does not require that the back pay remedy available here be considered equitable. The money damages sought are the type of relief usually awarded by courts of law. Affirmed.

CONCURRENCE: (Brennan, J.) The constitutional right to a jury trial should be decided on the basis of the relief sought. If the relief is legal in nature, the parties have a constitutional right to a trial by jury, unless Congress has permissibly delegated the particular dispute to a non-Article III decision-maker and jury trials would frustrate Congress' purposes in enacting a particular statutory scheme. Historically, jurisdictional lines between law and equity were primarily a matter of remedy.

CONCURRENCE: (Stevens, J.) Duty of fair representation suits are for the most part ordinary civil actions involving the stuff of contract and malpractice disputes. There is, accordingly, no ground for excluding these actions from the jury right.

DISSENT: (Kennedy, J.) The presence of monetary damages in this duty of fair representation action does not make it more analogous to a legal action than an equitable action. The trust analogy is the controlling one here, and a breach of trust historically carries no right of trial by jury. Furthermore, the Seventh Amendment right to a jury trial in civil cases, a right existing in 1791, cannot be preserved without looking to history to identify it.

EDITOR'S ANALYSIS: Part III-A of the majority opinion contained a two-part historical test customarily applied by the Court in deciding the right to a jury trial. The historical test first compared the statutory action to 18th-century actions brought in the courts of England prior to the merger of the courts of law and equity. Second, the test examined the remedy sought to determine whether it was legal or equitable in nature, with the second inquiry given more weight than the first. The Justices differed as to whether or not this historical test should now be abandoned.

[For more information on right to jury trial, see Casenote Law Outline on Civil Procedure, Chapter 9, § II, The Right to Jury Trial in Federal Court.]

NOTES:

GRANFINANCIERA, S.A. v. NORDBERG
492 U.S. 33 (1989).

NATURE OF CASE: Appeal from denial of a defendant's request for a jury trial in an action to recover damages for fraudulent monetary transfers.

FACT SUMMARY: After Nordberg (P), the bankruptcy trustee for Chase & Sanborn Corporation's Chapter 11 reorganization, filed this suit against Granfinanciera (D) for fraudulent transfer, Granfinanciera (D) requested a jury trial for all issues so triable, but the court denied the request.

CONCISE RULE OF LAW: When sued by the trustee in bankruptcy to recover an allegedly fraudulent monetary transfer, a person who has not submitted a claim against a bankruptcy estate has a right to a jury trial.

FACTS: After the Chase & Sanborn Corporation filed a petition for reorganization under Chapter 11 of the Bankruptcy Code, Nordberg (P), the bankruptcy trustee, filed suit against Granfinanciera, S.A. (D). The suit alleged that Granfinanciera (D) had received a large sum of money from Chase & Sanborn's corporate predecessor within one year of the date its bankruptcy petition was filed, without giving consideration or a reasonably equivalent value in return. Nordberg (P) sought to recover damages, costs, expenses, and interest. The district court referred the proceedings to the bankruptcy court. Granfinanciera (D) requested a trial by jury on all issues so triable. The bankruptcy judge denied the request. Following a bench trial, the court entered judgment for Nordberg (P). The district court affirmed, as did the court of appeals. Granfinanciera (D) appealed.

ISSUE: When sued by the trustee in bankruptcy to recover an allegedly fraudulent monetary transfer, does a person who has not submitted a claim against a bankruptcy estate have a right to a jury trial?

HOLDING AND DECISION: (Brennan, J.) Yes. When sued by the trustee in bankruptcy to recover an allegedly fraudulent monetary transfer, a person who has not submitted a claim against a bankruptcy estate has a right to a jury trial. Nordberg's (P) fraudulent conveyance action plainly seeks relief traditionally provided by law courts having both legal and equitable dockets. Unless Congress has withdrawn jurisdiction over that action by courts of law, the Seventh Amendment still guarantees a jury trial here, upon request. Congress may not deprive litigating parties of the guarantee of a jury trial, unless a legal cause of action involves "public rights"; however, the federal government need not be a party for a case to revolve around public rights. A bankruptcy trustee's right to recover a fraudulent conveyance is more accurately characterized as a private rather than a public right. Because Granfinanciera (D) has not filed claims against the estate, Nordberg's (P) fraudulent conveyance action does not arise as part of the processes of allowance and disallowance of claims. Congress cannot therefore divest Granfinanciera (D) of its right to a trial by jury. Affirmed.

CONCURRENCE: (Scalia, J.) A matter of public rights, whose adjudication Congress may assign to tribunals lacking the essential characteristics of Article III courts, must arise between the government and others. Until quite recently, this has also been the consistent view of the Court. However, the remainder of the Court's opinion is correct, as is its judgment.

DISSENT: (White, J.) Granfinanciera (D) has no Seventh Amendment right to a jury trial when Nordberg (P) seeks to avoid the fraudulent transfers Granfinanciera (D) received. Congress has defined actions such as the one in the instant case to be among the "core" of bankruptcy proceedings, triable in a bankruptcy court before a bankruptcy judge and without a jury. These decisions require deference.

DISSENT: (Blackmun, J.) Congress has legislated treacherously close to the constitutional line by denying a jury trial in a fraudulent conveyance action in which a defendant has no claim against the estate. Nonetheless, given the importance of permitting Congress to fashion a modern bankruptcy system, it cannot be said that Congress has crossed the constitutional line on the facts of this case. By holding otherwise, the Court today throws Congress into still another round of bankruptcy court reform, without compelling reason.

EDITOR'S ANALYSIS: When Congress creates new statutory public rights, it may assign their adjudication to an administrative agency with which a jury trial would be incompatible without violating the Seventh Amendment's injunction that jury trial is to be preserved in suits at common law. But Congress lacks the power to strip parties contesting matters of private right of their constitutional right to a trial by jury. Legal claims are not magically converted into equitable issues by their presentation to a court of equity, nor can Congress avoid the Seventh Amendment by mandating that traditional legal claims be brought there or taken to an administrative tribunal.

[For more information on right to jury trial, see Case-note Law Outline on Civil Procedure, Chapter 9, § II, The Right to Jury Trial in Federal Court.]

NOTES:

GALLOWAY v. UNITED STATES
319 U.S. 372 (1943).

NATURE OF CASE: Appeal of directed defense verdict denying military disability pay.

FACT SUMMARY: In Galloway's (P) action to obtain military disability pay, the court directed a defense verdict.

CONCISE RULE OF LAW: A directed verdict does not violate the Seventh Amendment.

FACTS: Galloway (P) served in World War I. During his stay in Europe, he demonstrated several episodes of bizarre behavior. Upon his return, his behavior became increasingly erratic. By 1930, he was diagnosed as psychotic and was put under the care of a guardian (whom he later married). In 1934, he filed a claim for military disability benefits. To qualify therefor, he had to have been mentally ill no later than 1919. His claim was denied, and he filed an action to obtain the benefits. At trial, he introduced virtually no evidence of his condition from 1923 to 1930. The trial court, finding that the lack of evidence for this period made an insufficient showing of mental disability, ordered a directed verdict for the Government (D). The court of appeals affirmed. The Supreme Court granted review.

ISSUE: Does a directed verdict violate the Seventh Amendment?

HOLDING AND DECISION: (Rutledge, J.) No. A directed verdict does not violate the Seventh Amendment. The Amendment preserves the right to jury trial in common law actions. However, the power of juries over the factual issues of a civil action had never been absolute. Further, at different times in the history of the common law, courts had exercised different levels of control over juries. It appears that the true purpose of the Seventh Amendment was to preserve the jury trial as a basic institution and to preserve its most fundamental elements. Judicial control by such procedural mechanisms as the directed verdict is permitted, when appropriate. Here, the evidence presented by Galloway (P) had such large gaps that any award in his favor could only have been based on specu-lation, an impermissible basis. Affirmed.

DISSENT: (Black, J.) The founders of our government thought that trial by jury was an essential bulwark of liberty. The language of the Seventh Amendment is clear, and the concept of the directed verdict constitutes an improper departure from the Amendment.

EDITOR'S ANALYSIS: The Court did not really need to address the issue it did. The present action was based on a statutory right not existing at common law. Statutory actions carry no right to jury trial. The Court acknowledged this but went ahead with its analysis anyway.

[For more information on directed verdicts, see Casenote Law Outline on Civil Procedure, Chapter 9, § V, Directed Verdicts.]

NOTES:

LAVENDER v. KURN
327 U.S. 645 (1946).

NATURE OF CASE: Action under Federal Employer's Liability Act.

FACT SUMMARY: Haney was killed while working for the St. Louis-San Francisco Railway Co. (D) and the Illinois Central Railroad (D) due to head injuries suffered on the job.

CONCISE RULE OF LAW: An appellate court's function in reviewing a jury verdict is exhausted as soon as it determines that there is an evidentiary basis for the jury's verdict, and only when it finds a complete absence of probative facts to support a verdict may the court reverse it as clearly erroneous.

FACTS: Lavender (P), as administrator of the estate of Haney, sued Kurn (D), as representative of the St. Louis-San Francisco Railway Co. (D) and the Illinois Central Railroad (D), under the Federal Employer's Liability Act. Haney died from head injuries suffered on his job while working as a switch-tender for the Railroad (D). At trial, Lavender (P) attempted to prove that Haney had been killed by a mail hook protruding from a moving train (i.e., negligence). This theory depended upon the jury's finding that Haney was standing exactly at one certain spot on a mound near the tracks so that the hook would have hit him at exactly 63½ inches above the ground. The Railroad's (D) defense was that Haney was murdered. The jury entered judgment for Haney. On appeal, the Missouri Supreme Court reversed the jury, stating, "it would be mere speculation and conjecture to say that Haney was struck by the mail hook," and such was not sufficient to sustain a verdict. Lavender (P) appealed.

ISSUE: May an appellate court reverse a jury verdict as erroneous merely because the jury may have engaged in "speculation and conjecture" in reaching its verdict?

HOLDING AND DECISION: (Murphy, J.) No. An appellate court's function in reviewing a jury verdict is exhausted as soon as it determines that there is an evidentiary basis for the jury's verdict, and only when it finds a complete absence of probative facts to support a verdict may the court reverse it as clearly erroneous. The jury is free to discard or disbelieve whatever facts are inconsistent with its conclusion. Whenever facts are in dispute or evidence is such that fair-minded men might draw different inferences, a measure of speculation and conjecture is required on the part of the jury, whose duty it is to choose the most reasonable inference. The appellate court was unjustified in reversing on such grounds. The judgment of the Missouri Supreme Court is reversed.

EDITOR'S ANALYSIS: The standard is that the court will not interfere with the judgment of the trier of fact unless it is "clearly erroneous." The jury is to be controlled only where its actions are so clearly out of line ("clearly erroneous") that justice cannot be served in any manner other than reversal. Compare this to the procedure "judgment n.o.v."

[For more information on standards of appellate review, see Casenote Law Outline on Civil Procedure, Chapter 10, § I, The Mechanics of Appeal.]

NOTES:

GUENTHER v. ARMSTRONG RUBBER CO.
406 F.2d 1315 (3d Cir. 1969).

NOTES:

NATURE OF CASE: Appeal of directed verdict in personal injury action.

FACT SUMMARY: In a personal injury action based on an allegedly defective tire, a directed defense award was made when Guenther (P) and his expert disagreed over the identity of the tire.

CONCISE RULE OF LAW: Whether or not a crucial piece of evidence is authentic is a jury issue.

FACTS: Guenther (P), a mechanic, was injured when a tire allegedly manufactured by Armstrong Rubber Co., Inc. (D) exploded. He filed a personal injury claim. At trial, disagreement arose between Guenther (P) and his expert as to the identity of the allegedly offending tire. The trial court entered a defense award, based on a failure to authenticate the tire. Guenther (P) appealed.

ISSUE: Is whether or not a crucial piece of evidence is authentic a jury issue?

HOLDING AND DECISION: (McLaughlin, J.) Yes. Whether or not a crucial piece of evidence is authentic is a jury issue. Where an issue of fact as to authentication exists, it is the jury's function to decide whether a proffered piece of evidence is that which it is claimed to be. Here, dispute exists as to whether the tire offered as evidence was in fact the same one that injured the plaintiff. This was an issue the jury could consider. Reversed.

EDITOR'S ANALYSIS: Guenther (P), in support of his offer of proof, noted that 80%–85% of the tires sold at the store at which he was hurt were manufactured by Armstrong (D). The court rejected this as a basis for authentication. Any conclusion based on this, said the court, would be speculation.

[For more information on the role of the judge at trial, see Casenote Law Outline on Civil Procedure, Chapter 9, § IV, The Role of Judge and Jury Before and During Trial.]

KEELER v. HEWITT
697 F.2d 8 (1st Cir. 1982).

NATURE OF CASE: Motion for a new trial following a defense verdict in a civil rights action.

FACT SUMMARY: Keeler (P) and Lewis (P) contended that a jury's verdict in favor of Hewitt (D) and the other officer (D) who had attempted to arrest them was against the clear weight of the evidence, requiring a new trial.

CONCISE RULE OF LAW: A jury verdict is to stand unless seriously erroneous; mere disagreement with the verdict will not justify the granting of a new trial.

FACTS: Hewitt (D), a fish and game officer, pulled his boat alongside Keeler's (P) and Lewis' (P) boat and demanded to see their fishing licenses. Lewis (P) did not have one, and Keeler's (P) was back on shore. Angry words were exchanged, and Hewitt (D) attempted to seize their fishing poles as evidence. That night, Hewitt (D) and Lyon (D), another officer, attempted to serve arrest warrants on them at the vacation home where they were staying. When one person in the party allegedly waved a gun, the officers (D) left. Hewitt (D) attempted, unsuccessfully, to arrest Keeler (P) at his office the next week. Lewis (P) and Keeler (P) were ultimately served with summonses and charged with fishing without a license, and Keeler (P) with interfering with an officer. Lewis (P) was acquitted, and Keeler (P) was convicted on the fishing charge only. They later filed a § 1983 action based on the attempted arrest at the vacation home, alleging warrantless, forcible entry, invasion of privacy, and public embarrassment. The jury returned a defense verdict. Lewis (P) and Keeler (P) moved for a new trial, contending that the verdict was against the clear weight of the evidence. The court, while commenting that it disagreed with the jury, denied the motion. Lewis (P) and Keeler (P) appealed.

ISSUE: Is a jury verdict to stand unless seriously erroneous?

HOLDING AND DECISION: (Campbell, J.) Yes. A jury verdict will stand unless it is seriously erroneous. A denial of a motion for a new trial will be reversed only if it was an abuse of discretion, and a denial is an abuse of discretion only if, under the evidence presented, the jury's verdict was seriously erroneous. Here, the various parties, not surprisingly, gave very different versions of the events. The officers' (D) version, which the jury elected to accept, supported the conclusion that the officers (D) had probable cause to believe Lewis (P) and Keeler (P) were in the house when they entered it, and the officers' (D) conduct was not per se unreasonable. The motion was therefore properly denied. Affirmed.

EDITOR'S ANALYSIS: Note the similarity between the new trial ruling based on the insufficiency of the evidence and a judgment n.o.v. (judgment notwithstanding the verdict). The standard here, however, for assessing new trial motions is not as onerous; the judge's power to overturn the jury's verdict is correspondingly much greater than that permitted for a directed verdict or judgment n.o.v. This is because the grant of a new trial does not implicate the right to a trial by jury, because the case is simply being sent to a second jury, not eliminating a jury verdict altogether.

[For more information on motion for a new trial, see Casenote Law Outline on Civil Procedure, Chapter 9, § VI, Post-verdict Motions.]

NOTES:

NEELY v. MARTIN K. EBY CONSTRUCTION CO., INC.
386 U.S. 317 (1967).

NATURE OF CASE: Review of appellate order dismissing wrongful death action.

FACT SUMMARY: A court of appeals, after reversing a denial of Martin K. Eby Construction Co.'s (D) motion for judgment n.o.v., entered an order of dismissal.

CONCISE RULE OF LAW: A court of appeals may, after reversing a defendant's motion for judgment n.o.v., enter an order of dismissal.

FACTS: Neely (P) brought a wrongful death action against Martin K. Eby Construction Co. (D), contending that the latter's negligent construction of a scaffold caused the decedent to fall to his death. A jury awarded $25,000. Eby Construction (D) unsuccessfully moved for judgment n.o.v. and then appealed. The court of appeals, finding that the evidence was not sufficient to have permitted the case to go to a jury, reversed and ordered the action dismissed. Neely (P) petitioned for review, contending that the court of appeals lacked the power to dismiss.

ISSUE: May a court of appeals, after reversing a denial of a motion for judgment n.o.v. by a defendant, enter an order of dismissal?

HOLDING AND DECISION: (White, J.) Yes. A court of appeals, after reversing a denial of a defendant's motion for judgment n.o.v., may enter an order of dismissal. Fed. R. Civ. P. 50(d) makes adequate provision for a party subjected to a court of appeals' reversal of a denial of a motion for judgment n.o.v. to present new grounds, either in his original brief or in a motion for reconsideration, for a new trial. To hold that, in the fare of this, a court of appeals lacks the power to enter a dismissal but rather must remand would constitute a waste of court time. Here, Neely (P) presented nothing in her brief before the court of appeals as to why, if the court reversed, a new trial should be granted. She did not file a motion for reconsideration either. In light of this, the court of appeals' action was proper. Affirmed.

DISSENT: (Black, J.) Fed. R. Civ. P. 50 should not be construed to remove from the verdict winner the opportunity of a new trial, as the trial judge is in a much better position than a court of appeals to decide if a new trial is warranted. At the very least, the matter should be remanded to the district court with an instruction that a new trial should be given. If the trial court has already denied a motion for a new trial, then perhaps an appellate court can dismiss. This has not occurred here.

EDITOR'S ANALYSIS: Neely (P) also made a Seventh Amendment argument. She claimed that to permit the court of appeals to do as it did violated her right to a jury under the Seventh Amendment. The Court rejected this without much comment, noting that an appellate court's granting of a judgment n.o.v. did not offend the Seventh Amendment any more than a trial court's doing so.

[For more information on posttrial motion procedure, see Casenote Law Outline on Civil Procedure, Chapter 9, § VI, Post-verdict Motions.]

NOTES:

DIMICK v. SCHIEDT
293 U.S. 474 (1935).

NATURE OF CASE: Writ of certiorari in action for negligence damages.

FACT SUMMARY: Dimick (P) claimed that the court's increase of his damage award without his consent and consequent denial of his motion for a new trial was a denial of his Seventh Amendment right to a jury trial.

CONCISE RULE OF LAW: Although the damages awarded by the jury may be deemed inadequate, the court has no power to increase them even though the defendant consents to such an increase.

FACTS: Dimick (P) sued Schiedt (D) for damages for personal injury allegedly caused by Schiedt's (D) negligent operation of an automobile. The jury returned a verdict for Dimick (P) for $500. Dimick (P) moved for a new trial. One of his arguments was that the damages allowed were inadequate. The trial court ordered a new trial unless Schiedt (D) would consent to an increase in damages to the sum of $1,500. Schiedt (D) consented, and the motion for a new trial was then automatically denied. Dimick (P) appealed, charging that he had not consented to the increase and that he had been denied his Seventh Amendment right to a jury trial. The appellate court reversed.

ISSUE: Where the verdict of the jury is deemed inadequate, can the court deny the plaintiff's motion for a new trial upon the defendant's consenting to pay greater damages than the jury awarded?

HOLDING AND DECISION: (Sutherland, J.) No. In order to determine the intent of the Seventh Amendment, it is necessary to examine the common law existing at the time of its adoption. A review of English law in that period shows that, while the practice of remitting excessive damages awarded by juries (i.e., remittitur) was mildly disapproved of in English law, increasing them (i.e., additur) was expressly prohibited. Without giving any real explanation, our courts have accepted remittitur since 1822. It is notable that they have never — in spite of numerous contrary arguments — granted an increase in damages. This would indicate a lack of judicial belief in the existence of the power to increase damages. A rational foundation can be found for remittitur since it does not consist of eliminating the jury verdict but of merely lopping off an increment when that verdict is excessive. However, when the verdict is too small, an increase by the court is an addition which in no sense can be found in the jury verdict. There is consequently a deprivation of the constitutional guarantee of trial by jury. What we are dealing with here is not merely the court's power to declare and effectuate an adaptation of common law but rather the question of the court's changing the Constitution. This the court cannot do. Therefore, even if the defendant should consent to an increase in damages, the court has no power to increase damages when the amount awarded by the jury is deemed inadequate. Affirmed.

DISSENT: (Stone, J.) First, the Court should not be limited by the fact that, by the time the Seventh Amendment was adopted, no English judge had denied a motion for a new trial in actions at law. The trial court's action here is not a procedure which would curtail the jury's essential function of deciding questions of fact. It is unquestionably within the discretion of the trial judge to deny the motion for a new trial without intruding on the province of the jury to decide questions of fact. Then surely he may also exercise his discretion in denying it when he knows the plaintiff will suffer no harm since he will receive a proper recovery and the defendant will suffer no harm since he consented to it.

EDITOR'S ANALYSIS: Additur occurs when the court grants a new trial but conditions its order by providing that if the defendant will consent to an increase in the amount of the verdict to a specified sum, then the motion for a new trial will be denied. Additur is not presently allowed in federal courts. In the above case, the Court rejected additur as violative of the plaintiff's right to a second jury trial on the issue of damages if the first award is inadequate. The position seems untenable since remittitur involves the same impairment of the right to jury trial and its constitutionality is not questioned. In any event, additur is permitted under various state statutes. Note that in some of these jurisdictions, the defendant need not be required to consent before a judge can increase the amount of a legally inadequate jury award.

[For more information on the process of additur, see Casenote Law Outline on Civil Procedure, Chapter 9, § VI, Post-verdict Motions.]

NOTES:

WHITLOCK v. JACKSON
754 F. Supp. 1384 (S.D. Ind. 1991).

NATURE OF CASE: Motion for a new trial on personal injury/civil rights action.

FACT SUMMARY: The estate administrator (P) for Gaisor, who had died in police custody, sought a new trial on the basis that the jury's answers to special interrogatories were inconsistent.

CONCISE RULE OF LAW: A jury's answers to interrogatories will not be a basis for overturning a verdict if any means of reconciling them with the verdict exists.

FACTS: Gaisor died of a brain aneurysm after an arrest in which he had been struck several times. Whitlock (P), his estate administrator, filed an action alleging wrongful death and assault and battery, as well as constitutional violations. The jury returned a special verdict finding liability for battery on the part of the officers (D), but no constitutional violations. It also found that the officers' (D) conduct had not proximately caused Gaisor's death. The jury awarded $29,700 collectively against the arresting officers (D) in the form of compensatory and punitive damages. Whitlock (P) moved for a new trial, contending that the verdict was internally inconsistent since if it awarded punitive damages, it had to have found a civil rights violation.

ISSUE: Will a jury's answers to interrogatories be a basis for overturning a verdict if any means of reconciling them with the verdict exists?

HOLDING AND DECISION: (McKinney, J.) No. A jury's answers to interrogatories will not be a basis for overturning a verdict if any means of reconciling them with the verdict exists. There will often be more than one way to view what a jury is saying when it renders a verdict, and if any one way is consistent with the law, the verdict will stand. Here, the jury found that the officers (D) battered Gaisor and awarded punitive damages but did not find the officers (D) used excessive force or denied medical treatment — both torts of constitutional magnitude. Contrary to Whitlock's (P) contentions, this is not inconsistent. Punitive damages can be awarded to deter other officers from battering suspects without finding that the conduct of the officers (D) here was constitutionally protected. Not every example of police battery rises to the level of a civil rights violation. The jury here apparently found that the police (D) had neither caused Gaisor's death nor violated his due process rights, but that they had been too liberal in the use of force. This was a legally acceptable verdict. Motion denied.

EDITOR'S ANALYSIS: Far and away the most common form of verdict in jury trials is the general verdict whereby the jury does not disclose any grounds for its final decision. However, in order to save appellate time that would otherwise be spent determining whether a jury decided its verdict based on inadmissible evidence, the Federal Rules provide for two additional forms of verdict: a special verdict where the jury answers certain factual questions and the judge then enters a judgment accordingly (Rule 49(1)); and a general verdict accompanied by written interrogatories (Rule 49(b)). The distinction between the two special verdicts was highlighted in the case above, since Rule 49(b) expressly provides that a plaintiff's failure to object to inconsistent jury answers constitutes waiver of the objection, while Rule 49(a) does not contain this waiver principle.

[For more information on motion for a new trial, see Casenote Law Outline on Civil Procedure, Chapter 9, § VI, Post-verdict Motions.]

NOTES:

SOPP v. SMITH
Cal. Sup. Ct., 59 Cal.2d 12, 377 P.2d 649 (1963).

NATURE OF CASE: Review of order denying motion for new trial.

FACT SUMMARY: Sopp (P) sought a new trial on the basis of a declaration from a juror that he had improperly conducted his own investigation into the case.

CONCISE RULE OF LAW: Affidavits of jurors may not be used to impeach a verdict.

FACTS: Sopp (P) filed a personal injury action based on an automobile accident. After the trial, he sought a new trial, submitting a declaration from a juror that he had conducted his own investigation of the accident scene, something the court had forbidden. The trial court denied the motion, and the California Supreme Court granted review.

ISSUE: May affidavits of jurors be used to impeach a verdict?

HOLDING AND DECISION: (Schauer, J.) No. Affidavits of jurors may not be used to impeach a verdict. The general rule, which admits few exceptions, is that a declaration from a juror that he had engaged in improper conduct after being empaneled may not be used to overturn a verdict. This rule exists due to the need to respect the finality of jury verdicts and to prevent postverdict juror harassment. The main exception to the rule involves disqualification due to a juror's lack of veracity on voir dire, a situation not present here. Affirmed.

DISSENT: (Peters, J.) The rule here is court-created on the basis that, in older times, a witness could not allege his own turpitude. This rule has been abandoned, and the rule followed today should also be.

EDITOR'S ANALYSIS: The jury process is imperfect at best. Hardly a trial goes by that there is not at least some technical impropriety. The need for finality must prevail over all but the most egregious examples of this imperfection.

[For more information on motion for a new trial, see Casenote Law Outline on Civil Procedure, Chapter 9, § VI, Post-verdict Motions.]

PEOPLE v. HUTCHINSON
Cal. Sup. Ct., 71 Cal.2d 342 (1969).

NATURE OF CASE: Appeal of denial of motion for new trial.

FACT SUMMARY: A trial court refused to consider a juror's affidavit of improper remarks by a bailiff to the jury trying Hutchinson (D).

CONCISE RULE OF LAW: Jurors may testify as to objective facts to impeach a verdict.

FACTS: Hutchinson (D) was prosecuted for and convicted of drug possession. Subsequently, in support of a motion for a new trial, Hutchinson (D) produced an affidavit from a juror to the effect that the bailiff had made remarks tending to pressure the jury into a guilty verdict. The trial court refused to consider the affidavit, ruling that a juror cannot impeach the verdict. The motion was denied. The court of appeal affirmed. The State Supreme Court granted review.

ISSUE: May jurors testify as to objective facts to impeach a verdict?

HOLDING AND DECISION: (Traynor, C.J.) Yes. Jurors may testify as to objective facts to impeach a verdict. The old rule to the contrary was based on an English maxim that one cannot impeach. In recent times, the justification for such a rule has been the discouragement of instability of verdicts, as well as fraud. This has been seen as more important a policy than prevention of the occasional injustice resulting from the rule. However, this court is of the view that individuals suffering such instances of injustice are entitled to more consideration. When a juror testifies as to matters capable of objective verification, the possibility of fraud is minimal. Therefore, jurors should be able to impeach a verdict when the grounds for impeachment are objectively verifiable. Here, the alleged remarks of the bailiff were verifiable, so the juror's affidavit should have been considered. Reversed.

EDITOR'S ANALYSIS: Jury verdicts are seldom overturned for misconduct. Generally speaking, only misconduct by forces extrinsic to the jury itself will lead to overturning a verdict. For instance, a verdict was upheld in Tanner v. United States, 483 U.S. 107 (1987), despite evidence of heavy alcohol and drug use during the trial by several jurors.

[For more information on misconduct by counsel or jury, see Casenote Law Outline on Civil Procedure, Chapter 9, § VI, Post-verdict Motions.]

NOTES

CHAPTER 9
CHOOSING THE FORUM - GEOGRAPHICAL LOCATION

QUICK REFERENCE RULES

1. **Constitutional Standards for Proper Notice.** Where the object of the action is to determine the personal rights and obligations of the parties, service by publication against nonresidents is ineffective to confer jurisdiction on the court. (Pennoyer v. Neff)

   [For more information on constitutional standards for proper notice, see Casenote Law Outline on Civil Procedure, Chapter 2, § III, Jurisdiction and Valid Judgments.]

2. **Quasi in Rem Jurisdiction.** A debtor's obligation to pay debt accompanies him wherever he goes, and the question of jurisdiction is not dependent on either the site of the debt or the nature of the debtor's stay in a state. (Harris v. Balk)

   [For more information on quasi in rem jurisdiction, see Casenote Law Outline on Civil Procedure, Chapter 3, Minimum Contacts Analysis, § I, Historical Background.]

3. **Notice Required by Due Process.** In advance of a nonresident's use of its highways, a state may require the nonresident to appoint one of the state's officials as his agent on whom process may be served in proceedings growing out of such highway use. (Hess v. Pawloski)

   [For more information on notice required by due process, see Casenote Law Outline on Civil Procedure, Chapter 2, § III, Jurisdiction and Valid Judgments.]

4. **Minimum Contacts Doctrine.** For a state to subject a nonresident defendant to in personam jurisdiction, due process requires that he have certain minimum contacts with it such that the maintenance of the suit does not offend traditional notions of fair play and substantial justice. (International Shoe Co. v. Washington)

   [For more information on the minimum contacts doctrine, see Casenote Law Outline on Civil Procedure, Chapter 3, § II, The Birth of Minimum Contacts Doctrine in International Shoe.]

5. **Specific Jurisdiction.** Due process requires only that in order to subject a nonresident defendant to the personal jurisdiction of the forum, he have certain minimum contacts with the forum and that maintenance of the suit does not offend traditional notions of fair play and substantial justice. (McGee v. International Life Insurance Company)

   [For more information on specific jurisdiction, see Casenote Law Outline on Civil Procedure, Chapter 3, §§ III and V.]

6. **"Long Arm" Jurisdiction.** Whether a nonresident activity within a state is adequate to subject it to the jurisdiction of that state depends upon the facts of each case, and the relevant inquiry is whether the defendant engaged in some act or conduct by which he invoked the benefits and protections of the forum. (Gray v. American Radiator & Standard Sanitary Corp.)

   [For more information on "long arm" jurisdiction, see Casenote Law Outline on Civil Procedure, Chapter 2, § II, Overview from Defendants' Perspective.]

7. **The "Stream of Commerce" Contact.** The sale of an automobile by a corporate defendant is not a sufficient purposeful availment of the benefits and protection of the laws of a state where the automobile is fortuitously driven there so as to constitute the requisite "minimum contacts" with that state for personal jurisdiction purposes. (World-Wide Volkswagen Corp. v. Woodson)

[For more information on the "stream of commerce" contact, see Casenote Law Outline on Civil Procedure, Chapter 3, § III, Further Development of Minimum Contacts Doctrine.]

8. **Purposeful Contacts.** Publication of a defamatory article in a state may create jurisdiction over the authors thereof. (Calder v. Jones)

    [For more information on purposeful contacts, see Casenote Law Outline on Civil Procedure, Chapter 3, § III, Further Development of Minimum Contacts Doctrine.]

9. **Reasonableness Factors for Specific Jurisdictions.** Where the circumstances establish a substantial and continuing relationship with a forum state and indicate that there was a fair notice that a nonresident might be subject to suit in the forum state, the assertion of personal jurisdiction over the nonresident by the forum state, if otherwise fair, does not offend due process. (Burger King v. Rudzewicz)

    [For more information on reasonableness factors for specific jurisdictions, see Casenote Law Outline on Civil Procedure, Chapter 3, § V, Step-by-Step Guide to Minimum Contacts Analysis.]

10. **Purposefulness of Minimum Contacts.** Minimum contacts sufficient to sustain jurisdiction are not satisfied simply by the placement of a product into the stream of commerce coupled with an awareness that its product would reach the forum state. (Asahi Metal Ind. Co., Ltd. v. Sup. Court of California)

    [For more information on purposefulness of minimum contacts, see Casenote Law Outline on Civil Procedure, Chapter 3, § V, Step-by-Step Guide to Minimum Contacts Analysis.]

11. **In Rem Jurisdiction.** Jurisdiction cannot be founded on property within a state unless there are sufficient contacts within the meaning of the test developed in International Shoe. (Shaffer v. Heitner)

    [For more information on in rem jurisdiction, see Casenote Law Outline on Civil Procedure, Chapter 3, § III, Further Development of Minimum Contacts Doctrine.]

12. **Jurisdiction.** Personal jurisdiction based on physical presence alone does not violate due process. (Burnham v. Superior Court)

    [For more information on jurisdiction, see Casenote Law Outline on Civil Procedure, Chapter 2, § III, Jurisdiction and Valid Judgments.]

13. **Relatedness of Minimum Contacts.** Purchases, even at regular intervals, do not subject a foreign corporation to state jurisdiction if the purchases are unrelated to the cause of action. (Helicopteros Nacionales de Colombia, S.A. v. Hall)

    [For more information on relatedness of minimum contacts, see Casenote Law Outline on Civil Procedure, Chapter 3, § V, Step-by-Step Guide to Minimum Contacts Analysis.]

14. **Consent.** A court may declare jurisdiction as a sanction for failure to comply with discovery. (Insurance Corp. of Ireland, Ltd. v. Compagnie des Bauxites de Guinee)

15. **Forum.** If reasonable, a forum selection clause in a form contract should control. (Carnival Cruise Lines v. Shute)

16. **Notice Requirements for Due Process.** In order to satisfy due process challenges, notice must be by means calculated to inform the desired parties, and, where they reside outside of the state and their names and addresses are available, notice by publication is insufficient. A court may declare jurisdiction as a sanction for failure to comply with discovery. (Mullane v. Central Hanover Bank & Trust Co.)

[For more information on notice requirements for due process, see Casenote Law Outline on Civil Procedure, Chapter 2, § III, Jurisdiction and Valid Judgments.]

17. **Federal Venue.** An action may be brought in a judicial district in which a substantial part of the events or omissions giving rise to the claim occurred. (Bates v. C & S. Adjusters, Inc.)

   [For more information on federal venue, see Casenote Law Outline on Civil Procedure, Chapter 4, § VI, Supplemental Jurisdiction.]

18. **Forum non Conveniens.** A plaintiff may not defeat a motion to dismiss for forum non conveniens merely by showing that the substantive law that would be applied in the alternative forum is less favorable to him than that of the present forum. (Piper Aircraft Co. v. Reyno)

   [For more information on forum non conveniens, see Casenote Law Outline on Civil Procedure, Chapter 2, § V, Other Constraints on Choice of Forum.]

PENNOYER v. NEFF
95 U.S. 714 (1877).

NATURE OF CASE: Action to recover possession of land.

FACT SUMMARY: Neff (P) alleged that Pennoyer's (D) deed from a sheriff's sale was invalid because the court ordering the sale had never obtained personal jurisdiction over Neff (P).

CONCISE RULE OF LAW: Where the object of the action is to determine the personal rights and obligations of the parties, service by publication against nonresidents is ineffective to confer jurisdiction on the court.

FACTS: Neff (P) owned real property in Oregon. Mitchell brought suit in Oregon to recover legal fees allegedly owed him by Neff (P). Neff (P), a nonresident, was served by publication, and Mitchell obtained a default judgment. The court ordered Neff's (P) land sold at a sheriff's sale to satisfy the judgment. Pennoyer (D) purchased the property. Neff (P) subsequently learned of the sale and brought suit in Oregon to recover possession of his property. Neff (P) alleged that the court ordering the sale had never acquired in personam jurisdiction over him. Therefore, the court could not adjudicate the personal rights and obligations between Neff (P) and Mitchell, and the default judgment had been improperly entered.

ISSUE: Where an action involves the adjudication of personal rights and obligations of the parties, is service by publication against a nonresident sufficient to confer jurisdiction?

HOLDING AND DECISION: (Field, J.) No. Every state possesses exclusive jurisdiction and sovereignty over persons and property within its territory. Following from this, no state can exercise direct jurisdiction and authority over persons or property outside of its territory. These are two well-established principles of public law respecting the jurisdiction of an independent state over persons and property. However, the exercise of jurisdiction which every state possesses over persons and property within it will often affect persons and property outside of it. A state may compel persons domiciled within it to execute, in pursuance of their contracts respecting property situated elsewhere, instruments transferring title. Likewise, a state may subject property situated within it which is owned by nonresidents to the payment of the demands of its own citizens. Substituted service by publication or by other authorized means may be sufficient to inform the parties of the proceedings where the property is brought under the control of the court or where the judgment is sought as a means of reaching such property or effectuating some interest therein. That is, such service is effectual in proceedings in rem. The law assumes that property is always in the possession of its owner or an agent. It proceeds upon the theory that a seizure of the property will inform the owner that he must look to any proceedings upon such seizure for the property's condemnation or sale. But where the entire object of the action is to determine personal rights and obligations, the action is in personam and service by publication is ineffectual to confer jurisdiction over the nonresident defendant upon the court. Process sent out of state to a nonresident is equally ineffective to confer personal jurisdiction. In an action to determine a defendant's personal liability, he must be brought within the court's jurisdiction by service of process within the state or by his voluntary appearance. Without jurisdiction, due process requirements are not satisfied. In the case herein, Neff (P) was not personally served, and he never appeared. Hence, the personal judgment obtained against Neff (P) was not valid, and the property could not be sold.

EDITOR'S ANALYSIS: This is the leading case on the extent of the court's power to compel a defendant's attendance. At common law, the presence of the defendant within the jurisdiction, plus service while there, were the indispensable ingredients for the acquisition of jurisdiction of the person of the defendant. It still remains the basic method of acquiring jurisdiction over the defendant. It does not matter how transient the defendant's presence is if she is served within the jurisdiction. One case held that service on a defendant while he was in an airplane passing over a state is sufficient. Of course, a voluntary appearance by a defendant also gives the court jurisdiction over her.

[For more information on constitutional standards for proper notice, see Casenote Law Outline on Civil Procedure, Chapter 2, § III, Jurisdiction and Valid Judgments.]

NOTES:

HARRIS v. BALK
198 U.S. 215 (1905).

NATURE OF CASE: Action to recover a debt.

FACT SUMMARY: Harris (D), a North Carolina resident, owed $180 to Balk (P), another North Carolina resident. While Harris (D) was in Maryland temporarily, Epstein brought suit to recover $300 which Harris (D) owed him. Balk's (P) debt was attached.

CONCISE RULE OF LAW: A debtor's obligation to pay debt accompanies him wherever he goes, and the question of jurisdiction is not dependent on either the site of the debt or the nature of the debtor's stay in a state.

FACTS: Harris (D) and Balk (P) were both North Carolina residents. Harris (D) owed Balk (P) $180. He also owed Epstein, a Maryland resident, $300. On August 6, 1896, while Harris (D) was temporarily in Maryland, Epstein brought suit and had issued a writ of attachment, attaching the debt due Balk (P). Harris (D) did not contest the process issued to garnish the debt due Balk (P). Judgment was entered for Epstein for $180, which Harris (D) paid. On August 11, 1896, Balk (P) brought this action to recover the $180 owed him. Harris (D) answered with Epstein's recovery in Maryland. The lower court entered judgment for Balk (P) on the ground that the Maryland court obtained no jurisdiction to attach or garnish the debt due Balk (P) because Harris (D) was in Maryland only temporarily and the situs of the debt was in North Carolina.

ISSUE: Is the question of jurisdiction dependent upon either the situs of the debt or the nature of the debtor's stay in the state?

HOLDING AND DECISION: (Peckham, J.) No. Power over the person of the garnishee (or debtor) confers jurisdiction on the courts of the state where a writ of attachment issues. Jurisdiction is not dependent upon the original situs of the debt or upon the character of the garnishee's stay in the state where attachment is issued. As for the situs, the obligation of the debtor to pay the debt accompanies him wherever he goes. He is as much bound to pay the debt in a foreign state when sued there by a creditor as he is in the state where the debt was contracted. Balk (P) had a right to sue Harris (D) in Maryland since, as a citizen of North Carolina, he is entitled to all the privileges and immunities of citizens of all the states. If the garnishee is found in a state and process is personally served on him there, the court thereby acquires jurisdiction over him and can garnish the debt due from him and condemn it, provided the garnishee could be sued by his creditor in that state. Hence, the judgment against Harris (D) in Maryland was valid because the court had jurisdiction over Harris (D) by personal service. Further, Balk (P) obviously had notice of the Maryland suit because he sued Harris (D) a few days later. He could have contested it in Maryland but did not. Judgment for Balk (P) is reversed, and the case is remanded.

EDITOR'S ANALYSIS: This case demonstrates how a debt may be seized. Since, for the purposes of garnishment, a debt clings to the debtor, quasi in rem jurisdiction can be obtained over the debt by personal service of process on the debtor. The problem becomes more complex when the debtor goes into another state or country or is a corporation who might be sued in many states. In Weitzel v. Weitzel, the plaintiff had a judgment for alimony against her husband, who was working in Mexico for a railroad company. She served a garnishee summons on the railroad in Arizona to reach the debt it owed her husband in Mexico. The court did not allow the garnishment on the ground that it was probable the Mexican courts would not respect the quasi in rem judgment of the Arizona court.

[For more information on quasi in rem jurisdiction, see Casenote Law Outline on Civil Procedure, Chapter 3, Minimum Contacts Analysis, § I, Historical Background.]

NOTES:

HESS v. PAWLOSKI
274 U.S. 352 (1927).

NATURE OF CASE: Action to recover damages for personal injuries.

FACT SUMMARY: A Massachusetts statute provided that nonresident motorists were deemed to have appointed a state official as their agent for service of process in cases growing out of accidents or collisions involving them. Pawloski (P) sued Hess (D), a nonresident, for damages due to an auto accident in Massachusetts.

CONCISE RULE OF LAW: In advance of a nonresident's use of its highways, a state may require the nonresident to appoint one of the state's officials as his agent on whom process may be served in proceedings growing out of such highway use.

FACTS: Pawloski (P) alleged that Hess (D) negligently drove a car on a Massachusetts highway, thereby injuring Pawloski (P). Hess (D) was a nonresident of Massachusetts. No personal service was made on him, and no property belonging to him was attached. A Massachusetts statute provided that nonresident motorists were deemed to have appointed the registrar of motor vehicles as their agent for service of process in cases arising out of accidents or collisions in which nonresidents were involved. The statute also required that notice of such service and a copy of the process be sent by registered mail to the defendant.

ISSUE: Does a state statute by which nonresident motorists are deemed to have appointed a state official as their agent for service of process in cases arising out of accidents involving them violate their due process?

HOLDING AND DECISION: (Butler, J.) No. Motor vehicles are dangerous vehicles. In the public interest, the state may make and enforce regulations reasonably calculated to promote care on the part of all who use its highways. The statute involved in this case limits the nonresident's implied consent to proceedings growing out of accidents or collisions on a highway involving the nonresident. It requires that he receive notice of the service and a copy of the process. It makes no hostile discrimination against nonresidents. The state's power to regulate the use of its highways extends to its use by nonresidents as well as residents. In advance of the operation of a motor vehicle on its highway by a nonresident, the state may require him to appoint one of its officials as his agent on whom process may be served in proceedings growing out of such use. Judgment for Hess (P) is affirmed.

EDITOR'S ANALYSIS: Other states were quick to pass similar nonresident motorist statutes and thus provide their citizens with local forums for injuries caused by nonresident motorists. Some passed statutes subjecting nonresident boat and airplane owners to local fora also. Under the reasoning of Hess, it was thought that in order to subject the nonresident to local jurisdiction the activity engaged in must be one subject to state regulations under its police power. Consequently, the first extensions of Hess were to such situations as the sale of securities, an industry subject to a real high degree of regulation, and the ownership of local real estate.

[For more information on notice required by due process, see Casenote Law Outline on Civil Procedure, Chapter 2, § III, Jurisdiction and Valid Judgments.]

NOTES:

INTERNATIONAL SHOE CO. v. WASHINGTON
326 U.S. 310 (1945).

NATURE OF CASE: Proceedings to recover unemployment contributions.

FACT SUMMARY: A state statute authorized the mailing of notice of assessment of delinquent contributions for unemployment compensation to nonresident employers. International Shoe Co. (D) was a nonresident corporation. Notice of assessment was served on one of its salespersons within the state and was mailed to International's (D) office.

CONCISE RULE OF LAW: For a state to subject a nonresident defendant to in personam jurisdiction, due process requires that he have certain minimum contacts with it such that the maintenance of the suit does not offend traditional notions of fair play and substantial justice.

FACTS: A Washington statute set up a scheme of unemployment compensation which required contributions by employers. The statute authorized the commissioner, Washington (P), to issue an order and notice of assessment of delinquent contributions by mailing the notice to nonresident employers. International (D), a Delaware corporation having its principal place of business in Missouri, employed 11 to 13 salespersons under the supervision of managers in Missouri. These salespeople resided in Washington and did most of their work there. They had no authority to enter into contracts or make collections. International (D) did not have any office in Washington and made no contracts there. Notice of assessment was served upon one of International's (D) Washington salespersons, and a copy of the notice was sent by registered mail to International's (D) Missouri address.

ISSUE: For a state to subject a nonresident defendant to in personam jurisdiction, does due process require only that he have certain minimum contacts with it, such that the maintenance of the suit does not offend notions of fair play and substantial justice?

HOLDING AND DECISION: (Stone, C.J.) Yes. Historically, the jurisdiction of courts to render judgment in personam is grounded on their power over the defendant's person, and his presence within the territorial jurisdiction of a court was necessary to a valid judgment. But now, due process requires only that in order to subject a defendant to a judgment in personam, if he is not present within the territorial jurisdiction, he have certain minimum contacts with the territory such that the maintenance of the suit does not offend traditional notions of fair play and substantial justice. The contacts must be such as to make it reasonable, in the context of our federal system, to require a defendant corporation to defend the suit brought there. An estimate of the inconveniences which would result to the corporation from a trial away from its "home" is relevant. To require a corporation to defend a suit away from home where its contact has been casual or isolated activities has been thought to lay too unreasonable a burden on it. However, even single or occasional acts may, because of their nature, quality, and circumstances, be deemed sufficient to render a corporation liable to suit. Hence, the criteria to determine whether jurisdiction is justified is not simply mechanical or quantitative. Satisfaction of due process depends on the quality and nature of the activity in relation to the fair and orderly administration of the laws. In this case, International's (D) activities were neither irregular nor casual. Rather, they were systematic and continuous. The obligation sued upon here arose out of these activities. They were sufficient to establish sufficient contacts or ties to make it reasonable to permit Washington (P) to enforce the obligations International (D) incurred there.

DISSENT: (Black, J.) The U.S. Constitution leaves to each state the power to tax and to open the doors of its courts for its citizens to sue corporations who do business in the state. It is a judicial deprivation to condition the exercise of this power on this Court's notion of "fair play."

EDITOR'S ANALYSIS: Before this decision, three theories had evolved to provide for suits by and against foreign corporations. The first was the consent theory. It rested on the proposition that since a foreign corporation could not carry on its business within a state without the permission of that state, the state could require a corporation to appoint an agent to receive service of process within the state. However, it soon became established law that a foreign corporation could not be prevented by a state from carrying on interstate commerce within its borders. The presence doctrine required that the corporation was "doing business" and "present" in the state. The third theory used either the present or consent doctrine, and it was necessary to determine whether the corporation was doing business within the state to decide whether its consent could property be implied or to discover whether the corporation was present.

[For more information on the minimum contacts doctrine, see Casenote Law Outline on Civil Procedure, Chapter 3, § II, The Birth of Minimum Contacts Doctrine in International Shoe.]

NOTES:

McGEE v. INTERNATIONAL LIFE INSURANCE CO.
355 U.S. 220 (1957).

NATURE OF CASE: Suit to enforce payment of life insurance proceeds.

FACT SUMMARY: McGee (P) was the beneficiary of a life insurance policy on the life of her son, a California resident. He had purchased the policy by mail from International Life (D) and was the only California policyholder. McGee (P) obtained a judgment for the proceeds in California which she attempted to enforce in Texas.

CONCISE RULE OF LAW: Due process requires only that in order to subject a nonresident defendant to the personal jurisdiction of the forum, he have certain minimum contacts with the forum and that maintenance of the suit does not offend traditional notions of fair play and substantial justice.

FACTS: McGee's (P) son purchased a policy of life insurance from International Life's (D) predecessor. When International (D) assumed the obligations of the predecessor, it mailed a certificate of insurance to the son, who resided in California. The son paid the premiums by mail to International (D) to its home office in Texas for two years. He was the only California policyholder, and International (D) solicited no other business in that state. Upon his death, McGee (P), as beneficiary, filed a claim which International (D) denied, claiming suicide. McGee (P) then sued in California and obtained a default judgment. No personal service was had on International (D), but it received actual notice and did not appear. McGee (P) then took the judgment to Texas for enforcement, which was denied on the basis that the California court had no jurisdiction over International (D).

ISSUE: May personal jurisdiction be exercised over a nonresident defendant on the basis of a single contact with the forum if such jurisdiction would not violate traditional notions of fair play and substantial justice?

HOLDING AND DECISION: (Black, J.) Yes. The increasing national character of commercial transactions and the rising practice of conducting business by mail have made dealings between persons of different states commonplace. Modern transportation has substantially eased the ability of nonresident defendants to come to states where they do business to defend suits against them. California has a substantial interest in providing an effective means for its residents to redress grievances against foreign insurers. This contract was delivered in California, and the premiums were payable there. The beneficiary and policyholders are California residents. It would work a great hardship on the California beneficiary to travel to other states to prosecute a claim. International (D) was in a better position to defend in California, particularly in view of the witnesses to substantiate or rebut its defense of suicide. International (D) had ample notice to defend the action. No impairment of contract would result in affirming this judgment since no substantial rights were affected, merely a remedial procedure. Texas must give full faith and credit enforcement to the California judgment.

EDITOR'S ANALYSIS: The McGee decision represents the farthest extension of the minimum contacts doctrine developed in the International Life decision. The fact of solicitation of the policy in California was a key element of this decision. That solicitation, albeit a single incident, could reasonably be thought to have put International Life (D) on notice that it might be sued in California. If, on the other hand, the insured had taken out the policy in Texas and then moved to California, where he was the sole policyholder, this foreseeability argument would be greatly diluted. However, if the insured was one of a number of California policyholders, the exercise of personal jurisdiction there could be expected.

[For more information on specific jurisdiction, see Casenote Law Outline on Civil Procedure, Chapter 3, §§ III and V.]

NOTES:

GRAY v. AMERICAN RADIATOR & STANDARD SANITARY CORPORATION

Ill. Sup. Ct., 22 Ill. 2d 432, 176 N.E.2d 761 (1961).

NATURE OF CASE: Action to recover damages for personal injury.

FACT SUMMARY: Gray (P), a resident of Illinois, alleged that Titan's (D), an Ohio corporation, negligent construction of a valve which it sold to American (D), which incorporated the valve into a water heater, caused an explosion which injured her.

CONCISE RULE OF LAW: Whether a nonresident activity within a state is adequate to subject it to the jurisdiction of that state depends upon the facts of each case, and the relevant inquiry is whether the defendant engaged in some act or conduct by which he invoked the benefits and protections of the forum.

FACTS: Gray (P), an Illinois resident, alleged that Titan (D), an Ohio corporation, negligently constructed a valve which it sold to American (D), which incorporated it into a water heater. Titan's (D) negligence, Gray (P) alleged, caused the heater to explode, thereby injuring her. Titan (D) did no business in Illinois and had no agent physically present there.

ISSUE: Where a nonresident's only contact with a state is an injury, is that contact adequate to subject the nonresident to jurisdiction of the state without violating due process?

HOLDING AND DECISION: (Klingbiel, J.) Yes. The court first decided that a tortious act is committed where the resulting damage occurs. Since the Pennoyer decision, the power of a state to exert jurisdiction over nonresidents has been greatly expanded, particularly with respect to foreign corporations. Since the International Shoe decision, the requirements for jurisdiction have further relaxed. Now it is sufficient if the act or transaction itself has a substantial connection with the state. It is no longer necessary that the business done by the foreign corporation be of a substantial volume. Hence, it has been held sufficient for due process requirements where the action was based on a contract which had a substantial connection with the state. Continuous activity is not required, and the commission of a single tort within the state has been held sufficient to sustain jurisdiction. Whether the activity conducted within the state is adequate to satisfy due process depends upon the facts in the particular case. In application of this flexible test, the relevant question is whether the defendant engaged in some act or conduct by which he invoked the benefits and protections of the law of the state. In this case, Titan (D) does not claim that the present use of its product in Illinois is an isolated instance. It is a reasonable inference that its commercial transactions, like those of other manufacturers, result in substantial use and consumption in Illinois. To the extent that its businesses may be directly affected by transactions occurring in Illinois, it enjoys benefits from the laws of this state. The fact that the benefit Titan (D) derives from Illinois' law is an indirect one does not make it any less essential to the conduct of its business. It is not unreasonable, where a cause of action arises from alleged defects in a nonresident's product, to say that the use of such product in the ordinary course of commerce is sufficient contact with the state to justify that the nonresident defend there. Further, witnesses on the issues of injury, damages, etc., will be most likely found where the accident occurred. Titan's (D) contact with Illinois is sufficient to support the exercise of jurisdiction.

EDITOR'S ANALYSIS: After the International Shoe decision, states began to enact "long-arm" statutes. The Illinois statute (which was involved in this case) was the first to be passed. The primary purpose of these statutes is to provide local fora for local plaintiffs on locally generated causes of action. The chief barrier to an undue extension of long-arm jurisdiction is the Fourteenth Amendment. It is reinforced by the First Amendment in libel suits where free speech and free press are involved. In those cases, greater contact with the state must be shown.

[For more information on "long arm" jurisdiction, see Casenote Law Outline on Civil Procedure, Chapter 2, § II, Overview from Defendants' Perspective.]

NOTES:

WORLD-WIDE VOLKSWAGEN CORP. v. WOODSON
444 U.S. 286 (1980).

NATURE OF CASE: Appeal from denial of writ of prohibition restraining exercise of in personam jurisdiction.

FACT SUMMARY: The Robinsons bought a new Audi in New York from Seaway and while traveling in Oklahoma were involved in a fiery crash allegedly aggravated by Audi's negligent placement of the gas tank. The district court asserted personal jurisdiction over Seaway and World-Wide (P), another dealer.

CONCISE RULE OF LAW: The sale of an automobile by a corporate defendant is not a sufficient purposeful availment of the benefits and protection of the laws of a state where the automobile is fortuitously driven there so as to constitute the requisite "minimum contacts" with that state for personal jurisdiction purposes.

FACTS: The Robinsons purchased a new Audi from Seaway, a dealer, in New York. Then they left New York for a new home in Arizona but en route were involved in a fiery crash in Oklahoma. Alleging that the injuries sustained were aggravated by Audi's negligent placement of the gas tank and other fuel system design defects, the Robinsons brought an action in federal court in Oklahoma against Seaway and another dealer, World-Wide (P). Both were located in New York, and neither had an office in Oklahoma nor conducted any business in that state. No evidence was adduced that any of the cars sold by either had ever entered Oklahoma on any prior occasion, until the Robinsons' mishap. The district court rejected World-Wide's (P) constitutional objections to any assertion of personal jurisdiction over it and Seaway. World-Wide (P) then applied to the Oklahoma Supreme Court for a writ of prohibition against District Judge Woodson (D), restraining him from exercising personal jurisdiction over it. The court denied the writ, and the U.S. Supreme Court granted certiorari.

ISSUE: Is the sale of an automobile by a corporate defendant a sufficient purposeful availment of the benefits and protections of the laws of a state where the automobile is fortuitously driven so as to constitute the requisite "minimum contacts" with that state for purposes of personal jurisdiction?

HOLDING AND DECISION: (White, J.) No. The Due Process Clause limits the power of a state court to render a valid personal judgment against a nonresident defendant. It has long been held that for such a judgment to be rendered, the nonresident defendant must have "minimum contacts" with the forum state. There is a total absence in this case of any affiliating circumstances with Oklahoma. No sales were closed there nor services provided. While it is argued that the "minimum contacts" test is satisfied by the foreseeability that the car would enter other states, the mere unilateral activity of a purchaser in moving the automobile from New York to Oklahoma cannot satisfy the requirement. The defendant must "purposely avail" itself of the benefits and protections of the laws of the forum state, and this neither Seaway nor World-Wide (P) did. The sale of an automobile by a corporate defendant is not a sufficiently pur-

poseful availment of the benefits and protections of the laws of a state where the automobile is fortuitously driven so as to constitute the requisite "minimum contacts" with that state for personal jurisdiction purposes. Denial of writ of prohibition reversed.

DISSENT: (Marshall, J.) The majority takes too narrow a view of the importance of World-Wide's (P) forum-related conduct. World-Wide (P) and Seaway take part in a nationwide or even global network for the sales and service of automobiles. By knowingly selling and thereby deriving pecuniary benefit from automobiles sold to persons who will travel to other states, the petitioners here subjected themselves to the possibility of lawsuits in other jurisdictions.

EDITOR'S ANALYSIS: The "purposeful availment of the benefits and protections of the laws of the forum state" involves some action designed to benefit the actor through an effect in the state asserting jurisdiction. In this case, the court found that the car was "fortuitously" in Oklahoma, negating the inference that the sale of the car brought revenue to World-Wide (P) in anticipation that the car would be driven there.

[For more information on the "stream of commerce" contact, see Casenote Law Outline on Civil Procedure, Chapter 3, § III, Further Development of Minimum Contacts Doctrine.]

NOTES:

CALDER v. JONES
465 U.S. 783 (1984).

NATURE OF CASE: Review of denial of motion to quash.

FACT SUMMARY: In a defamation action, a state court in the jurisdiction in which the offending article was published exercised jurisdiction over out-of-state authors.

CONCISE RULE OF LAW: Publication of a defamatory article in a state may create jurisdiction over the authors thereof.

FACTS: The National Enquirer (D), a weekly tabloid of nationwide circulation, published an unflattering article concerning Jones (P), a well-known actress. Also named as defendants were Calder (D), the Enquirer's (D) editor, and South (D), the article's author. All defendants were located in Florida. Calder (D) and South (D) moved to quash, alleging no personal jurisdiction. Neither had visited California, where the suit was filed, to research the article. Neither had a substantial presence in California. Nonetheless, the state court denied the motion, and the state appellate court affirmed. The Supreme Court granted review.

ISSUE: May publication of a defamatory article in a state create jurisdiction over the authors thereof?

HOLDING AND DECISION: (Rehnquist, J.) Yes. Publication of a defamatory article in a state may create jurisdiction over the authors thereof. It has long been held that the standard for personal jurisdiction over an out-of-state defendant is whether the defendant has such contacts with the forum state that he could reasonably expect to be brought into court in that state. When a defendant purposely engages in a series of actions that are likely to have an effect in that state, it is not unreasonable to expect him to face court process there. Here, Calder (D) and South (D) knew that Jones (P) lived in California and that their article would be published there, having its effect on Jones (P) there. This being the case, jurisdiction over Calder (D) and South (D) was proper in this action. Affirmed.

EDITOR'S ANALYSIS: The National Enquirer (D) did not contest jurisdiction in this matter. It sold over 500,000 issues in California, and it conceded jurisdiction. The Supreme Court has upheld jurisdiction in instances of much smaller distribution figures. In Keeton v. Hustler Magazine, Inc., 465 U.S. 770 (1984), jurisdiction was upheld on the basis of a circulation of no more that 15,000 issues.

[For more information on purposeful contacts, see Casenote Law Outline on Civil Procedure, Chapter 3, § III, Further Development of Minimum Contacts Doctrine.]

BURGER KING CORPORATION v. RUDZEWICZ
471 U.S. 462 (1985).

NATURE OF CASE: Appeal from decision reversing assertion of personal jurisdiction over nonresident in action for breach of contract.

FACT SUMMARY: Burger King Corporation (P) (BKC) appealed from a decision of the court of appeals finding that the district court erred in asserting personal jurisdiction over Rudzewicz (D) without reasonable notice of the prospect of franchise litigation in Florida and thus violated due process fairness concerns.

CONCISE RULE OF LAW: Where the circumstances establish a substantial and continuing relationship with a forum state and indicate that there was a fair notice that a nonresident might be subject to suit in the forum state, the assertion of personal jurisdiction over the nonresident by the forum state, if otherwise fair, does not offend due process.

FACTS: BKC (P) oversaw its franchise operations through a two-tiered administrative structure. Governing contracts provided that franchise relationships were established in Miami and were governed by Florida law. All fees were paid to the Miami office, where BKC (P), a Florida corporation, was headquartered. Major problems were resolved through the Miami office. The day-to-day monitoring of the franchises, which were subject to exacting regulation and supervision by BKC (P) under the franchising contracts, was conducted through a network of offices. Rudzewicz (D), a Michigan resident, and MacShara applied at the regional office in Michigan for a franchise, and the application was forwarded to the Miami office. A preliminary agreement was entered into by BKC (P); it was decided that Rudzewicz (D) and MacShara would take over an existing facility in Drayton Plains, Michigan. They purchased restaurant equipment from a division of BKC (P) in Miami, and MacShara attended required management courses in Miami. Disputes arose, with Rudzewicz (D) and MacShara negotiating with both the regional and the Miami offices. Operations were begun in June 1979, with Rudzewicz (D) personally becoming liable for over $1 million in payments over the 20-year franchise relationship. Rudzewicz (D) and MacShara fell behind in their payments, and an extended period of negotiations between them, the regional office, and the Miami office ensued. BKC (P) eventually terminated the franchise, but Rudzewicz (D) refused to vacate the premises, continuing to operate the restaurant as a Burger King. Florida's long-arm statute extended jurisdiction over nonresidents resulting from breaches of contract formed in Florida and breached for failure to perform required acts in Florida. BKC (P) brought suit in the Southern District of Florida, and Rudzewicz (D) made special appearances, contending that since they were nonresidents and the claim did not arise within the Southern District of Florida, the district court lacked personal jurisdiction. The district court disagreed, and after trial judgment was entered in favor of BKC (P). On appeal, the court of appeals reversed, stating that the assertion of jurisdiction was unfair under the circumstances since Rudzewicz (D) was bereft of notice of the

Continued on next page

prospect of franchise litigation in Florida. From this decision, BKC (P) appealed.

ISSUE: Where the circumstances establish a substantial and continuing relationship with a forum state and indicate that there was fair notice that a nonresident might be subject to suit in the forum state, does the assertion of personal jurisdiction over the nonresident by the forum state, if otherwise fair, offend due process?

HOLDING AND DECISION: (Brennan, J.) No. Where the circumstances establish a substantial and continuing relationship with the forum state and indicate that there was fair notice that a nonresident might be subject to suit in the forum state, the assertion of personal jurisdiction over the nonresident by the forum state, if otherwise fair, does not offend due process. When determining whether it is fair to determine that a nonresident reasonably could anticipate out-of-state litigation, a court should look to see if the nonresident purposefully availed himself of the benefits and privileges of conducting activities within that state. Once minimum contacts are established, other factors that may make the assertion of jurisdiction unfair can be considered in order to comport with fundamental fairness and substantial justice. Substantial evidence exists to support a finding of jurisdiction in the present case. The existence of the contract with BKC (P), a Florida corporation, is not sufficient to support the assertion of Florida jurisdiction over Rudzewicz (D). The prior negotiation of the contract, the terms of the contract itself, the consequences of the contract, and the parties' actual course of dealings must all be evaluated to determine whether a nonresident has established minimum contacts with the forum state. Rudzewicz (D), in the present case, entered into a highly structured 20-year relationship with BKC (P) involving continuing and wide-reaching contacts with Burger King (P) in Florida. Negotiations were made with the Miami office, not the regional office. His actions in refusing to vacate the premises and continuing to use the Burger King (P) trademarks after termination caused foreseeable injuries to BKC (P). Surely, Rudzewicz's (D) connection with Florida cannot be seen as "random, fortuitous, or attenuated." Further, the contract specified that the agreements were made in and enforced from Miami, and the negotiations which led to the litigation came from the Miami office. Choice of law analysis is distinct from minimum contacts jurisdiction analysis, and to hold that such choice should be ignored in determining whether a nonresident has purposefully availed himself of the benefits of the state confuses the two. Rudzewicz (D) has not pointed to any other factors that outweigh the considerations favoring a finding of jurisdiction and certainly no factors establishing the unconstitutionality of the Florida long-arm statute. All parties involved were experienced in business, and there is no indication that Rudzewicz (D) was under any economic duress. No mechanical rule can be applied in these cases, and each case must be scrutinized individually. Here, jurisdiction was properly asserted pursuant to the Florida long-arm statute. Reversed and remanded.

DISSENT: (White, J.) No hearing is required to protect the debtor.

The creditor has a "property" interest deserving of as much protection as the debtor's. The debtor, who will not be interested in a speedy resolution of the matter, at the least should be required to continue to make payment (into a court trust) upon which his right to possession is conditioned. A hearing should also not be required because credit documents will most likely be rewritten so that there will be a waiver of hearing upon a default, and the requirement of a hearing will just make credit that much more expensive to obtain.

DISSENT: (Stevens, J.) Rudzewicz's (D) only contacts with BKC (P) were conducted through the regional Michigan office. He only did business in Michigan. There is nothing in the record to establish that he purposefully availed himself of the benefits and protections of Florida law. His activities gave him no notice of the possibility of franchise litigation in Florida for which he was financially unprepared. The unequal bargaining positions of the parties further accentuate the unfairness of hauling Rudzewicz (D) into Florida courts.

EDITOR'S ANALYSIS: There is some question among the Circuits as to what extent a choice of law provision in a contract also implies a choice of forum. Even though it is clear that mechanical tests will not be applied in making these determinations, the contrasting factual viewpoints of the majority and the dissent in the present case make it quite likely that future opinions in this area will be inconsistent.

[For more information on reasonableness factors for specific jurisdictions, see Casenote Law Outline on Civil Procedure, Chapter 3, § V, Step-by-Step Guide to Minimum Contacts Analysis.]

NOTES:

ASAHI METAL INDUSTRY CO., LTD. v.
SUPERIOR COURT OF CALIFORNIA, SOLANO COUNTY
480 U.S. 102 (1987).

NATURE OF CASE: Appeal from discharge of writ quashing service of summons.

FACT SUMMARY: Asahi (P) appealed from a decision of the California Supreme Court discharging a peremptory writ issued by the appeals court quashing service of summons in Cheng Shin's indemnity action, contending that there did not exist minimum contacts between California and Asahi (P) sufficient to sustain jurisdiction.

CONCISE RULE OF LAW: Minimum contacts sufficient to sustain jurisdiction are not satisfied simply by the placement of a product into the stream of commerce coupled with an awareness that its product would reach the forum state.

FACTS: Asahi (P), a Japanese corporation, manufactured tire valve assemblies in Japan, selling some of them to Cheng Shin, a Taiwanese company who incorporated them into the motorcycles it manufactured. Zurcher was seriously injured in a motorcycle accident, and a companion was killed. He sued Cheng Shin, alleging the motorcycle tire, manufactured by Cheng Shin was defective. Cheng Shin sought indemnity from Asahi (P), and the main action settled. Asahi (P) moved to quash service of summons, contending that jurisdiction could not be maintained by California, the state in which Zurcher filed his action, consistent with the Due Process Clause of the Fourteenth Amendment. The evidence indicated Asahi's (P) sales to Cheng Shin took place in Taiwan, and shipments went from Japan to Taiwan. Cheng Shin purchased valve assemblies from other manufacturers. Sales to Cheng Shin never amounted to more than 1.5% of Asahi's (P) income. Approximately 20% of Cheng Shin's sales in the United States are in California. In declaration, an attorney for Cheng Shin stated he made an informal examination of tires in a bike shop in Solano County, where Zurcher was injured, finding approximately 20% of the tires with Asahi's (P) trademark (25% of the tires manufactured by Cheng Shin). The Superior Court (D) denied the motion to quash, finding it reasonable that Asahi (P) defend its claim of defect in its product. The court of appeals issued a peremptory writ commanding the Superior Court (D) to quash service of summons. The state supreme court reversed and discharged the writ, finding that Asahi's (P) awareness that some of its product would reach California by placing it in the stream of commerce satisfied minimum contacts sufficient to sustain jurisdiction. From this decision, Asahi (P) appealed.

ISSUE: Are minimum contacts sufficient to sustain jurisdiction satisfied by the placement of a product into the stream of commerce, coupled with the awareness that its product would reach the forum state?

HOLDING AND DECISION: (O'Connor, J.) No. Minimum contacts sufficient to sustain jurisdiction are not satisfied by the placement of a product in the stream of commerce, coupled with the awareness that its product would reach the forum state. To satisfy minimum contacts, there must be some act by which the defendant purposefully avails itself of the privilege of conducting activities within the forum state. Although the courts that have squarely addressed this issue have been divided, the better view is that the defendant must do more than place a product in the stream of commerce. The unilateral act of a consumer's bringing the product to the forum state is not sufficient. Asahi (P) has not purposefully availed itself of the California market. It does not do business in the state, conduct activities, maintain offices or agents, or advertise. Nor did it have anything to do with Cheng Shin's distribution system, which brought the tire valve assembly to California. Assertion of jurisdiction based on these facts exceeds the limits of Due Process. [The Court went on to consider the burden of defense on Asahi (P) and the slight interests of the state and Zurcher, finding the assertion of jurisdiction unreasonable and unfair.] Reversed and remanded.

CONCURRENCE: (Brennan, J.) The state supreme court correctly concluded that the stream of commerce theory, without more, has satisfied minimum contacts in most courts which have addressed the issue, and it has been preserved in the decision of this Court.

CONCURRENCE: (Stevens, J.) The minimum contacts analysis is unnecessary; the Court has found by weighing the appropriate factors that jurisdiction under these facts is unreasonable and unfair.

EDITOR'S ANALYSIS: The Brennan concurrence is quite on point in criticizing the plurality for its characterization that this case involves the act of a consumer in bringing the product within the forum state. The argument presented in World-Wide Volkswagen Corp. v. Woodson, 444 U.S. 286 (1980), cited by the plurality, seems more applicable to distributors and retailers than to manufacturers of component parts.

[For more information on purposefulness of minimum contacts, see Casenote Law Outline on Civil Procedure, Chapter 3, § V, Step-by-Step Guide to Minimum Contacts Analysis.]

NOTES:

SHAFFER v. HEITNER
433 U.S. 186 (1977).

NATURE OF CASE: Appeal from a finding of state jurisdiction.

FACT SUMMARY: Heitner (P) brought a derivative suit against Greyhound (D) directors for antitrust losses it had sustained in Oregon. The suit was brought in Delaware, Greyhound's (D) state of incorporation.

CONCISE RULE OF LAW: Jurisdiction cannot be founded on property within a state unless there are sufficient contacts within the meaning of the test developed in International Shoe.

FACTS: Heitner (P) owned one share of Greyhound (D) stock. Greyhound (D) had been subjected to a large antitrust judgment in Oregon. Heitner (P), a nonresident of Delaware, brought a derivative suit in Delaware, the state of Greyhound's (D) incorporation. Jurisdiction was based on sequestration of Greyhound (D) stock which was deemed to be located within the state of incorporation. The Delaware sequestration statute allowed property within the state to be seized ex parte to compel the owner to submit to the in personam jurisdiction of the court. None of the stock was actually in Delaware, but a freeze order was placed on the corporate books. Greyhound (D) made a special appearance to challenge the court's jurisdiction to hear the matter. Greyhound (D) argued that the sequestration statute was unconstitutional under the line of cases beginning with Sniadach. Greyhound (D) also argued that there were insufficient contacts with Delaware to justify an exercise of jurisdiction. The Delaware courts found that the sequestration statute was valid since it was not a per se seizure of the property and was merely invoked to compel out-of-state residents to defend actions within the state. Little or no consideration was given to the "contact" argument based on a finding that the presence of the stock within the state conferred quasi-in-rem jurisdiction.

ISSUE: May a state assume jurisdiction over an issue merely because defendant's property happens to be within the state?

HOLDING AND DECISION: (Marshall, J.) No. Mere presence of property within a state is insufficient to confer jurisdiction on a court absent independent contacts within the meaning of International Shoe, which would make acceptance constitutional. The Court expressly rejected that line of cases represented by Harris v. Balk, which permits jurisdiction merely because the property happens to be within the state. If sufficient contacts do not exist to assume jurisdiction absent the presence of property within the state, it cannot be invoked on the basis of property within the court's jurisdiction. This decision is based on the fundamental concepts of justice and fair play required under the Due Process and Equal Protection Clauses of the Fourteenth Amendment. Here, the stock is not the subject of the controversy. There is no claim to ownership of it or injury caused by it. The defendants do not reside in Delaware or have any contacts there. The injury occurred in Oregon. No activities complained of were done within the forum. Finally, Heitner (P) is not even a Delaware resident. Jurisdiction was improperly granted. Reversed.

CONCURRENCE: (Powell, J.) The Court errs only in regard to cases involving property permanently within the state, e.g., real property. Such property should confer jurisdiction.

CONCURRENCE: (Stevens, J.) Purchase of stock in the marketplace should not confer in rem jurisdiction in the state of incorporation.

CONCURRENCE AND DISSENT: (Brennan, J.) The Court reasons correctly regarding the use of a minimum contacts test but misapplies it in this case. The Delaware sequestration statute's sole purpose is to force in personam jurisdiction through a quasi-in-rem seizure. The opinion is purely advisory in that if the court finds the statute invalid, the rest of the opinion is not required. Delaware never argued that it was attempting to obtain in rem jurisdiction. Further, a derivative suit may be brought in the state of incorporation. Greyhound's (D) choice of incorporation in Delaware is a prima facie showing of submission to its jurisdiction.

EDITOR'S ANALYSIS: While the corporation could be sued in its state of incorporation under the dissent's theory, the suit is against the directors, and neither the site of the wrong nor the residence of a defendant is in Delaware. The decision will only have a major impact in cases such as herein where the state really has no reason to want to adjudicate the issue. Of course, real property would still be treated as an exception.

[For more information on in rem jurisdiction, see Casenote Law Outline on Civil Procedure, Chapter 3, § III, Further Development of Minimum Contacts Doctrine.]

NOTES:

BURNHAM v. SUPERIOR COURT OF CALIFORNIA
495 U.S. 604 (1990).

NATURE OF CASE: Denial of motion to quash service of process in divorce proceeding.

FACT SUMMARY: After he was personally served with a summons while visiting San Francisco, Burnham (P) contended that California (D) lacked personal jurisdiction over him because his only contacts with the state were a few short visits there to conduct business and to visit his children.

CONCISE RULE OF LAW: Personal jurisdiction based on physical presence alone does not violate due process.

FACTS: Burnham (P) and his wife separated in 1987, and she moved with the children from New Jersey to California. She then brought suit for divorce in California state court (D). While Burnham, a New Jersey resident, was in California on business, he visited San Francisco to see his children. While he was returning one of the children to his wife's home there, he was served with a California court (D) summons and a copy of his wife's divorce petition. He moved to quash the service of process on the ground that the California court (D) lacked personal jurisdiction over him because he lacked "minimum contacts" with the state. The superior court (D) denied the motion, and the appellate court affirmed. The Supreme Court granted review.

ISSUE: Does personal jurisdiction based on physical presence alone violate due process?

HOLDING AND DECISION: (Scalia, J.) No. Personal jurisdiction based on physical presence alone does not violate due process. A firmly established principle of personal jurisdiction is that state courts have jurisdiction over nonresidents who are physically present in the state. Furthermore, a formidable body of precedent holds that personal service upon a physically present nonresident is sufficient to confer jurisdiction, regardless of whether he was only briefly in the state or whether the cause of action was related to his activities there. Continuous and systematic contacts with the forum are not necessary. The "minimum contacts" requirement developed in International Shoe Co. v. Washington, 326 U.S. 310 (1945), only applies to situations in which the defendant is not present within the territory of the forum. Therefore, the Due Process Clause does not prohibit the California court (D) from exercising jurisdiction over Burnham (P) based on in-state service of process.

CONCURRENCE: (White, J.) The rule allowing jurisdiction to be obtained over a nonresident by personal service in the forum state is so widely accepted that I could not possibly strike it down, either facially or as applied here.

CONCURRENCE: (Brennan, J.) I would not rely on a jurisdictional rule's pedigree to determine whether it comports with due process but would instead undertake an independent inquiry to determine if it is consistent with traditional notions of fair play and substantial justice.

CONCURRENCE: (Stevens, J.) The historical evidence, the considerations of fairness, and common sense all combine to make

affirmance an easy decision.

EDITOR'S ANALYSIS: Regardless of the rationale used to uphold "transient" jurisdiction, everyone agrees that a nonresident who is fraudulently enticed to enter a state may defeat such jurisdiction. For example, if a defendant, prior to being sued, enters a state to engage in settlement negotiations, and the plaintiff does not warn him that he may be served, the defendant will be able to quash service of process. See also Wyman v. Newhouse, 93 F.2d 313 (2d Cir. 1937), in which a woman urged her lover to visit her in Florida one last time, then slapped him with a fraudulent-promise-of-marriage suit. A New York court later ruled that he had been enticed.

[For more information on jurisdiction, see Casenote Law Outline on Civil Procedure, Chapter 2, § III, Jurisdiction and Valid Judgments.]

NOTES:

HELICOPTEROS NACIONALES DE COLOMBIA, S.A. v. HALL
466 U.S. 408 (1984).

NATURE OF CASE: Review of damages awarded for personal injury.

FACT SUMMARY: A Texas state court exercised jurisdiction over Helicopteros Nacionales (D) on the basis of its regular purchases in the state.

CONCISE RULE OF LAW: Purchases, even at regular intervals, do not subject a foreign corporation to state jurisdiction if the purchases are unrelated to the cause of action.

FACTS: Four Americans were killed when a helicopter crashed on them while they were working on the ground. The helicopter was owned and operated by Helicopteros Nacionales de Colombia, S.A. (D). Survivors filed a personal injury action in Texas. Helicopteros (D) regularly purchased products in Texas, although these purchases were unrelated to the incident in question. The Texas court held personal jurisdiction to exist. A jury awarded $1 million, and the Texas Supreme Court affirmed. The U.S. Supreme Court granted review.

ISSUE: Do purchases at regular intervals subject a foreign corporation to state jurisdiction if the purchases are unrelated to the cause of action?

HOLDING AND DECISION: (Blackmun, J.) No. Purchases at regular intervals do not subject a foreign corporation to state jurisdiction if the purchases are unrelated to the cause of action. When a defendant's contacts with a forum state are unrelated to a cause of action, the contacts must be sufficiently substantial that a defendant can expect to be haled into court there. Purchases alone do not constitute the sort of exploitation of a state's facilities to be considered such a substantial contact. Only when the purchases are not so related can the contact be considered substantial and therefore jurisdiction be proper. Affirmed.

DISSENT: (Brennan, J.) The cause of action did not arise out of the purchases but was related to the purchases. The Court does not make this distinction, as it should have.

EDITOR'S ANALYSIS: The Court in this action reaffirmed Rosenberg Bros. & Co. v. Curtis Brown Co. 260 U.S. 516 (1923). Rosenberg's rule was the same as that established here. Rosenberg predates the "minimum contacts" theory of personal jurisdiction, but the Court felt it was still valid. Regular purchases by themselves, said the Court, will not constitute minimum contacts.

[For more information on relatedness of minimum contacts, see Casenote Law Outline on Civil Procedure, Chapter 3, § V, Step-by-Step Guide to Minimum Contacts Analysis.]

INSURANCE CORPORATION OF IRELAND, LTD. v. COMPAGNIE DES BAUXITES DE GUINEE
456 U.S. 694 (1982).

NATURE OF CASE: Review of jurisdiction declared by way of discovery sanctions in a declaratory relief action regarding insurance coverage.

FACT SUMMARY: A district court held jurisdiction to exist over nonresident corporations when they failed to comply with discovery orders.

CONCISE RULE OF LAW: A court may declare jurisdiction as a sanction for failure to comply with discovery.

FACTS: A dispute arose between a U.S. corporation and certain foreign insurers as to whether a certain loss was covered. The U.S. corporation, Compagnie des Bauxites de Guinee (P), filed a declaratory relief action in the district court in Pennsylvania. The foreign insurers (D) objected to jurisdiction and moved for summary judgment thereon. In the meantime, the foreign insurers (D) refused to comply with discovery orders. The court, under its sanctioning power, declared the jurisdictional objections of the foreign insurers (D) waived. The Supreme Court accepted the insurer's interlocutory appeal.

ISSUE: May a court declare jurisdiction as a sanction for failure to comply with discovery?

HOLDING AND DECISION: (White, J.) Yes. A court may declare jurisdiction as a sanction for failure to comply with discovery. Rules regarding personal jurisdiction are rights related to personal liberty held by individuals. Such rights may be waived, either voluntarily or otherwise. When a defendant specially appears in an action contesting jurisdiction, it is bound to follow all court orders until the jurisdictional issue is settled. Refusal to do so can constitute a waiver of jurisdictional objections. Here, the refusal to provide discovery hampered resolution of the jurisdictional issue, so the sanction was appropriate. Affirmed.

EDITOR'S ANALYSIS: A defendant objecting to jurisdiction has an alternative path to that taken by the insurers (D) here. He can ignore the action, allow a default to be taken, and challenge the default in a collateral proceeding. This is a risky course of action, as a failure in the collateral proceeding leaves a defendant with a default judgment against him.

CARNIVAL CRUISE LINES, INC. v. SHUTE
499 U.S. 585 (1991).

NATURE OF CASE: Review of order reversing dismissal of personal injury action.

FACT SUMMARY: In a personal injury suit filed by the Shutes (P), Carnival Cruise Lines (D) sought to enforce a forum selection clause appearing in fine print on its tickets.

CONCISE RULE OF LAW: If reasonable, a forum selection clause in a form contract should control.

FACTS: The Shutes (P) booked passage on a Carnival Cruise Lines (D) ship. After paying the fare, they received the tickets, which stated that no refunds were allowed. The tickets also contained a clause stating that any litigation arising out of the cruise would be held in Florida, where Carnival (D) had its principal place of business. Ms. Shute (P) was injured while on the cruise. The Shutes (P) filed suit in district court in Washington, where they resided. The district court granted Carnival's (D) motion to dismiss based on the forum selection clause. The Ninth Circuit reversed on the grounds that the forum selection clause was nonnegotiable. The court also found that the Shutes (P) were physically and financially unable to litigate in Florida. Carnival (D) appealed, and the Supreme Court granted certiorari.

ISSUE: Will a forum selection clause in a form contract control if reasonable?

HOLDING AND DECISION: (Blackmun, J.) Yes. If reasonable, a forum selection clause in a form contract will control. In light of present-day commercial realities and the increasingly interstate and international nature of trade, a forum selection clause can be a legitimate tool for parties to promote stability in their commercial relationships. To be reasonable, such a clause must not exist for the sole or primary purpose of evading litigation, for example, by citing a foreign forum to which a plaintiff has no realistic recourse. Here, the forum selected is Florida. It is a U.S. forum and the home state of Carnival (D), and many of its cruises depart from and return there. Since the Shutes (P) did not claim lack of notice of the clause, they have not satisfied the heavy burden of proof required to set aside the clause on grounds of inconvenience. Reversed.

EDITOR'S ANALYSIS: In a portion of the decision not excerpted in the casebook, the Shutes (P) also cited 46 U.S.C. App. § 183c, which prohibited ship operators from restricting passengers' right to sue in a "court of competent jurisdiction." The court rejected that argument, however, insofar as it concluded that Florida was in fact a competent jurisdiction. That issue had an unusual post-decision legislative history. Soon after the above decision was rendered, Congress overruled it by statute. Soon after that, however, the original language of the operative statute, 46 U.S.C. § 183c, was restored, arguably adopting the Supreme Court's interpretation in Carnival Cruise Lines as to the enforceability of forum selection clauses.

NOTES:

MULLANE v. CENTRAL HANOVER BANK AND TRUST CO.
339 U.S. 306 (1950).

NATURE OF CASE: Constitutional challenge of the sufficiency of the notice provision of a statute relating to beneficiaries of common trust funds.

FACT SUMMARY: Central Hanover Bank (D) pooled a number of small trust funds, and beneficiaries (some of whom lived out of state) were notified by publication in a local newspaper.

CONCISE RULE OF LAW: In order to satisfy due process challenges, notice must be by means calculated to inform the desired parties, and, where they reside outside of the state and their names and addresses are available, notice by publication is insufficient.

FACTS: A New York statute allowed corporate trustees to pool the assets of numerous small trusts administered by them, allowing more efficient and economical administration of the funds. Each participating trust shared ratably in the common fund, but the trustees held complete control of all assets. A periodic accounting of profits, losses, and assets was to be submitted to the courts for approval. Beneficiaries were to be notified of the accounting so that they might object to any irregularities in the administration of the common fund. Once approved by the court, their claims would be barred. A guardian was appointed to protect the interests of principal and income beneficiaries. Central Hanover Bank (D) established a common fund by consolidating the corpus of 113 separate trusts under their control. Notice of the common fund was sent to all interested parties along with the relevant portions of the statute. Notice of accountings were by publication in a local New York newspaper. Mullane (P), the appointed guardian for all parties known and unknown who had an interest in the trust's income, objected to the sufficiency of the statutory notice provisions, claiming that they violated the Due Process Clause of the Fourteenth Amendment. Notice by publication was not a reasonable method of informing interested parties that their rights were being affected, especially with regard to out-of-state beneficiaries. Mullane's (P) objections were overruled in state courts, and he appealed.

ISSUE: Is notice by publication sufficient to satisfy due process challenges where the parties to be informed reside out of state and an alternative means, better calculated to give actual notice, is available?

HOLDING AND DECISION: (Jackson, J.) No. The purpose of a notice requirement is to inform parties that their rights are being affected. Therefore, the method chosen should, if at all possible, be reasonably designed to accomplish this end. Notice in a New York legal paper is not reasonably calculated to provide out-of-state residents with the desired information. While the state has a right to discharge trustees of their liabilities through the acceptance of their accounting, it must also provide beneficiaries with adequate notice so that their rights to contest the accounting are not lost. In cases where the identity or whereabouts of beneficiaries or future interest holders is unknown, then publication is the most viable alternate means available for giving notice. Publication is only a supplemental method of giving notice. However, the court will approve its use where alternative methods are not reasonably possible or practical. Where alternative methods, better calculated to give actual notice, are available, publication is an impermissible means of providing notice. Notice to known beneficiaries via publication is inadequate not because it, in fact, fails to inform everyone but because under the circumstances, it is not readily calculated to reach those who could easily be informed by other means at hand. Since publication to known beneficiaries is ineffective, the statutory requirement violates the Due Process Clause of the Fourteenth Amendment. These parties have, at least potentially, been deprived of property without due process of law. With respect to remote future interest holders and unknown parties, publication is permissible.

EDITOR'S ANALYSIS: Ineffective notice provisions violate procedural due process rights. As in all due process challenges, there must be a legitimate state interest, and the means selected must be reasonably adapted to accomplish the state's purpose. While in Mullane the state's ends were permissible, the method of giving notice was unreasonable as it pertained to known parties. As has been previously stated, publication is only a supplementary method for giving notice. It is normally used in conjunction with other means when personal service by hand is unavailable or impractical. Mullane has been applied to condemnation cases where a known owner of property was never personally served. Schroeder v. City of New York, 371 U.S. 208. Factors considered by the court involve the nature of the action, whether the party's whereabouts or identity are known or unknown, whether he is a resident, and whether or not he has attempted to avoid personal service. If an attempt to avoid service is made, then constructive service by publication in conjunction with substitute service by mail is permitted. Finally, foreign corporations are generally required to appoint resident agents authorized to accept service of process.

[For more information on notice requirements for due process, see Casenote Law Outline on Civil Procedure, Chapter 2, § III, Jurisdiction and Valid Judgments.]

NOTES:

PIPER AIRCRAFT COMPANY v. REYNO
454 U.S. 235 (1982).

NATURE OF CASE: Appeal from dismissal on the basis of forum non conveniens.

FACT SUMMARY: Reyno (P), the representative of five victims of an air crash, brought suit in California even though the location of the crash and the homes of the victims were in Scotland.

CONCISE RULE OF LAW: A plaintiff may not defeat a motion to dismiss for forum non conveniens merely by showing that the substantive law that would be applied in the alternative forum is less favorable to him than that of the present forum.

FACTS: Reyno (P) was the representative of five air crash victims' estates and brought suit for wrongful death in United States district court in California, even though the accident occurred and all the victims resided in Scotland. Piper (D) moved to dismiss for forum non conveniens, contending that Scotland was the proper forum. Reyno (P) opposed the motion on the basis that the Scottish laws were less advantageous to her than American laws. The district court granted the motion, while the court of appeals reversed. The Supreme Court granted certiorari.

ISSUE: May a plaintiff defeat a motion to dismiss for forum non conveniens merely on the basis that the laws of the alternative forum are less advantageous?

HOLDING AND DECISION: (Marshall, J.) No. A plaintiff may not defeat a motion to dismiss for forum non conveniens merely by showing that the substantive law of the alternative forum is less advantageous than that of the present forum. In this case, all the evidence, witnesses, and interests were in Scotland. Thus, the most convenient forum was there. As a result, the motion was properly granted. Reversed.

EDITOR'S ANALYSIS: The Court in this case specifically noted that under some circumstances, the fact that the chosen state's laws are less attractive to the defendant could be used to defeat a motion to dismiss for forum non conveniens. If the state chosen by the plaintiff has the only adequate remedy for the wrong alleged, then the motion may be denied.

[For more information on forum non conveniens, see Casenote Law Outline on Civil Procedure, Chapter 2, § V, Other Constraints on Choice of Forum.]

BATES v. C & S ADJUSTERS, INC.
980 F.2d 865 (2d Cir. 1992).

NATURE OF CASE: Appeal from dismissal of a complaint due to improper venue.

FACT SUMMARY: After Bates (P) received a collection notice, which C & S (D) had sent to Bates' (P) old address in Pennsylvania but which had been forwarded to his new address in New York, Bates (P) brought this action in New York, alleging violations of the Fair Debt Collection Practices Act.

CONCISE RULE OF LAW: An action may be brought in a judicial district in which a substantial part of the events or omissions giving rise to the claim occurred.

FACTS: Bates (P) incurred a debt while he was a resident of the western district of Pennsylvania. The creditor, a corporation with its principal place of business in that district, referred the account to C & S (D), a local collection agency which transacted no regular business in New York. Meanwhile, Bates (P) had moved to the western district of New York. When C & S (D) mailed a collection notice to Bates (P) at his Pennsylvania address, it was forwarded to his new address in New York. When he received the collection notice, Bates (P) filed this action in the western district of New York, alleging violations of the Fair Debt Collection Practices Act. The district court dismissed because of improper venue. Bates (P) appealed.

ISSUE: May an action be brought in a judicial district in which a substantial part of the events or omissions giving rise to the claim occurred?

HOLDING AND DECISION: (Newman, J.) Yes. An action may be brought in a judicial district in which a substantial part of the events or omissions giving rise to the claim occurred. In adopting the Fair Debt Collection Practices Act, Congress was concerned about the harmful effect of abusive debt-collection practices on consumers. The harm does not occur until receipt of the collection notice, which is a substantial part of the events giving rise to a claim under the Act. If the bill collector prefers not to be challenged for its collection practices outside the district of a debtor's original residence, the envelope containing the notice can be marked "do not forward." Here, because C & S Adjusters, Inc. (D) appears not to have marked the notice with instructions not to forward and has not objected to the assertion of personal jurisdiction, trial in the western district of New York would not be unfair. Reversed and remanded.

EDITOR'S ANALYSIS: Prior to 1966, venue was proper in federal question cases, absent a special venue statute, only in the defendant's state of citizenship. From 1966 to 1990, 28 U.S.C. § 1391 allowed for venue in the judicial district in which the claim arose. This language gave rise to a variety of conflicting interpretations. Before Congress' 1990 amendment of § 1391(b), applied in the instant case, most courts applied at least a form of the weight of contacts test.

[For more information on federal venue, see Casenote Law Outline on Civil Procedure, Chapter 4, § VII, Federal Venue.]

10

CHAPTER 10
CHOOSING THE FORUM — STATE v. FEDERAL COURT

QUICK REFERENCE RULES OF LAW

1. **Diversity Jurisdiction and One's Domicile.** A party's mere residence in a state, even if the party has no intention of returning to his state of citizenship, will not create citizenship for purposes of federal diversity jurisdiction. (Mas v. Perry)

   [For more information on diversity jurisdiction and one's domicile, see Casenote Law Outline on Civil Procedure, Chapter 4, § IV, The Diversity Jurisdiction of the District Courts.]

2. **Federal Question Jurisdiction.** Alleging an anticipated constitutional defense in the complaint does not give a federal court jurisdiction if there is no diversity of citizenship between the litigants. (Louisville & Nashville R.R. Co. v. Mottley)

   [For more information on federal question jurisdiction, see Casenote Law Outline on Civil Procedure, Chapter 4, § III, The Federal Question Jurisdiction of the District Courts.]

3. **Implied Private Rights of Action.** Federal jurisdiction does not exist where an action involves a federal standard, but Congress had not intended that a federal private right of action be created. (Merrell Dow Pharmaceuticals, Inc. v. Thompson)

   [For more information on implied private rights of action, see Casenote Law Outline on Civil Procedure, Chapter 4, § III, The Federal Question Jurisdiction of the District Courts.]

4. **Pendant Jurisdiction.** Under pendant jurisdiction, federal courts may decide state issues which are closely related to the federal issues being litigated. (United Mine Workers of America v. Gibbs)

   [For more information on pendant jurisdiction, see Casenote Law Outline on Civil Procedure, Chapter 6, § V, Supplemental Jurisdiction in Aid of Liberal Joinder in the Federal Courts.]

5. **Ancillary Jurisdiction.** In a diversity case, the federal court does not have ancillary jurisdiction over the plaintiff's claims against a third-party defendant who is a citizen of the same state. (Owens Equipment & Erection Co. v. Kroger)

   [For more information on ancillary jurisdiction, see Casenote Law Outline on Civil Procedure, Chapter 6, § V, Supplemental Jurisdiction in Aid of Liberal Joinder in the Federal Courts.]

6. **Pendant Claims.** When parties and their various causes of action are linked to a claim properly before a federal court, the court may hear those claims even if the federal claim is dismissed. (Palmer v. Hospital Authority of Randolph County)

   [For more information on pendant claims, see Casenote Law Outline on Civil Procedure, Chapter 6, § I, Joinder of Claims.]

7. **Removal Jurisdiction.** In a removed action, the defendant shall answer or present the other defenses or objections available within twenty days after the receipt through service or otherwise of a copy of the initial pleading. (Apache Nitrogen Products, Inc. v. Harbor Ins. Co.)

   [For more information on removal jurisdiction, see Casenote Law Outline on Civil Procedure, Chapter 4, § V, Removal Jurisdiction.]

NOTES

LOUISVILLE & NASHVILLE R.R. v. MOTTLEY
211 U.S. 149 (1908).

NATURE OF CASE: Appeal of a decision overruling a demurrer in an action for specific performance of a contract.

FACT SUMMARY: Mottley (P) was injured on a train owned by Louisville & Nashville Railroad (D), which granted Mottley (P) a lifetime free pass which he sought to enforce.

CONCISE RULE OF LAW: Alleging an anticipated constitutional defense in the complaint does not give a federal court jurisdiction if there is no diversity of citizenship between the litigants.

FACTS: In 1871, Mottley (P) and his wife were injured while riding on the Louisville & Nashville R.R. (D). The Mottleys (P) released their claims for damages against the Louisville & Nashville R.R. (D) upon receiving a contract granting free transportation during the remainder of their lives. In 1907, the Louisville & Nashville R.R. (D) refused to renew the Mottleys' (P) passes, relying upon an act of Congress which forbade the giving of free passes or free transportation. The Mottleys (P) filed an action in a circuit court of the United States for the western district of Kentucky. The Mottleys (P) and the Louisville & Nashville R.R. (D) were both citizens of Kentucky. Therefore, the Mottleys (P) attempted to establish federal jurisdiction by claiming that the Louisville & Nashville R.R. (D) would raise a constitutional defense in its answer, thus raising a federal question. The Louisville & Nashville R.R. (D) filed a demurrer to the complaint for failing to state a cause of action. The demurrer was denied. On appeal, the Supreme Court did not look at the issue raised by the litigants but on its own motion raised the issue of whether the federal courts had jurisdiction to hear the case.

ISSUE: Does an allegation in the complaint that a constitutional defense will be raised in the answer raise a federal question which would give a federal court jurisdiction if no diversity of citizenship is alleged?

HOLDING AND DECISION: (Moody, J.) No. The Supreme Court reversed the lower court's ruling and remanded the case to that court with instructions to dismiss the suit for want of jurisdiction. Neither party to the litigation alleged that the federal court had jurisdiction in this case, and neither party challenged the jurisdiction of the federal court to hear the case. Because the jurisdiction of the circuit court is defined and limited by statute, the Supreme Court stated that it is their duty to see that such jurisdiction is not exceeded. Both parties to the litigation were citizens of Kentucky, and so there was no diversity of citizenship. The only way that the federal court could have jurisdiction in this case would be if there were a federal question involved. Mottley (P) did allege in his complaint that the Louisville & Nashville R.R. (D) based its refusal to renew the free pass on a federal statute. Mottley (P) then attempted to allege information that would defeat the defense of the Louisville & Nashville R.R. (D). This is not sufficient. The plaintiff's complaint must be based upon the federal laws of the Constitution to confer jurisdiction on the federal courts. Mottley's (P) cause of action was not based on any federal laws or constitutional privileges; it was based on a contract. Even though it is evident that a federal question will be brought up at the trial, plaintiff's cause of action must be based on a federal statute or the Constitution in order to have a federal question which would grant jurisdiction to the federal courts.

EDITOR'S ANALYSIS: If Mottley (P) could have alleged that he was basing his action on a federal right, it would have been enough to have given the federal court jurisdiction. The federal court would have had to exercise jurisdiction at least long enough to determine whether there actually was such a right. If the federal court ultimately concludes that the claimed federal right does not exist, the complaint would be dismissed for failure to state a claim upon which relief can be granted rather than for lack of jurisdiction. The court has the power to determine the issue of subject matter jurisdiction on its own motion as it did in this case. Subject matter jurisdiction can be challenged at any stage of the proceeding.

[For more information on federal question jurisdiction, see Casenote Law Outline on Civil Procedure, Chapter 4, § III, The Federal Question Jurisdiction of the District Courts.]

NOTES:

MAS v. PERRY
489 F.2d 1396 (5th Cir. 1974).

NATURE OF CASE: Jurisdictional appeal of damages awarded for invasion of privacy.

FACT SUMMARY: Mas (P), temporarily in Louisiana with no intention of returning to her home in Mississippi, sued Perry (D), a Louisiana citizen, in the federal district court of Louisiana.

CONCISE RULE OF LAW: A party's mere residence in a state, even if the party has no intention of returning to his state of citizenship, will not create citizenship for purposes of federal diversity jurisdiction.

FACTS: Jean Paul Mas (P) was a citizen of France. Judy Mas (P) was a U.S. citizen from Mississippi. They resided in Louisiana while studying. Judy Mas (P) did not intend to return to Mississippi, and did not intend to remain in Louisiana, as the couple was undecided where they intended to move after their studies were finished. After discovering that Perry (D), their landlord, spied on them through a two-way mirror, they sued in Louisiana district court. Perry (D), a Louisiana citizen, appealed the damages awarded based on a jurisdictional objection, contending that Judy Mas (P) was a citizen of Louisiana.

ISSUE: Does a party's residence in a state, if the party has no intention of returning to his state of citizenship, create citizenship for purposes of federal diversity jurisdiction?

HOLDING AND DECISION: (Ainsworth, J.) No. A party's mere residence in a state, even if the party has no intention of returning to his state of citizenship, will not create citizenship for purposes of federal diversity jurisdiction. For such purposes, a party is considered a citizen of the state of domicile. "Domicile" means a fixed residence coupled with the intention of remaining. A move from the state of domicile cannot be considered a change of domicile unless an intention to remain exists. Until such an intention is formed, domicile remains in the last state where such an intention existed, even if no intention to return exists. Here, although Judy Mas (P) had no intention of returning to Mississippi, her state of domicile, she had not formed new domiciliary intentions. Consequently, she remained a citizen of Mississippi. Affirmed.

EDITOR'S ANALYSIS: Perry (D) also argued that Judy Mas (P) had lost her Mississippi citizenship due to her marriage to a foreign national. Unlike Jean Paul Mas (P), who by statute could sue in district court, Judy (P) would not be able to do so, as she was not an alien. The court rejected this out of hand, noting that one forfeits no citizenship rights by reason of marriage alone.

[For more information on diversity jurisdiction and one's domicile, see Casenote Law Outline on Civil Procedure, Chapter 4, § IV, The Diversity Jurisdiction of the District Courts.]

MERRELL DOW PHARMACEUTICALS, INC. v. THOMPSON
478 U.S. 804 (1986).

NATURE OF CASE: Review of denial of motion to remand an action to state court.

FACT SUMMARY: A personal injury lawsuit involved a federal standard for which no federal private action had been created.

CONCISE RULE OF LAW: Federal jurisdiction does not exist where an action involves a federal standard, but Congress had not intended that a federal private right of action be created.

FACTS: Thompson (P) and others filed a state action in Ohio against Merrell Dow Pharmaceuticals, Inc. (D), alleging that a drug manufactured by them had caused personal injury. Among the allegations were violations of the Federal Food, Drug and Cosmetic Act. Merrell (D) successfully petitioned for removal. Thompson (P) unsuccessfully moved to remand. The district court then dismissed on forum non conveniens grounds. The Sixth Circuit reversed, holding that, since the FFDC created no private right of action, the motion to remand should have been granted. The Supreme Court accepted review.

ISSUE: Does federal jurisdiction exist where an action involves a federal standard but Congress had not intended that a federal private right of action be created?

HOLDING AND DECISION: (Stevens, J.) No. Federal jurisdiction does not exist where an action involves a federal standard but Congress had not intended that a federal private right of action be created. Under 28 U.S.C. § 1331, jurisdiction exists if an action "arises under" a U.S. law. It has long been recognized that a suit arises under that law which creates a cause of action. Where federal law does not create the cause of action, the suit does not arise under federal law. Further, to hold that federal jurisdiction exists when no federal private right of action was intended would undercut Congress' intention not to create a federal private right of action. For these reasons, only the presence of a federal claim, not merely a federal standard, can confer federal jurisdiction. Affirmed.

DISSENT: (Brennan, J.) Where a plaintiff's right to relief depends upon the construction of a federal law, federal jurisdiction is proper.

EDITOR'S ANALYSIS: 28 U.S.C. § 1331 was enacted pursuant to Article III, § 2 of the Constitution. This section granted jurisdiction to all cases arising under the Constitution, statutes, or treaties. Section 1331 essentially mirrors the language of Article III, § 2. Nonetheless, § 1331 has largely been construed more narrowly than its constitutional counterpart.

[For more information on implied private rights of action, see Casenote Law Outline on Civil Procedure, Chapter 4, § III, The Federal Question Jurisdiction of the District Courts.]

UNITED MINE WORKERS OF AMERICA v. GIBBS
383 U.S. 715 (1966).

NATURE OF CASE: Action to recover damages for violation of § 303 of the Labor Management Relations Act and for interference with a business interest.

FACT SUMMARY: Gibbs (P) lost his job as superintendent of a coal mining company because of alleged unlawful influence of United Mine Workers (D).

CONCISE RULE OF LAW: Under pendant jurisdiction, federal courts may decide state issues which are closely related to the federal issues being litigated.

FACTS: There was a dispute between United Mine Workers (D) and the Southern Labor Union over who should represent the coal miners in that area. Tennessee Consolidated Coal Company closed down a mine where over 100 men belonging to United Mine Workers (D) were employed. Later, Grundy Company, a wholly owned subsidiary of Tennessee Consolidated Coal Company, hired Gibbs (P) to open a new mine using members of the Southern Labor Union. Gibbs (P) was also given a contract to haul the mine's coal to the nearest railroad loading point. Members of Local 5881 of the United Mine Workers (D) forcibly prevented the opening of the mine. Gibbs (P) lost his job and never entered into performance of his haulage contract. He soon began to lose other trucking contracts and mine leases he held in the area. Gibbs (P) claimed this was a result of a concerted union plan against him. He filed suit in the United States District Court for the Eastern District of Tennessee for violation of § 303 of the Labor Management Relations Act and a state law claim, based on the doctrine of pendant jurisdiction, that there was an unlawful conspiracy and boycott aimed at him to interfere with his contract of employment and with his contract of haulage. The jury's verdict was that the United Mine Workers (D) had violated both § 303 and the state law. On motion, the trial court set aside the award of damages for the haulage contracts and entered a verdict for United Mine Workers (D) on the issue of violation of § 303, which was the federal claim. The award as to the state claim was sustained. The court of appeals affirmed.

ISSUE: Can federal courts decide state issues that are closely related to the federal issues being litigated?

HOLDING AND DECISION: (Brennan, J.) Yes. When there are both state and federal claims involved in the same set of facts and the claims are such that the plaintiff would ordinarily be expected to try them all in one judicial proceeding, the federal court has the power to hear both the state and the federal claims. The federal claims must have substance sufficient to confer subject matter jurisdiction on the court. This is the doctrine of pendant jurisdiction. The court is not required to exercise this power in every case. It has consistently been recognized that pendant jurisdiction is a doctrine of discretion, not of plaintiff's right. The court should look at judicial economy, convenience, and fairness to litigants in deciding whether to exercise jurisdiction over the state claims. If the factual relationship between the state and federal claims is so close that they ought to be litigated at the same trial, the court ought to grant pendant jurisdiction in order to save an extra trial. If the issues are so complicated that they are confusing to the jury, then the court probably should dismiss the state claims. The issue of whether pendant jurisdiction has been properly assumed is one which remains open throughout the litigation. If, before the trial, the federal claim is dismissed, then the state claim should also be dismissed. If it appears that a state claim constitutes the real body of a case, then it may fairly be dismissed. [The Court went on to hold that the plaintiff could not recover damages for conspiracy under the state claim.] Reversed.

EDITOR'S ANALYSIS: This case helped clarify the law that had been established by the case of Hurn v. Oursler, 289 U.S. 238. This case set the rule for determining if a federal court could hear the state claim. If a case had two distinct grounds in support of a single cause of action, one of which presents a federal question, then the court could hear the state claim. But if a case had two separate and distinct causes of action and only one was a federal question, then the court could not hear the state claim. Now the state and federal claims can state separate causes of action as long as they are factually closely related.

[For more information on pendant jurisdiction, see Casenote Law Outline on Civil Procedure, Chapter 6, § V, Supplemental Jurisdiction in Aid of Liberal Joinder in the Federal Courts.]

NOTES:

OWEN EQUIPMENT & ERECTION v. KROGER
437 U.S. 365 (1978).

NATURE OF CASE: Action for damages for wrongful death.

FACT SUMMARY: Kroger (P) brought a wrongful death action in federal court against a defendant of diverse citizenship and then amended her complaint to include an impleaded third-party defendant, Owen (D), even though they were citizens of the same state.

CONCISE RULE OF LAW: In a diversity case, the federal court does not have ancillary jurisdiction over the plaintiff's claims against a third-party defendant who is a citizen of the same state.

FACTS: Kroger's (P) husband was electrocuted when the boom of a steel crane owned and operated by Owen (D), and next to which he was walking, came too close to a high tension electric power line of the Omaha Public Power District (OPPD). Kroger (P) brought a wrongful death action against OPPD in federal court in Nebraska, she being a resident of Iowa. However, OPPD filed a third-party complaint against Owen (D), alleging its negligence had caused the electrocution. Eventually, OPPD's motion for summary judgment was granted, and Owen (D) was the only defendant left in the case. During trial, it was discovered that Owen (P), a Nebraska corporation, had its principal place of business in Iowa and was therefore a citizen of the same state as Kroger (P). The district court denied Owen's (D) motion to dismiss the complaint for lack of jurisdiction, and the jury returned a verdict in favor of Kroger (P). The court of appeals affirmed.

ISSUE: Can a federal court exercise ancillary jurisdiction over a plaintiff's claims against a third-party defendant who is a citizen of the same state in a diversity case?

HOLDING AND DECISION: (Stewart, J.) No. The concept of ancillary jurisdiction is not so broad as to permit a federal court in a diversity case to exercise jurisdiction over the plaintiff's claims against a third-party defendant who is a citizen of the same state. 28 U.S.C. § 1332(a)(1) requires complete diversity of citizenship. To allow ancillary jurisdiction in a case like this would be to allow circumvention of that requirement by the simple expedient of suing only those defendants who were of diverse citizenship and waiting for them to implead nondiverse defendants. Reversed.

DISSENT: (White, J.) Section 1332 requires complete diversity only between the plaintiff and those parties he actually brings into the suit, which would not include Owen (D) in this case. Beyond that, the district court has the power to entertain all claims among the parties arising from the same nucleus of operative fact as the plaintiff's original, jurisdiction-conferring claim against the original defendant. Thus, ancillary jurisdiction existed in this case.

EDITOR'S ANALYSIS: Fed. R. Civ. P. 14 permits ancillary jurisdiction. In amending it, the Advisory Committee stated that any attempt by a plaintiff to amend his complaint to assert a claim against an impleaded third party would be unavailing, by majority view, where the third party could not have been joined by the plaintiff

originally due to jurisdictional limitations. Congress reenacted § 1332 without relevant change and with knowledge of the aforementioned view. The majority opinion took this as evidence of congressional approval of that view.

[For more information on ancillary jurisdiction, see Casenote Law Outline on Civil Procedure, Chapter 6, § V, Supplemental Jurisdiction in Aid of Liberal Joinder in the Federal Courts.]

NOTES:

PALMER v. HOSPITAL AUTHORITY OF RANDOLPH COUNTY
22 F.3d 1559 (11th Cir. 1994).

NATURE OF CASE: Appeal from dismissal of federal statutory claim and related state-law wrongful death and medical malpractice claims.

FACT SUMMARY: Upon dismissing Palmer's (P) federal cause of action upon which federal jurisdiction had been based, the court dismissed all related state law claims and parties.

CONCISE RULE OF LAW: When parties and their various causes of action are linked to a claim properly before a federal court, the court may hear those claims even if the federal claim is dismissed.

FACTS: Palmer's (P) wife and unborn child died following medical care at a Randolph County Hospital (D). Palmer (P) filed an action in Georgia District Court against Patterson Hospital (D) and Dr. Bates (D). All parties were originally Georgia citizens; Palmer (P) resided in Alabama at the time of the claim. Federal question jurisdiction was based on 42 U.S.C. § 1395dd, the patient "anti-dumping" protection provisions of COBRA. Several state-law causes of action were also asserted. Bates (D) moved to dismiss on the ground that 42 U.S.C. § 13955dd did not create a cause of action against private physicians. The court agreed and dismissed the claim. It then proceeded to dismiss all the state-law claims for lack of subject matter jurisdiction. Palmer (P) appealed, arguing that the court could retain jurisdiction over the state-law claims under supplemental jurisdiction.

ISSUE: When parties and their various causes of action are linked to a claim properly before a federal court, may the court hear those claims even if the federal claim is dismissed as to those parties?

HOLDING AND DECISION: (Birch, J.) Yes. When parties and their various causes of action are linked to a claim properly before a federal court, the court may hear those claims even if the federal claim is dismissed as to those parties. 28 U.S.C. § 1367 provides that a district court shall have supplemental jurisdiction over both additional claims and additional parties when these claims or parties are so related to the federal claim as to be part of the same case or controversy. That § 1367 allows a state claim against a party against whom a federal claim has been asserted is without question. The issue here is whether a state-law claim can be assessed against a party related to a federal claim properly before the court but against whom the federal claim is not applicable. The jurisdiction of the federal judiciary is set by Congress within constitutional restrictions. Section 1367(a) allows jurisdiction up to the full extent allowed by the Constitution, which requires that a party or a claim is within the same case or controversy. Palmer (P), as an Alabama citizen, is legitimately before the court on claims against Patterson Hospital (D). Bates (D) is within the court's jurisdictional reach on the state-law claims of Palmer (P) as a Georgia citizen. Finally, the claims asserted against Bates (D) are nearly identical whether Palmer's (P) residence is Georgia or Alabama. The same facts, occurrences, witnesses, and evidence are present in all these claims. Each state-law claim is linked, finally, to the surviving COBRA claim. Therefore, the district court has the power, subject to its discretion, to exercise jurisdiction in this case. Reversed and remanded for a determination whether to exercise supplemental jurisdiction.

EDITOR'S ANALYSIS: Section 1367(a) was a codification of a series of Supreme Court decisions, most notably United Mine Workers v. Gibbs, 393 U.S. 715 (1966). These cases had introduced the concept of pendant jurisdiction in which related state-law claims could be joined to a federal claim. Also codified was ancillary jurisdiction, which allowed related parties to be joined.

[For more information on pendant claims, see Casenote Law Outline on Civil Procedure, Chapter 6, § I, Joinder of Claims.]

NOTES:

APACHE NITROGEN PRODUCTS, INC. v.
HARBOR INSURANCE CO.
145 F.R.D. 674 (D. Ariz. 1993).

NATURE OF CASE: Action by a manufacturer seeking declaratory relief and damages against insurance companies for refusal of coverage.

FACT SUMMARY: When Apache's (P) insurers removed to federal district court after receiving a courtesy copy of Apache's (P) complaint, Apache (P) requested an entry of default for failure to answer within the stipulated twenty-day period, even though the insurers had not received service of process.

CONCISE RULE OF LAW: In a removed action, the defendant shall answer or present the other defenses or objections available within twenty days after the receipt through service or otherwise of a copy of the initial pleading.

FACTS: Because Apache (P) was being investigated for potential violations of CERCLA, Apache (P) repeatedly demanded that its eighteen liability insurers extend coverage in relation to the investigation. When all its insurers refused Apache's (P) demands, it filed suit, seeking declaratory relief and damages. Instead of immediately initiating service of process, Apache (P) mailed courtesy copies of the complaint to Continental (D) and Stonewall (D). Although service had not yet been effectuated, the insurers removed to federal court. When they had not answered within twenty days after removal, as prescribed by Fed. R. Civ. P. 81(c), Apache (P) requested an entry of default, which was granted. Both insurers moved to set aside the default.

ISSUE: In a removed action, shall the defendant answer or present the other defenses or objections available within twenty days after the receipt through service or otherwise of a copy of the initial pleading?

HOLDING AND DECISION: (Bilby, J.) Yes. In a removed action, the defendant shall answer or present the other defenses or objections available within twenty days after the receipt through service or otherwise of a copy of the initial pleading. Receipt "otherwise" does not eliminate the requirement that process be served before the thirty day period set by 28 U.S.C. § 1446(b) commences to run. Since Rule 81(c) must be interpreted in harmony with § 1446(b), the twenty-day response time under Rule 81(c) does not commence to run until service has been effectuated. If Apache's (P) liability insurers are allowed to remove and answer before Apache (P) has effectuated service, then its right to amend once as of right will be eliminated. Accordingly, the entry of default against Stonewall (D) and Continental (D) must be set aside.

EDITOR'S ANALYSIS: The use of the "service or otherwise" language in both Rule 81(c) and 28 U.S.C. § 1446(b) was a conscious legislative effort to create consistency in the law governing removal. The majority view of the "or otherwise" language is that the defendant must both be served with process and receive a copy of the initial pleading before the clock starts ticking. But a significant minority holds that the clock starts ticking upon receipt of a copy of the initial pleading, regardless of whether service has been effectuated. This was the approach argued for by Apache (P).

[For more information on removal jurisdiction, see Casenote Law Outline on Civil Procedure, Chapter 4, § V, Removal Jurisdiction.]

NOTES:

CHAPTER 11
CHOOSING THE LAW TO BE APPLIED IN FEDERAL COURT

QUICK REFERENCE RULES OF LAW

1. **Choice-of-law Questions.** Federal courts sitting in diversity are not obligated to follow state decisional precedent. (Swift v. Tyson)

    [For more information on choice-of-law questions, see Casenote Law Outline on Civil Procedure, Chapter 4, § VIII, The Erie Doctrine.]

2. **The Erie Doctrine.** Although the 1789 Rules of Decision Act left federal courts unfettered to apply their own rules of procedure in common law actions brought in federal court, state law governs substantive issues. State law includes not only statutory law but case law as well. (Erie Railroad Co. v. Tompkins)

    [For more information on the Erie doctrine, see Casenote Law Outline on Civil Procedure, Chapter 4, § VIII, The Erie Doctrine.]

3. **The Erie Doctrine.** Where a state statute that would completely bar recovery in state court has significant affect on the outcome determination of the action, even though the suit be brought in equity, the federal court is bound by the state law. (Guaranty Trust Co. of New York v. New York)

    [For more information on developments of the Erie doctrine, see Casenote Law Outline on Civil Procedure, Chapter 4, § VIII, The Erie Doctrine.]

4. **Balancing State and Federal Interests.** A federal court sitting in diversity need not follow state law allocating the fact-finding roles of judge and jury. (Byrd v. Blue Ridge Rural)

    [For more information on balancing state and federal interests, see Casenote Law Outline on Civil Procedure, Chapter 4, § VIII, The Erie Doctrine.]

5. **Supremacy of the Federal Rules.** The Erie doctrine mandates that federal courts are to apply state substantive law and federal procedural law, but, where matters fall roughly between the two and are rationally capable of classification as either, the Constitution grants the federal court system the power to regulate its practice and pleading (procedure). (Hanna v. Plumer)

    [For more information on the supremacy of the Federal Rules, see Casenote Law Outline on Civil Procedure, Chapter 4, § VIII, The Erie Doctrine.]

6. **Expanding Role of the Federal Rules.** A state law mandating sanctions for an unsuccessful appeal shall not be applicable in a federal diversity action. (Burlington Northern R.R. v. Woods)

    [For more information on the expanding role of the Federal Rules, see Casenote Law Outline on Civil Procedure, Chapter 4, § VIII, The Erie Doctrine.]

7. **State vs. Federal Law.** In a diversity action, state law regarding when an action is commenced shall be followed. (Walker v. Armco Steel Corp.)

    [For more information on state vs. federal law, see Casenote Law Outline on Civil Procedure, Chapter 4, § VIII, The Erie Doctrine.]

8. **Supremacy of the Federal Rules.** A state supreme court ruling on an issue need not be followed by a federal court sitting in diversity if that ruling has lost its vitality. (Mason v. American Emery Wheel Works)

[For more information on the supremacy of the Federal Rules, see Casenote Law Outline on Civil Procedure, Chapter 4, § VIII, The Erie Doctrine.]

9. **State Courts and Federal Procedure.** Though federal claims may be adjudicated by state courts, state laws are never controlling on the question of what the incidents of any federal right may be. (Dice v. Akron, Canton & Youngstown R.R. Co.)

   [For more information on state courts and federal procedure, see Casenote Law Outline on Civil Procedure, Chapter 4, § VIII, The Erie Doctrine.]

10. **Supremacy of the Federal Rules.** The priority of the FHA and SBA as creditors is to be governed by federal standards adopting the priority rules of the forum states. (United States v. Kimbell Foods, Inc.)

    [For more information on the supremacy of the Federal Rules, see Casenote Law Outline on Civil Procedure, Chapter 4, § VIII, The Erie Doctrine.]

11. **Implied Constitutional and Statutory Remedies.** A federal agent's violation of the Fourth Amendment gives rise to a cause of action for damages. (Bivens v. Six Unknown Named Agents of the Federal Bureau of Narcotics)

SWIFT v. TYSON
41 U.S. (16 Pet.) 1 (1842).

NATURE OF CASE: Review of action seeking to enforce a bill of exchange.

FACT SUMMARY: The result in a diversity federal action depended upon whether the district court was obligated to follow state decisional precedent.

CONCISE RULE OF LAW: Federal courts sitting in diversity are not obligated to follow state decisional precedent.

FACTS: In an action seeking to enforce a bill of exchange, an issue arose as to whether the district court was obligated to follow New York common law or was free to apply general principles of common law. [The casebook excerpt did not state the decision in the district court.]

ISSUE: Are federal courts sitting in diversity obligated to follow state decisional precedent?

HOLDING AND DECISION: (Story, J.) No. Federal courts sitting in diversity are not obligated to follow decisional precedent. The Rules Decision Act, found at 28 U.S.C. § 1652, mandates that federal courts sitting in diversity follow state law. However, the decisions of courts are not laws; they are interpretations thereof and can be reexamined, qualified, or reversed by courts themselves. Consequently, while federal courts sitting in diversity must follow state statutes, state court decisions need not be. [The casebook excerpt did not note how the rule affected the case in question.]

EDITOR'S ANALYSIS: This decision was reversed almost a century later in Erie Railroad Co. v. Tompkins, 304 U.S. 64 (1938). Swift was decided purely as a matter of statutory construction. Erie found the creation of federal general common law to be unconstitutional.

[For more information on choice-of-law questions, see Casenote Law Outline on Civil Procedure, Chapter 4, § VIII, The Erie Doctrine.]

NOTES:

ERIE RAILROAD CO. v. TOMPKINS
304 U.S. 64 (1938).

NATURE OF CASE: Action to recover damages for personal injury allegedly caused by negligent conduct.

FACT SUMMARY: In a personal injury suit, a federal district court trial judge refused to apply applicable state law because such law was "general" (judge-made) and not embodied in any statute.

CONCISE RULE OF LAW: Although the 1789 Rules of Decision Act left federal courts unfettered to apply their own rules of procedure in common law actions brought in federal court, state law governs substantive issues. State law includes not only statutory law but case law as well.

FACTS: Tompkins (P) was walking in a right-of-way parallel to some railroad tracks when an Erie Railroad (D) train came by. Tompkins (P) was struck and injured by what he would, at trial, claim to be an open door extending from one of the railcars. Under Pennsylvania case law (the applicable law since the accident occurred there), state courts would have treated Tompkins (P) as a trespasser in denying him recovery for other than wanton or willful misconduct on Erie's (D) part. Under "general" law, recognized in federal courts, Tompkins (P) would have been regarded as a licensee and would only have been obligated to show ordinary negligence. Because Erie (D) was a New York corporation, Tompkins (P) brought suit in a federal district court in New York, where he won a judgment for $30,000. Upon appeal to a federal circuit court, the decision was affirmed.

ISSUE: Was the trial court in error in refusing to recognize state case law as the proper rule of decision in deciding the substantive issue of liability?

HOLDING AND DECISION: (Brandeis, J.) Yes. The Court's opinion is in four parts: (1) Swift v. Tyson, 41 U.S. (16 Pet.) 1 (1842), which held that federal courts exercising jurisdiction on the ground of diversity of citizenship need not, in matters of general jurisprudence, apply the unwritten law of the state as declared by its highest court, is overruled. Section 34 of the federal Judiciary Act of 1789, c. 20, 28 U.S.C. § 725, requires that federal courts in all matters except those where some federal law is controlling apply as their rules of decision the law of the state, unwritten as well as written. Up to this time, federal courts had assumed the power to make "general law" statutes. (2) Swift had numerous political and social defects. The hoped-for uniformity among state courts had not occurred; there was no satisfactory way to distinguish between local and general law. On the other hand, Swift introduced grave discrimination by noncitizens against citizens. The privilege of selecting the court for resolving disputes rested with the noncitizen, who could pick the more favorable forum. The resulting far-reaching discrimination was due to the broad province accorded "general law" in which many matters of seemingly local concern were included. Furthermore, local citizens could move out of the state and bring suit in a federal court if they were disposed to do so; corporations, similarly, could simply reincorporate in another state. More than

statutory relief is involved here; the unconstitutionality of Swift is clear. (3) Except in matters governed by the federal Constitution or by acts of Congress, the law to be applied in any case is the law of the state. There is no federal common law. The federal courts have no power derived from the Constitution or by Congress to declare substantive rules of common law applicable in a state whether they be "local" or "general" in nature. (4) The federal district court was bound to follow the Pennsylvania case law, which would have denied recovery to Tompkins (P).

DISSENT: (Butler, J.) Since no constitutional question was presented or argued in the lower court, and a 1937 statute which required notice to the Attorney General whenever the constitutionality of an Act of Congress was raised was not followed, the court's conduct was improper.

CONCURRENCE AND DISSENT: (Reed, J.) It is unnecessary to go beyond interpreting the meaning of "laws" in the Rules of Decision Act. Article III and the Necessary and Proper Clause of Article I of the Constitution might provide Congress with the power to declare rules of substantive law for federal courts to follow.

EDITOR'S ANALYSIS: Erie can fairly be characterized as the most significant and sweeping decision on civil procedure ever handed down by the U.S. Supreme Court. As interpreted in subsequent decisions, Erie held that while federal courts may apply their own rules of procedure, issues of substantive law must be decided in accord with the applicable state law — usually the state in which the federal court sits. Note, however, how later Supreme Court decisions have made inroads into the broad doctrine enunciated here.

[For more information on the Erie doctrine, see Casenote Law Outline on Civil Procedure, Chapter 4, § VIII, The Erie Doctrine.]

NOTES:

GUARANTY TRUST CO. OF NEW YORK v. YORK
326 U.S. 99 (1945).

NATURE OF CASE: Class action alleging fraud and misrepresentation.

FACT SUMMARY: York (P), barred from filing suit in state court because of the state statute of limitations, brought an equity action in federal court based upon diversity of citizenship jurisdiction.

CONCISE RULE OF LAW: Where a state statute that would completely bar recovery in state court has significant affect on the outcome determination of the action, even though the suit be brought in equity, the federal court is bound by the state law.

FACTS: Van Swerigen Corporation, in 1930, issued notes and named Guaranty Trust Co. (D) as trustee with power and obligations to enforce the rights of the note holders in the assets of the corporation and the Van Swerigens. In 1931, when it was apparent that the corporation could not meet its obligations, Guaranty (D) cooperated in a plan for the purchase of the outstanding notes for 50% of the notes' face value and an exchange of 20 shares of the corporation's stock for each $1,000 note. In 1934, York (P) received some cash, her donor not having accepted the rate of exchange. In 1940, three accepting note holders sued Guaranty (D), charging fraud and misrepresentation, in state court. York (P) was not allowed to intervene. Summary judgment in favor of Guaranty (D) was affirmed. In 1942, York (P) brought a class-action suit in federal court based on diversity of citizenship and charged Guaranty (D) with breach of trust. Guaranty (D) moved for, and was granted, summary judgment on the basis of the earlier state decision. The court of appeals reversed on the basis that the earlier state decision did not foreclose this federal court action, and held that, even though the state statute of limitations had run, the fact that the action was brought in equity releases the federal court from following the state rule.

ISSUE: Does a state statute of limitations, which would bar a suit in state court, also act as a bar to the same action if the suit is brought in equity in federal court and jurisdiction being based on diversity of citizenship?

HOLDING AND DECISION: (Frankfurter, J.) Yes. Erie Railroad Co. v. Tompkins overruled a particular way of looking at law after its inadequacies had been laid bare. Federal courts have traditionally given state-created rights in equity greater respect than rights in law since the former are more frequently defined by legislative enactment. Even though federal equity may be thought of as a separate legal system, the substantive right is created by the state, and federal courts must respect state law which governs that right. While state law cannot define the remedies which a federal court must give simply because a federal court in diversity jurisdiction is available as an alternative, a federal court may afford an equitable remedy for a substantive right recognized by a state even though a state court cannot give it. Federal courts enforce state-created substantive rights if the mode of proceeding and remedy were consonant with the traditional body of equitable remedies, practice, and procedure. Matters of "substance" and of "procedure" turn on different considerations. Here, since the federal court is adjudicating a state-created right solely because of diversity of citizenship of the parties is, in effect, only another court of the state, it cannot afford recovery if the right to recovery is made unavailable by the state. The question is not whether a statute of limitation is "procedural" but whether the statute so affects the result of litigation as to be controlling in state law. It is, therefore, immaterial to make a "substantive-procedure" dichotomy — Erie Railroad Co. v. Tompkins was not an endeavor to formulate scientific legal terminology but rather an expression of a policy that touches the distribution of judicial power between state and federal courts. Erie insures that insofar as legal rules determine the outcome of litigation, the result should not be any different in a federal court extending jurisdiction solely on the basis of diversity of citizenship. Through diversity jurisdiction, Congress meant to afford out-of-state litigants another tribunal and not another body of law.

EDITOR'S ANALYSIS: Guaranty Trust, which clarified Erie, may itself be in the process of being slowly eroded by modern courts. Hanna v. Plumer, 380 U.S. 460 (1965), held that where state law conflicts with the Federal Rules of Civil Procedure, the latter prevails regardless of the effect on outcome of the litigation. And in Byrd v. Blue Ridge Elec. Cooperative, 356 U.S. 525 (1958), the Court suggested that some constitutional doctrines (there, the right to a jury trial in federal court) are so important as to be controlling over state law once again, the outcome notwithstanding.

[For more information on developments of the Erie doctrine, see Casenote Law Outline on Civil Procedure, Chapter 4, § VIII, The Erie Doctrine.]

NOTES:

HANNA v. PLUMER
380 U.S. 460 (1965).

NATURE OF CASE: Appeal of summary judgment in federal diversity tort action.

FACT SUMMARY: Plumer (P) filed a tort action in federal court in Massachusetts, where Hanna (D) resided, for an auto accident that occurred in South Carolina.

CONCISE RULE OF LAW: The Erie doctrine mandates that federal courts are to apply state substantive law and federal procedural law, but, where matters fall roughly between the two and are rationally capable of classification as either, the Constitution grants the federal court system the power to regulate its practice and pleading (procedure).

FACTS: Hanna (P), a citizen of Ohio, filed a tort action in federal court in Massachusetts against Plumer (D), the executor of the estate of Louise Plumer Osgood, a Massachusetts citizen. It was alleged that Osgood caused injuries to Hanna (P) in an auto accident in South Carolina. Service on Plumer (D) was accomplished pursuant to Fed. R. Civ. P. 4(d)(1) by leaving copies of the summons with Plumer's (D) wife. At trial, motion for summary judgment by Plumer (D) was granted on the grounds that service should have been accomplished pursuant to Massachusetts law (by the Erie doctrine), which required service by hand to the party personally. On appeal, Hanna (P) contended that Erie should not affect the application of the Federal Rules of Civil Procedure to this case. Plumer (D), however, contended that (1) a substantive law question under Erie is any question in which permitting application of federal law would alter the outcome of the case (the so-called outcome determination test); (2) the application of federal law here (i.e., 4(d)(1)) will necessarily affect the outcome of the case (from a necessary dismissal to litigation); and, so, therefore, (3) Erie requires that the state substantive law requirement of service by hand be upheld along with the trial court's summary judgment.

ISSUE: Does the Erie doctrine classification of "substantive law questions" extend to embrace questions involving both substantive and procedural considerations merely because such a question might have an effect on the determination of the substantive outcome of the case?

HOLDING AND DECISION: (Warren, C.J.) No. The Erie doctrine mandates that federal courts are to apply state substantive law and federal procedural law, and, where matters fall roughly between the two and are rationally capable of classification as either, the Constitution grants the federal court system the power to regulate its practice and pleading (procedure). It is well settled that the Enabling Act for the Federal Rules of Civil Procedure requires that a procedural effect of any rule on the outcome of a case be shown to actually "abridge, enlarge, or modify" the substantive law in a case for the Erie doctrine to come into play. Where, as here, the question only goes to procedural requirements (i.e., service of summons, a dismissal for improper service here would not alter the substantive right of Hanna [P] to serve Plumer [D] personally and refile or effect the substantive law of negligence in the case), Article III and the Necessary and Proper Clause provide that Congress has a right to provide rules for the federal court system such as Fed. R. Civ. P. 4(d)(1). "Outcome determination analysis was never intended to serve as a talisman" for the Erie doctrine. Reversed.

CONCURRENCE: (Harlan, J.) Though the Court was correct to reject the outcome determination test, it was wrong in stating that anything arguably procedural is constitutionally placed within the province of the federal government to regulate. The test for "substantive" would be whether "the choice of rule would substantially affect those primary decisions respecting human conduct which our constitutional system leaves to state regulation."

EDITOR'S ANALYSIS: This case points up a return to the basic rationales of Erie R.R. Co. v. Tompkins. First, the Court asserts that one important consideration in determining how a particular question should be classified (substantive or procedural) is the avoidance of "forum shopping" (the practice of choosing one forum such as federal to file in in order to gain the advantages of one), which permits jurisdictions to infringe on the substantive law defining powers of each other. Second, the Court seeks to avoid inequitable administration of the laws which would result from allowing jurisdictional considerations to determine substantive rights. Chief Justice Warren here, in rejecting the "outcome determination" test, asserts that any rule must be measured ultimately against the Federal Rules Enabling Act and the Constitution.

[For more information on the supremacy of the Federal Rules, see Casenote Law Outline on Civil Procedure, Chapter 4, § VIII, The Erie Doctrine.]

NOTES:

BYRD v. BLUE RIDGE RURAL ELECTRIC COOPERATIVE, INC.
356 U.S. 525 (1958).

NATURE OF CASE: Appeal of reversal of damages awarded for personal injury.

FACT SUMMARY: In a diversity action, a court of appeals felt constrained to apply state law making certain factual determinations the province of the court alone.

CONCISE RULE OF LAW: A federal court sitting in diversity need not follow state law allocating the fact-finding roles of judge and jury.

FACTS: Byrd (P), injured while working on power lines owned and operated by Blue Ridge Rural Electric Cooperative, Inc. (D), sued Blue Ridge (D) for damages. Blue Ridge (D) claimed that a certain statutory defense applied. The district court, sitting in diversity, rejected its application, and a jury awarded damages. The court of appeals reversed, holding that the defense applied and was per state law an issue to be decided by the court. The court held the defense meritorious and entered judgment for Blue Ridge (D). Byrd (P) appealed.

ISSUE: Must a federal court sitting in diversity follow state law allocating the fact-finding roles of judge and jury?

HOLDING AND DECISION: (Brennan, J.) No. A federal court sitting in diversity need not follow state law allocating the fact-finding roles of judge and jury. The precedents of this Court mandate that federal courts sitting in diversity apply the law of the forum state. A major reason for this is to avoid different outcomes in federal and state courts. However, state laws that affect the basic functions of federal courts in how they operate do not require strict adherence. Where the application of state law would greatly upset the basic functions of the federal judiciary, the law should not be applied. Here, the fact-finding roles of the judge and jury are integral to the federal judiciary, in fact implicating the Constitution by virtue of the Seventh Amendment. Therefore, state law making determination of the statutory defense a factual issue for the court should not have been followed. Reversed.

EDITOR'S ANALYSIS: The Court, in a brief passage, mentioned that the fact-finding allocation of the statute was a "form and mode" of enforcing the statutory immunity and was not integral to the rights of the parties. The import of this passage is unclear. Further, the Court did not appear to base its decision on this observation so much as upon the structural argument outlined above.

[For more information on balancing state and federal interests, see Casenote Law Outline on Civil Procedure, Chapter 4, § VIII, The Erie Doctrine.]

BURLINGTON NORTHERN RAILROAD CO. v. WOODS
480 U.S. 1 (1987).

NATURE OF CASE: Review of sanctions awarded pursuant to statute in an action seeking damages for personal injury.

FACT SUMMARY: A court of appeals, pursuant to a state statute, assessed a 10% penalty for an unsuccessful appeal in a diversity action.

CONCISE RULE OF LAW: A state law mandating sanctions for an unsuccessful appeal shall not be applicable in a federal diversity action.

FACTS: Woods (P) sued Burlington Northern Railroad Co. (D) for personal injury in a district court sitting in Alabama, jurisdiction being based on diversity. A jury awarded Woods (P) over $300,000. Burlington (D) appealed. The Eleventh Circuit affirmed and, pursuant to an Alabama statute, assessed a mandatory sanction of 10%. Burlington (D) sought review of the sanctions.

ISSUE: Shall a state law mandating sanctions for an unsuccessful appeal be applicable in a federal diversity action?

HOLDING AND DECISION: (Marshall, J.) No. A state law mandating sanctions for an unsuccessful appeal shall not be applicable in a federal diversity action. Fed. R. App. P. 38 makes the imposition of sanctions discretionary, not mandatory. This Court's precedents have held that when a federal rule is arguably procedural and does not impair a substantive state-created right, it shall be constitutional to apply it rather than conflicting state law. Here, Fed. R. App. P. 38 is certainly at least arguably procedural. Further, it appears to this Court's satisfaction that the imposition of sanctions is not a substantive right under the statute in question. This being so, Fed. R. App. P. 38 shall prevail in this matter. Reversed.

EDITOR'S ANALYSIS: The seminal case to deal with conflicts between state law and federal rules in diversity cases was Hanna v. Plumer, 380 U.S. 460 (1965). There, a state law conflicted with Fed. R. Civ. P. 4(d)(1). The rule of presumptive validity, which means that if a state law conflicts with an arguably procedural federal rule the latter will be presumptively valid, was established here.

[For more information on the expanding role of the Federal Rules, see Casenote Law Outline on Civil Procedure, Chapter 4, § VIII, The Erie Doctrine.]

WALKER v. ARMCO STEEL CORP
446 U.S. 740 (1980).

NATURE OF CASE: Review of dismissal of federal diversity action.

FACT SUMMARY: Because state law applicable to a diversity action provided that an action commenced only upon service of process, a district court dismissed the case in question because service was not effected until after the statute of limitations had run.

CONCISE RULE OF LAW: In a diversity action, state law regarding when an action is commenced shall be followed.

FACTS: Walker (P) brought a federal diversity action against Armco Steel Corp. (D). The complaint was filed less than two years after the cause of action arose, but more than two years elapsed before service was effected. Under state law, the statute of limitations was two years, and an action was not considered to be commenced until process was served. The district court granted Armco's (D) motion for summary judgment on the grounds the statute of limitations had expired, and this was affirmed. The Supreme Court accepted review.

ISSUE: In a diversity action, shall state law regarding when an action is commenced be followed?

HOLDING AND DECISION: (Marshall, J.) Yes. In a diversity action, state law regarding when an action is commenced shall be followed. State substantive law is to be followed in federal courts sitting in diversity. When an action is considered to be commenced is not a matter of procedure. It is a statement of a substantive decision by a state that actual service upon a defendant is necessary to initiate an action. Fed. R. Civ. P. 3, which deals with service, does not address this issue, so there is no need to even consider a possible conflict between state and federal rules. Affirmed.

EDITOR'S ANALYSIS: Fed. R. Civ. P. 3 deals with service of process. As implied by the Court here, it deals strictly with the procedural aspects of effecting service. It is silent regarding the ramifications of service as to statutes of limitation.

[For more information on state vs. federal law, see Casenote Law Outline on Civil Procedure, Chapter 4, § VIII, The Erie Doctrine.]

MASON v. AMERICAN EMERY WHEEL WORKS
241 F.2d 106 (4th Cir. 1957).

NATURE OF CASE: Appeal of dismissal of action for damages for personal injury.

FACT SUMMARY: A federal court sitting in diversity held itself obligated to follow an old Mississippi Supreme Court decision regarding standing to sue in a products liability case.

CONCISE RULE OF LAW: A state supreme court ruling on an issue need not be followed by a federal court sitting in diversity if that ruling has lost its vitality.

FACTS: Mason (P), injured by an emery wheel manufactured by American Emery Wheel Works (D), sued in federal court, jurisdiction being based on diversity. Mason (P) had not obtained the wheel directly from American (D). The district court, following a 1928 Mississippi Supreme Court decision holding that privity of contract was necessary to sue a product manufacturer for injuries, granted summary judgment in favor of American (D). Mason (P) appealed.

ISSUE: Must a state supreme court ruling on an issue be followed by a federal court sitting in diversity, even if that ruling has lost its vitality?

HOLDING AND DECISION: (Magruder, C.J.) No. A state supreme court ruling on an issue need not be followed by a federal court sitting in diversity if that ruling has lost its vitality. There is no question but that a federal court sitting in diversity must follow state law. Generally speaking, a pronouncement of a state supreme court will be final on a given issue. Where, however, the decision appears to have lost its vitality, it is up to the district court to try to decide how the state court would rule on that issue today. Here, there has been a major shift in products liability law since 1928, and it is unlikely that the Mississippi Supreme Court would follow its own precedent. This is borne out by dicta in at least one case indicating dissatisfaction with the 1928 precedent. In light of this, it seems relatively clear that the true state of the law in Mississippi is not to require contractual privity. Reversed.

CONCURRENCE: (Hartigan, J.) The decision today was made much easier by the dicta to which reference was made in the opinion. It is much less clear how far a federal court in diversity can go in rejecting state supreme court precedent which has not been undercut in subsequent decisions.

EDITOR'S ANALYSIS: Obviously, not every issue that comes before a federal court sitting in diversity will have been ruled upon by the state supreme court. When this occurs, the role of a federal court becomes much like a state trial court. It must search through other state precedent to rule on an issue.

[For more information on the supremacy of the Federal Rules, see Casenote Law Outline on Civil Procedure, Chapter 4, § VIII, The Erie Doctrine.]

DICE v. AKRON, CANTON & YOUNGSTOWN R.R. CO.
342 U.S. 359 (1952).

NATURE OF CASE: Negligence action under Federal Employer's Liability Act.

FACT SUMMARY: Dice (P), a railroad fireman, was injured in an accident involving a train of the Railroad (D).

CONCISE RULE OF LAW: Though federal claims may be adjudicated by state courts, state laws are never controlling on the question of what the incidents of any federal right may be.

FACTS: Dice (P), a railroad fireman injured when an engine of the Railroad (D) jumped the track, sued in an Ohio state court under the Federal Employers Liability Act, charging negligence. At trial, the Railroad (D) offered in defense a document signed by Dice (P) which purported to release the Railroad (D) of all liability over and above $924.63, which Dice (P) had already received. Dice (P) contended that he had not read the statement before signing it, relying on fraudulent representations of the Railroad (D) that the document was merely a receipt for the $924.63. The jury found for Dice (P), but the trial court entered judgment n.o.v. for the Railroad (D) on the grounds that under Ohio state law, Dice (P) could not escape responsibility for signing the release. Under Ohio law, he was under a duty to read the document before signing it. The Ohio Court of Appeals reversed the trial judge on the grounds that federal law (that a finding of fraud will preclude the use of a release such as the one in this case) should have been applied. The Ohio Supreme Court reversed again, and this appeal followed.

ISSUE: In adjudicating a claim arising out of federal law, may a state court properly apply state law?

HOLDING AND DECISION: (Black, J.) No. Though federal claims may be adjudicated by state courts, state laws are never controlling on the question of what the incidents of any federal right may be. Federal rights according relief to injured railroad employees could be defeated if states were permitted to have the final say as to what defenses could and could not be interposed here. It is true that Ohio normally allows the judge in an action to resolve all issues of fraud in a negligence action, and that, in itself, is a perfectly acceptable procedure. But it is well settled that the federal right to a jury trial is an essential one, which Ohio may not infringe upon. Reversed.

DISSENT: (Frankfurter, J.) Requiring federal standards for the determination of fraud unconstitutionally invades the state's reserved power to maintain the common law division between law (i.e., negligence determined by a jury) and equity (fraud relieved by a judge).

EDITOR'S ANALYSIS: This case points up the general rule for the treatment of federal rights in state courts. In short, they are always governed by federal law. The Seventh Amendment right to a civil jury trial is an exclusively federal right. It is not a fundamental right incorporated in the Fourteenth Amendment and extended to the states. As such, states may properly provide that certain issues are to be determined by judges. When a federal right is involved, however, such discretion ceases. The federal standard of the Seventh Amendment must prevail.

[For more information on state courts and federal procedure, see Casenote Law Outline on Civil Procedure, Chapter 4, § VIII, The Erie Doctrine.]

NOTES:

CASENOTE LEGAL BRIEFS — CIVIL PROCEDURE

UNITED STATES v. KIMBELL FOODS, INC.
440 U.S. 715 (1979).

NATURE OF CASE: Review of consolidated actions between private and federal creditors.

FACT SUMMARY: Appellate decisions were rendered holding that the SBA's and FHA's priority as creditors was governed by a uniform federal standard.

CONCISE RULE OF LAW: The priority of the FHA and SBA as creditors is to be governed by federal standards adopting the priority rules of the forum states.

FACTS: A pair of actions involved security disputes between, respectively, the FHA and SBA and private creditors. In both actions, the FHA and SBA and private creditors sought priority, but the circuit courts hearing the matters established uniform federal standards giving priority to the governmental lienors. The Supreme Court accepted review.

ISSUE: Is the priority of the SBA and FHA as creditors to be governed by federal standards adopting the priority rules of the forum states?

HOLDING AND DECISION: (Marshall, J.) Yes. The priority of the SBA and FHA as creditors is to be governed by federal standards adopting the priority rules of the forum states. It is well established that federal law governs questions of rights of the Government (D) in the application of its programs. It does not follow, however, that a uniform national standard is necessary. Only when a uniform national standard is necessary to properly effect the Congressional purposes behind the program at issue will such a standard be compelled. Here, the Court is dealing with a situation where local creditors tend to rely on local rules in making their decisions. The FHA and SBA both have local offices which are familiar with the local rules where they are located. To adopt a national standard would throw an unnecessary inflexibility into situations at the local level. Therefore, although the standards to be applied to the SBA and FHA at the local level will be federal, they shall borrow from the applicable local standards. No uniform national standard should be promulgated. Reversed.

EDITOR'S ANALYSIS: The rule created by the Court is subject to congressional override anytime Congress chooses. The Court was careful to point out that the rule was to apply only when the law creating the program in question is silent as to standards. If Congress wants a uniform standard, it may so provide.

[For more information on the supremacy of the Federal Rules, see Casenote Law Outline on Civil Procedure, Chapter 4, § VIII, The Erie Doctrine.]

BIVENS v. SIX UNKNOWN NAMED AGENTS OF THE FEDERAL BUREAU OF NARCOTICS
403 U.S. 388 (1971).

NATURE OF CASE: Review of dismissal of action seeking damages for civil rights violation.

FACT SUMMARY: Bivens (P) brought an action for damages based on violation of the Fourth Amendment.

CONCISE RULE OF LAW: A federal agent's violation of the Fourth Amendment gives rise to a cause of action for damages.

FACTS: Federal agents effected a search of Bivens' (P) residence, who later brought an action for damages based on an alleged Fourth Amendment violation. A court of appeals held that an alleged Fourth Amendment violation did not give rise to a private cause of action for damages, and dismissed. Bivens (P) appealed.

ISSUE: Does a federal agent's violation of the Fourth Amendment give rise to a cause of action for damages?

HOLDING AND DECISION: (Brennan, J.) Yes. A federal agent's violation of the Fourth Amendment gives rise to a private cause of action for damages. The alternative would simply be a cause of action under state law. However, this would improperly equate the trespasses of a private citizen with those of a federal agent acting under color of authority. An agent acting in his capacity, albeit unconstitutionally, possesses far greater capacity for wrongdoing than a private citizen. Further, a guarantee that citizens shall be protected against unreasonable search and seizure is meaningless if it gives no form of redress. Damages are a logical form of such redress. Finally, violations of federal rights should be adjudicated in federal courts when possible. For all these reasons, the court of appeals erred. Reversed.

CONCURRENCE: (Harlan, J.) It is not necessary for Congress to create a right of action for constitutional violations. The Constitution may create them itself.

DISSENT: (Burger, C.J.) In the absence of an explicit provision in the Constitution or a statute creating a right of action, one should not be inferred.

DISSENT: (Black, J.) Congressional inaction in creating a right of action should be given deference.

EDITOR'S ANALYSIS: Subsequent to this decision, Congress enacted a law giving a right of action for Fourth Amendment violations. The law happened to coincide with Bivens, so no problem was created. It is unclear what the result would be if Congress were to enact a law limiting its application.

CHAPTER 12
APPEALS

QUICK REFERENCE RULES OF LAW

1. **The Requirement of Finality.** A court's determination that an action may not be maintained as a class action under the Federal Rules of Civil Procedure is not a "final decision" and is therefore not appealable as a matter of right. (Coopers & Lybrand v. Livesay)

    [For more information on the requirement of finality, see Casenote Law Outline on Civil Procedure, Chapter 10, § III, The Federal Courts and the Model of Finality.]

2. **The Requirement of Finality.** A district court order holding that state law requiring an undertaking prior to filing suit would not be applied in federal court is appealable. (Cohen v. Beneficial Indus. Loan Corp.)

    [For more information on exceptions to the requirement of finality, see Casenote Law Outline on Civil Procedure, Chapter 10, § III, The Federal Courts and the Model of Finality.]

3. **Reviewability of Decisions.** Refusal to enforce a settlement agreement claimed to shelter a party from suit altogether does not supply the basis for an immediate appeal. (Digital Equipment Corp. v. Desktop Direct, Inc.)

    [For more information on reviewability of decisions, see Casenote Law Outline on Civil Procedure, Chapter 10, § I, The Mechanics of Appeal.]

4. **Interlocutory Appeals.** An interlocutory appeal should not be permitted where the regular appellate process would be as expeditious. (Cardwell v. Chesapeake & Ohio Ry. Co.)

    [For more information on interlocutory appeals, see Casenote Law Outline on Civil Procedure, Chapter 10, § III, The Federal Courts and the Model of Finality.]

5. **Review by Extraordinary Writ.** Appellate review, except in certain narrowly defined circumstances, should be postponed until after final judgment has been rendered by the court, and, therefore, a higher court should not grant appellate review by the extraordinary remedy of mandamus against a lower court where there is nothing in the record to demonstrate that the case is a really extraordinary one amounting to a judicial usurpation of power. (Will v. United States)

    [For more information on review by extraordinary writ, see Casenote Law Outline on Civil Procedure, Chapter 10, § III, The Federal Courts and the Model of Finality.]

6. **Review for Correctness.** A district court's determination of the finality of an adjudication of an issue in a multi-issue litigation will be reversed only if clearly erroneous. (Curtiss-Wright Corp. v. General Elec. Co.)

    [For more information on review for correctness, see Casenote Law Outline on Civil Procedure, Chapter 10, § III, The Federal Courts and the Model of Finality.]

7. **Discretionary Jurisdiction.** Orders concerning stays of legal proceedings on equitable grounds are not automatically appealable. (Gulfstream Aerospace Corp. v. Mayacamas Corp.)

    [For more information on discretionary jurisdiction, see Casenote Law Outline on Civil Procedure, Chapter 10, § III, The Federal Courts and the Model of Finality.]

8. **Standards of Review.** In a defamation action regarding a public figure, an appellate court must perform a de novo review of a district court's finding of reckless disregard of the truth. (Bose Corp. v. Consumers Union of United States, Inc.)

[For more information on standards of review, see Casenote Law Outline on Civil Procedure, Chapter 10, § I, The Mechanics of Appeal.]

9. **The Standing Doctrine.** An individual school board member does not have standing to appeal a declaratory judgment against the board. (Bender v. Williamsport Area School District)

   [For more information on the standing doctrine, see Casenote Law Outline on Civil Procedure, Chapter 4, § I, General Principles of Federal Subject-Matter Jurisdiction.]

10. **Standards of Review for Appeal.** A party may appeal on an issue which, while not raised at trial, was raised in a motion for a directed verdict. (Wratchford v. S.J. Groves & Sons Co.)

   [For more information on standards of review for appeal, see Casenote Law Outline on Civil Procedure, Chapter 10, § I, The Mechanics of Appeal.]

COOPERS & LYBRAND v. LIVESAY
437 U.S. 463 (1978).

NATURE OF CASE: Appeal from an adverse class determination.

FACT SUMMARY: The court in which Livesay (P) brought suit against Coopers & Lybrand (D), alleging violations of the federal securities laws, determined that it could not be maintained as a class action, and Livesay (P) appealed that decision.

CONCISE RULE OF LAW: A court's determination that an action may not be maintained as a class action under the Federal Rules of Civil Procedure is not a "final decision" and is therefore not appealable as a matter of right.

FACTS: Livesay (P) brought an action based on the allegation that Coopers & Lybrand (D) had certified incorrect financial statements in a prospectus issued in connection with a public offering of securities in Punta Gorda Isles and that he had relied thereon in purchasing the securities on which he lost $2,650. Contending federal securities laws were violated by Coopers & Lybrand (D) and others, Livesay (P) sought to have the court declare a class action on behalf of similarly situated purchasers. When the court determined that the action was not maintainable as a class action under the Federal Rules of Civil Procedure, Livesay (P) attempted to appeal the decision. Federal law made only "final decisions" appealable as a matter of right.

ISSUE: If a court determines that an action may not be maintained as a class action under the Federal Rules of Civil Procedure, is that a "final decision" so as to make it appealable as a matter of right?

HOLDING AND DECISION: (Stevens, J.) No. A court's determination that an action may not be maintained as a class action under the Federal Rules of Civil Procedure is not a "final decision" and is therefore not appealable as a matter of right. Generally, a decision must end the litigation on the merits and leave nothing for the court to do but execute the judgment before it is appealable. Of course, there is an exception as to decisions that conclusively determine the disputed question, resolve an important issue completely separate from the merits of the case, and are effectively unreviewable on appeal from a final decision. None of these criteria fit a decision on a request for class certification, so this "collateral order" exception would not apply. Some jurisdictions have found a decision like the one in this case appealable as a matter of right under the "death knell" doctrine, which assumes that without the incentive of possible group recovery the individual plaintiff may find it economically imprudent to pursue his lawsuit to final judgment and then seek appellate review of an adverse class determination. This suggests a need to make certain factual determinations in order to avoid a waste of judicial resources which the "final decision" rule of appealability was designed to prevent. Thus, the "death knell" rationale is not a sufficient reason for finding adverse class determinations to be "final decisions" appealable as a matter of right, meaning the appeal in this case must be dismissed.

EDITOR'S ANALYSIS: This case is an indication of the present view of the Court against expansion on the concept of "final decision." For some time prior, the Court had been undergoing expansion inasmuch as it had taken to a "pragmatic" test for appealability, which underlies the "death knell" doctrine.

[For more information on the requirement of finality, see Casenote Law Outline on Civil Procedure, Chapter 10, § III, The Federal Courts and the Model of Finality.]

NOTES:

DIGITAL EQUIPMENT CORP. v. DESKTOP DIRECT, INC.
_U.S._, 114 S. Ct. 1992 (1994).

NATURE OF CASE: Appeal from a district court ruling to vacate a dismissal of a trade name dispute.

FACT SUMMARY: The district court granted Desktop Direct, Inc.'s (P) motion to vacate a dismissal order, the court of appeals upheld this decision, and Digital Equipment Corp. (D) appealed to the Supreme Court.

CONCISE RULE OF LAW: Refusal to enforce a settlement agreement claimed to shelter a party from suit altogether does not supply the basis for an immediate appeal.

FACTS: Desktop (P) sued Digital (D) in U.S. District Court for unlawful use of a trade name. After the parties reached a confidential settlement agreement, Desktop (P) filed a notice of dismissal in the district court. Several months later, Desktop (P) moved to vacate the dismissal and rescind the settlement agreement because Digital (D) had allegedly misrepresented material facts during the settlement negotiations. The district court granted the motion to vacate the dismissal and denied Digital's (D) request that they reconsider their ruling or stay the order vacating dismissal. Digital (D) appealed this ruling on the grounds that its contracted right to trial immunity made this order immediately appealable. The court of appeals found the order not appealable, and Digital (D) appealed to the Supreme Court.

ISSUE: Does a court's refusal to enforce a settlement agreement claimed to shelter a party from suit altogether supply the basis for an immediate appeal?

HOLDING AND DECISION: (Souter, J.) No. Refusal to enforce a settlement agreement claimed to shelter a party from suit altogether does not supply the basis for an immediate appeal. Section 1291 of the Judicial Code entitles a party to appeal from a district court decision that ends the litigation on the merits and leaves nothing more for the court to do but execute the judgment. In addition, the collateral order doctrine makes a narrow class of nonfinal decisions appealable under § 1291. These decisions must be conclusive and resolve important legal questions completely separate from the merits. They must render such important questions effectively unreviewable on appeal from a final judgment in the underlying action. Digital (D) claimed that its privately negotiated settlement established a right to immunity from suit that was confirmed by the district court's dismissal. It claimed that the order to vacate the dismissal should be immediately appealable as a final order to avoid the injustice of forcing it to stand trial. However, the privately negotiated right to trial immunity cannot be considered more important than the societal interests advanced by the ordinary operation of final judgment principles. Policy favors upholding trial immunity rights that are guaranteed by the Constitution or by statute. Extending this guarantee to private contract would be against public policy. Affirmed.

EDITOR'S ANALYSIS: The purpose of § 1291 is the efficient administration of justice in the federal courts. The collateral order doctrine applied in the case above is not considered an exception to § 1291's final decision rule, but rather a practical construction of it. Although such collateral decisions do not actually end litigation, they are nonetheless treated as final in the interest of "achieving a healthy legal system."

[For more information on reviewability of decisions, see Casenote Law Outline on Civil Procedure, Chapter 10, § I, The Mechanics of Appeal.]

NOTES:

COHEN v. BENEFICIAL INDUSTRIAL LOAN CORPORATION
337 U.S. 541 (1948).

NATURE OF CASE: Appeal of order denying request that security bond be posted.

FACT SUMMARY: Beneficial Industrial (D) appealed an order holding that a state law requiring an undertaking prior to filing suit would not be applied in federal court.

CONCISE RULE OF LAW: A district court order holding that state law requiring an undertaking prior to filing suit would not be applied in federal court is appealable.

FACTS: Cohen (P), minor shareholder of Beneficial Industrial Loan Corp. (D), brought a derivative action in federal court, based on diversity. A law of the forum state provided that a minor shareholder, prior to filing a derivative action, had to post a bond. Beneficial (D) moved for an order requiring such an undertaking. This was denied. The court of appeals affirmed. The Supreme Court granted review and first discussed the issue of appealability.

ISSUE: Is a district court order holding that state law requiring an undertaking prior to filing suit would not be applied in federal court appealable?

HOLDING AND DECISION: (Jackson, J.) Yes. A district court order holding that state law requiring an undertaking prior to filing suit would not be applied in federal court is appealable. 28 U.S.C. § 1291 permits appeals of "final decisions" of district courts only. Generally, this means that only a decision having a final and irreparable effect on a party to an action is subject to appeal. Put another way, only decisions which are not tentative steps to the final judgment are appealable. Generally, this means only final judgments are appealable. However, an order prior to this stage of litigation which conclusively determines rights within the litigation are also appealable. Here, the decision was made that a board was unnecessary. This order settled this particular issue, and no subsequent event in the action could affect this determination. This being so, the order was appealable. [The Court, on the merits, reversed, holding the state law to be applicable.]

EDITOR'S ANALYSIS: Generally speaking, only final judgments are appealable. Exceptions such as this case are uncommon. The purpose of this rule is to avoid protracted and piecemeal litigation in the appellate courts. For truly egregious lower court errors, the possibility of extraordinary review by mandamus exists.

[For more information on exceptions to the requirement of finality, see Casenote Law Outline on Civil Procedure, Chapter 10, § III, The Federal Courts and the Model of Finality.]

CARDWELL v. CHESAPEAKE & OHIO RAILWAY CO.
504 F.2d 444 (6th Cir. 1974).

NATURE OF CASE: Interlocutory appeal in a personal injury action.

FACT SUMMARY: The district court certified for interlocutory appeal an issue upon which a motion for judgment notwithstanding the absence of a verdict was decided.

CONCISE RULE OF LAW: An interlocutory appeal should not be permitted where the regular appellate process would be as expeditious.

FACTS: Cardwell (P) sued Chesapeake & Ohio Railway Co. (D) for injuries and death to her husband. Trial lasted four days. The jury awarded $10,500 for the dependent's injuries but was unable to agree on the causal connection between the injury and death. Chesapeake (D) moved for judgment notwithstanding the absence of a verdict, contending that there was insufficient evidence for the death issue to have gone to the jury in the first instance. The motion was denied, but the district court certified the issue for interlocutory appeal.

ISSUE: Should an interlocutory appeal be permitted where the regular appellate process would be as expeditious?

HOLDING AND DECISION: (McCree, J.) No. An interlocutory appeal should not be permitted where the regular appellate process would be as expeditious. 28 U.S.C. § 1292(b) permits a district court to certify for interlocutory appeal a ruling on a legal issue that is controlling and a ruling which would materially advance the ultimate termination of the litigation. Section 1292(b) was intended to be sparingly used. When the nature of an action is such that legal issues can be decided on direct appeal as easily as by interlocutory appeal, the regular appellate process should be permitted to work. Here, the trial was already over, and a normal appeal was close to being possible. An interlocutory appeal was an inappropriate procedure. [The court went on to rule on the interlocutory appeal anyway and affirmed.]

EDITOR'S ANALYSIS: Generally speaking, only a final judgment is subject to appeal. Thus, an erroneous ruling at the pleading stage can result in a protracted litigation based on an erroneous original ruling. Section 1292(b) was partially intended to prevent this.

[For more information on interlocutory appeals, see Casenote Law Outline on Civil Procedure, Chapter 10, § III, The Federal Courts and the Model of Finality.]

WILL v. UNITED STATES
389 U.S. 90 (1967).

NATURE OF CASE: On writ of certiorari in a criminal tax evasion case.

FACT SUMMARY: The Government (P) requested a writ of mandamus ordering District Judge Will (D) to vacate his order that the Government (P) furnish information to a defendant in an income tax evasion case.

CONCISE RULE OF LAW: Appellate review, except in certain narrowly defined circumstances, should be postponed until after final judgment has been rendered by the court, and, therefore, a higher court should not grant appellate review by the extraordinary remedy of mandamus against a lower court where there is nothing in the record to demonstrate that the case is a really extraordinary one amounting to a judicial usurpation of power.

FACTS: In a motion for a bill of particulars, the defendant in a criminal tax evasion case in the U.S. District Court for the Northern District of Illinois requested certain information concerning oral statements by him which were being relied upon by the Government (P). The requested information included the names and addresses of the persons to whom the statements were made as well as the times and places at which they were made. Judge Will (D), the district judge, ordered the Government (P) to furnish this information, but it refused to comply with the order. Judge Will (D) then indicated his intention to dismiss the indictment because of the Government's (P) refusal to comply with his order. The circuit court of appeals then granted the Government's (P) application for a stay of proceedings and subsequently a writ of mandamus directing Judge Will (D) to vacate his order requiring the Government (P) to furnish the requested information.

ISSUE: When there is nothing in the record to demonstrate that a case is truly extraordinary, should the court grant appellate review by the extraordinary means of a writ of mandamus against a lower court?

HOLDING AND DECISION: (Warren, C.J.) No. The peremptory writ of mandamus has traditionally been used in the federal courts only "to confine an interior court to the lawful exercise of its authority when it is its duty to do so." It is basic that appellate review, except in certain narrowly defined circumstances, should be postponed until after final judgment has been rendered by the court, and, therefore, a higher court should not grant appellate review by the extraordinary writ of mandamus against a lower court where there is nothing in the record to demonstrate that the case is really an extraordinary one amounting to judicial usurpation of power. Examples of writs granted in the past to curtail abuses are where unwarranted judicial action threatened to embarrass the execution aim of the government in conducting foreign relations and where a judicial judge displayed a persistent disregard for the Rules of Civil Procedure promulgated by this Court. The general policy against piecemeal appeals takes on added weight in criminal charges where the defendant is entitled to a speedy resolution of the charges against him. While the writ of mandamus may — in some circumstances — be used to review procedural orders in criminal cases, this Court has never approved its use to review an interlocutory procedural order in a criminal case which did not have the effect of dismissal. The Constitution not only grants a man the right to a speedy trial but also forbids that he be placed twice in jeopardy for the same offense. There is nothing in the record to reflect that Judge Will (D) — as the Government (P) suggested — adopted a policy of deliberate disregard for the criminal discovery rules or that his policies were disruptive of justice. The case does not, therefore, fall into the category of one demanding this extraordinary writ. Hence, the writ is vacated, and the cause is remanded to the court of appeals for further proceedings not inconsistent with this opinion.

EDITOR'S ANALYSIS: There persists in our judicial system an antipathy to governmental right of review in criminal cases, and appeal by the government is unusual and not favored. Piecemeal appeals are generally not permitted, and those statutory exceptions are addressed either in terms or by necessity solely to civil actions. The extraordinary writ has never been approved or used by the court to control a procedural order in a criminal case, within the district court's jurisdiction, which did not deprive the prosecution of its right to trial permitted by law or to the results of a proper conviction. The authority to issue the writ has been sparingly used to confine an inferior court to a lawful exercise of its prescribed jurisdiction or to compel it to exercise its authority where it is its duty to do so.

[For more information on review by extraordinary writ, see Casenote Law Outline on Civil Procedure, Chapter 10, § III, The Federal Courts and the Model of Finality.]

NOTES:

CURTISS-WRIGHT CORPORATION v. GENERAL ELECTRIC COMPANY
446 U.S. 1 (1980).

NATURE OF CASE: Appeal of award of damages for breach of contract.

FACT SUMMARY: The court of appeals, disagreeing with the district court's balancing of the equities of holding an adjudication of a certain issue to be appealable, held the order to be nonfinal.

CONCISE RULE OF LAW: A district court's determination of the finality of an adjudication of an issue in a multi-issue litigation will be reversed only if clearly erroneous.

FACTS: Curtiss-Wright Corporation (P) sued General Electric Company (D) for breach of contract. General Electric (D) counterclaimed on certain contractual theories as well. General Electric (D) did not dispute that a certain amount was owed to Curtiss-Wright (P) but did contend that until its counterclaim was adjudicated, its obligation to pay did not arise. The district court granted summary judgment to Curtiss-Wright (P), holding the judgment to be final. The court of appeals reversed, holding that, absent a clear showing of prejudice, the presence of a counterclaim prevented a judgment on the main claim from becoming final. The Supreme Court granted review.

ISSUE: Will a district court's determination of the finality of an adjudication of an issue in a multi-issue litigation be reversible unless clearly erroneous?

HOLDING AND DECISION: (Burger, C.J.) No. A district court's determination of the finality of an adjudication of an issue in a multi-issue litigation will be reversed only if clearly erroneous. Fed. R. Civ. P. 54(b) allows a court dealing with multiple issues to direct the entry of final judgment as to less than all issues if no just reason for delay exists. The Rule vests in the district court its sound discretion in this matter. This discretion will be disturbed only if clearly erroneous. Here, the court of appeals appeared to fashion a per se rule that a counterclaim will defeat the finality of judgment on the main claim. This constituted an interference with the discretion of the district court and was improper. Reversed.

EDITOR'S ANALYSIS: In this case, the district court based its judgment on the fact that the legal rate of interest was much lower than the current market rates. It basically decided that Curtiss-Wright (P) should get the benefit of the rate differential, not General Electric (D). The Court noted that this was the type of discretion particularly to be exercised by trial courts.

[For more information on review for correctness, see Casenote Law Outline on Civil Procedure, Chapter 10, § III, The Federal Courts and the Model of Finality.]

GULFSTREAM AEROSPACE CORPORATION v. MAYACAMAS CORPORATION
108 S. Ct. 1133 (1988).

NATURE OF CASE: Review of dismissal of appeal of order denying application for stay of federal action.

FACT SUMMARY: Gulfstream Aerospace (D) contended that an order denying a stay of a federal action at law which had been based on equitable grounds was automatically appealable.

CONCISE RULE OF LAW: Orders concerning stays of legal proceedings on equitable grounds are not automatically appealable.

FACTS: Gulfstream Aerospace (D) sued Mayacamas Corp. (P) in state court for breach of contract. Mayacamas (P) in turn sued Gulfstream (D) in federal court on the same underlying transaction. Gulfstream (D) moved to stay the federal action pending resolution of the state action. This was denied, and the court of appeals dismissed the appeal, holding the order nonappealable. The Supreme Court granted review.

ISSUE: Are orders concerning stays of legal proceedings on equitable grounds automatically appealable?

HOLDING AND DECISION: (Marshall, J.) No. Orders concerning stays of legal proceedings on equitable grounds are not automatically appealable. Orders relating to stays generally are neither final judgments appealable under 28 U.S.C. § 1291 nor interlocutory orders appealable under § 1292. However, because of the historical division of legal and equitable courts, a curious exception has arisen. Injunctions or denials thereof have been appealable under § 1292. Consequently, an injunction staying a legal proceeding was, when law and equity were separate, appealable. With the merger of law and equity, the rule has arisen that when a legal action is stayed on equitable grounds, § 1292 permitted an appeal, as it would have under the old law-equity dichotomy. However, to continue this rule in modern times no longer serves any practical purposes. It is contrary to any coherent appeals policy and constitutes nothing more than a failure to recognize modern circumstances. Therefore, this Court now holds that orders regarding stays are appealable under no circumstances and that the law-equity merger has effectively abolished the exception detailed above. Affirmed.

EDITOR'S ANALYSIS: Section 1292 relates to interlocutory orders. Such orders are generally unappealable. Certain types, however, such as those enumerated in § 1292, are. The injunction is one of those orders found in § 1292, and the rule abolished in this decision was generally regarded as an unintended anomalous result of this inclusion.

[For more information on discretionary jurisdiction, see Casenote Law Outline on Civil Procedure, Chapter 10, § III, The Federal Courts and the Model of Finality.]

BOSE CORPORATION v. CONSUMERS UNION OF UNITED STATES, INC.
466 U.S. 485 (1984).

NATURE OF CASE: Review of reversal of determination of liability in defamation action.

FACT SUMMARY: A court of appeals performed a de novo review of a district court's finding of reckless disregard of truth in a defamation action.

CONCISE RULE OF LAW: In a defamation action regarding a public figure, an appellate court must perform a de novo review of a district court's finding of reckless disregard of truth.

FACTS: Bose Corporation (P) sued Consumers Union (D), publisher of "Consumer Reports," for product disparagement. The district court found Bose (P) to be a public figure, thus implicating the First Amendment. The district court found Consumers Union (D) to have published with a reckless disregard of truth, a sufficient finding to establish liability. The court of appeals, performing a de novo review of the facts, reversed. Bose (P) petitioned for review, contending that the proper scope of review was a "clearly erroneous" standard.

ISSUE: In a defamation action regarding a public figure, must an appellate court perform a de novo review of a district court's finding of reckless disregard of truth?

HOLDING AND DECISION: (Stevens, J.) Yes. In a defamation action regarding a public figure, an appellate court must perform a de novo review of a district court's finding of reckless disregard of truth. Generally speaking, under Fed. R. Civ. P. 52(a), a reviewing court must give special deference to the factual findings of a trial court and upset the factual findings only when they are clearly erroneous. However, this Court has established that in actions implicating the First Amendment, appellate courts must exercise a de novo review of the entire record and satisfy themselves that the factual determinations regarding the crucial issues were in fact within constitutional restrictions. Rule 52(a)'s deferential standard will not be applied in defamation actions implicating the First Amendment. This being so, the court of appeals' standard of review here was proper. Affirmed.

DISSENT: (Rehnquist, J.) Appellate courts are ill-equipped to make the sort of mens rea determinations concerning malice that are at issue in defamation actions implicating the First Amendment.

EDITOR'S ANALYSIS: "Clearly erroneous" is one of the more deferential standards of review used by appellate courts. Under it, an appellate court may not reverse a trial court merely because it would have reached a contrary result. Rather, it must be clearly convinced that an incorrect result was reached.

[For more information on standards of review, see Casenote Law Outline on Civil Procedure, Chapter 10, § I, The Mechanics of Appeal.]

BENDER v. WILLIAMSPORT AREA SCHOOL DISTRICT
475 U.S. 534 (1986).

NATURE OF CASE: Appeal of order reversing declaratory judgment.

FACT SUMMARY: Youngerman, a member of the Williamsport Board of Education (D), appealed a district court ruling that a religious group could hold meetings on school grounds.

CONCISE RULE OF LAW: An individual school board member does not have standing to appeal a declaratory judgment against the board.

FACTS: A group of students within the jurisdiction of the Williamsport Board of Education (D) requested that they be permitted to form an officially recognized school organization which would be religious in nature. Acting on advice of counsel that the group's presence on campus would violate the First Amendment, the request was refused. A declaratory relief action was filed against the Board (D). The district court held that the group's presence on campus was constitutionally permissible. The Board (D) elected not to appeal. Youngerman, a Board (D) member, appealed on behalf of the Board (D). The court of appeals reversed. The Supreme Court granted certiorari.

ISSUE: Does an individual school board member have standing to appeal a declaratory judgment against the board?

HOLDING AND DECISION: (Stevens, J.) No. An individual school board member does not have standing to appeal a declaratory judgment against the board. Article III of the Constitution requires a party who invokes a federal court's authority to show that he has personally suffered some real or threatened injury as a result of the alleged conduct of another. This rule of standing applies at all levels of a litigation. To take an appeal, one must have an individual stake in the outcome of a litigation. A declaratory relief action against a school board does not put any of its individual members in any sort of jeopardy, and therefore no individual member has a right to appeal an adverse verdict. Here, Youngerman, a board member only, had no standing to appeal. Reversed and appeal dismissed.

CONCURRENCE: (Marshall, J.) Contrary to the dissent, Youngerman's ex post facto declaration that he was a parent of a child within the school district could not invoke standing to appeal.

DISSENT: (Burger, C.J.) The merits should be reached, as Youngerman's status as a parent provides a personal stake in the outcome sufficient to confer standing.

EDITOR'S ANALYSIS: "Standing" grows out of Article III's "case or controversy" requirement. For a party to be involved in a case or controversy, he must have a personal stake in the outcome. The doctrine is usually relevant at the outset of a suit but, as the Court notes, is applicable at all levels.

[For more information on the standing doctrine, see Casenote Law Outline on Civil Procedure, Chapter 4, § I, General Principles of Federal Subject-Matter Jurisdiction.]

WRATCHFORD v. S.J. GROVES & SONS COMPANY
405 F.2d 1061 (4th Cir. 1969).

NATURE OF CASE: Appeal of denial of damages for personal injury.

FACT SUMMARY: Wratchford (P), on appeal, raised a contention not made at the trial level although made in a motion for a directed verdict.

CONCISE RULE OF LAW: A party may appeal on an issue which, while not raised at trial, was raised in a motion for a directed verdict.

FACTS: Wratchford (P) sued S.J. Groves & Sons Company (D) for personal injury. At trial, all sides assumed that state standards of sufficiency of evidence applied in this federal diversity action. The jury returned a defense verdict. In a motion for a directed verdict, Wratchford (P) for the first time argued that a more liberal federal standard was appropriate. The court denied the motion, and Wratchford (P) appealed.

ISSUE: May a party appeal on an issue which, while not raised at trial, was raised in a motion for a directed verdict?

HOLDING AND DECISION: (Haynsworth, J.) Yes. A party may appeal on an issue which, although not raised at trial, was raised in a motion for a directed verdict. Normally, an issue not raised at trial is waived for appellate purposes. However, when a district court is fully briefed on an issue in a posttrial motion and rules upon its merits, no reason exists why appellate review would be improper. Here, the district court did rule on the merits, so this appeal was proper. [On the merits, the court reversed, holding a federal law applicable.]

EDITOR'S ANALYSIS: In reversing the district court, the Fourth Circuit looked to the importance of a sufficiency-of-evidence standard to the federal system. It found that nonuniformity would disrupt the federal system. Under Byrd v. Blue Ridge Rural Electrical Coop., 356 U.S. 525, this demanded a federal standard.

[For more information on standards of review for appeal, see Casenote Law Outline on Civil Procedure, Chapter 10, § I, The Mechanics of Appeal.]

CHAPTER 13
PRECLUSIVE EFFECTS OF JUDGMENTS

QUICK REFERENCE RULES OF LAW

1. **Res Judicata Doctrine.** One may not bring an action subsequent to final judgment in another action which, although based on a different cause of action, involved essentially the same facts. (Manego v. Orleans Board of Trade)

   [For more information on the res judicata doctrine, see Casenote Law Outline on Civil Procedure, Chapter 12, § I, Res Judicata Defined.]

2. **Res Judicata Doctrine.** Res judicata bars relitigation of an unappealed adverse judgment where other plaintiffs in similar actions against common defendants successfully appealed the judgments against them. (Federated Dept. Stores, Inc. v. Moitie)

   [For more information on the res judicata doctrine, see Casenote Law Outline on Civil Procedure, Chapter 12, § I, Res Judicata Defined.]

3. **The Application of Res Judicata.** The dismissal of a complaint for failure to state a claim, which does not specify whether it is with prejudice, is res judicata on a subsequent claim alleging the same facts. (Rinehart v. Locke)

   [For more information on the application of res judicata, see Casenote Law Outline on Civil Procedure, Chapter 12, § I, Res Judicata Defined.]

4. **Intersystem Preclusion.** A state court judgment's preclusive effect on a federal antitrust claim shall be governed by the law of the state in which the initial judgment was rendered. (Marrese v. American Academy of Orthopaedic Surgeons)

   [For more information on intersystem preclusion, see Casenote Law Outline on Civil Procedure, Chapter 12, § III, Unique Problems of Inter-system Preclusion.]

5. **Estoppel by Verdict.** A previous justice court judgment constitutes estoppel by verdict to a subsequent action, involving the same parties, issues, and transaction. (Little v. Blue Goose Motor Coach Co.)

   [For more information on estoppel by verdict, see Casenote Law Outline on Civil Procedure, Chapter 12, § II, Collateral Estoppel or Issue Preclusion.]

6. **Collateral Estoppel.** Collateral estoppel may not be applied when the fact finder based its decision on one of several possible bases. (Hardy v. Johns-Manville Sales Corp.)

   [For more information on collateral estoppel, see Casenote Law Outline on Civil Procedure, Chapter 12, § II, Collateral Estoppel or Issue Preclusion.]

7. **Collateral Estoppel.** Where two cases involve taxes in different taxable years, collateral estoppel will be confined to situations where the matter raised in the second suit is identical in all respects with that decided in the first proceeding and where the controlling facts and applicable legal rules remain unchanged. (Commissioner of Internal Revenue v. Sunnen)

   [For more information on collateral estoppel, see Casenote Law Outline on Civil Procedure, Chapter 12, § II, Collateral Estoppel or Issue Preclusion.]

8. **Collateral Estoppel.** When a prior judgment adjudicating one a bankrupt rests on two or more alternative grounds, it is not conclusive to discharge issues if less than all grounds in the bankruptcy adjudication involved such issues. (Halpern v. Schwartz)

> *[For more information on collateral estoppel, see Casenote Law Outline on Civil Procedure, Chapter 12, § II, Collateral Estoppel or Issue Preclusion.]*

9. **Issue Preclusion.** An identity of legal representation and witnesses is not sufficient to permit issue preclusion. (Benson and Ford, Inc. v. Wanda Petroleum Co.)

> *[For more information on issue preclusion, see Casenote Law Outline on Civil Procedure, Chapter 12, § II, Collateral Estoppel or Issue Preclusion.]*

10. **The Mutuality Doctrine.** A nonparty to a prior equitable action may assert collateral estoppel in a subsequent action at law. (Parklane Hosiery Co., Inc. v. Shore)

> *[For more information on the mutuality doctrine, see Casenote Law Outline on Civil Procedure, Chapter 12, § II, Collateral Estoppel or Issue Preclusion.]*

11. **Mutuality of Estoppel.** Where a district court erroneously dismisses a plaintiff's legal claims in an action combining both equitable and legal claims, collateral estoppel does not preclude relitigation of the same issues before a jury in the context of the plaintiff's legal claims. (Lytle v. Household Mfg., Inc.)

> *[For more information on mutuality of estoppel, see Casenote Law Outline on Civil Procedure, Chapter 12, § II, Collateral Estoppel or Issue Preclusion.]*

12. **Collateral Estoppel Against the Government.** Nonmutual offensive use of collateral estoppel may not be had against the federal government. (United States v. Mendoza)

> *[For more information on the use of collateral estoppel against the government, see Casenote Law Outline on Civil Procedure, Chapter 12, § II, Collateral Estoppel or Issue Preclusion.]*

FEDERATED DEPARTMENT STORES, INC. v. MOITIE
452 U.S. 394 (1981).

NATURE OF CASE: Appeal from reversal of dismissal of antitrust action.

FACT SUMMARY: Federated (D) contended that the doctrine of res judicata barred relitigation of an unappealed adverse judgment where other plaintiffs in similar actions had successfully appealed judgments against them.

CONCISE RULE OF LAW: Res judicata bars relitigation of an unappealed adverse judgment where other plaintiffs in similar actions against common defendants successfully appealed the judgments against them.

FACTS: In 1976, the Government (P) brought an antitrust action against Federated (D), alleging that it had violated § 1 of the Sherman Act by agreeing to fix the retail price of women's clothing sold in Northern California. Seven parallel civil actions were subsequently filed by private plaintiffs seeking treble damages on behalf of proposed classes of retail purchasers, including that of Moitie (P) (Moitie I) in state court and Brown (P) (Brown I) in federal district court. Each of these complaints tracked almost verbatim the allegations of the Government's (P) complaint, although the Moitie I complaint referred solely to state law. All of the actions, including Moitie I, were assigned to a single federal judge, who dismissed all of the actions because of pleading defects. The plaintiffs in five of the suits appealed that judgment to the federal court of appeals, while the single counsel representing Moitie (P) and Brown (P) chose not to appeal and instead refiled the two actions in state court, Moitie II and Brown II. Federated (D) removed the new actions to federal district court, where they were dismissed on the grounds of res judicata. However, the court of appeals reversed, such as was obtained by the other five plaintiffs, when their position is closely interwoven with that of the appealing parties. Federated (D) appealed.

ISSUE: Does res judicata bar relitigation of an unappealed adverse judgment where other plaintiffs in similar actions against common defendants successfully appealed the judgments against them?

HOLDING AND DECISION: (Rehnquist, J.) Yes. Res judicata bars relitigation of an unappealed adverse judgment where other plaintiffs in similar actions against common defendants successfully appealed the judgments against them. A final judgment on the merits of an action precludes the parties or their privies from relitigating issues that were, or could have been, raised in that action. A judgment merely voidable because it is based upon an erroneous view of the law is not open to collateral attack but can be corrected only by a direct review and not by bringing another action upon the same cause of action. Here, both Brown I and Moitie I were final judgments on the merits and involved the same claims and the same parties as Brown II and Moitie II. Both those parties seek to be the windfall beneficiaries on an appellate reversal procured by other independent parties, and it is further apparent that Brown (P) and Moitie (P) made a calculated choice to forgo their appeals. Reversed and remanded.

CONCURRENCE: (Blackmun, J.) Brown I is res judicata on Brown's (P) state law claims. Even if the state and federal claims are distinct, Brown's (P) failure to allege the state claims in Brown I manifestly bars their allegation in Brown II.

DISSENT: (Brennan, J.) The Court today disregards statutory restrictions on federal court jurisdiction and, in the process, confuses rather than clarifies long-established principles of res judicata.

EDITOR'S ANALYSIS: The Court, in a footnote, agreed with the court of appeals that at least some of the claims had a sufficient federal character, such as would support removal to the federal court. Both the district court and the court of appeals had found that Brown (P) and Moitie (P) had attempted to avoid removal jurisdiction by artfully casting their essentially federal law claims as state-law claims.

————————

[For more information on the res judicata doctrine, see Casenote Law Outline on Civil Procedure, Chapter 12, § I, Res Judicata Defined.]

NOTES:

MANEGO v. ORLEANS BOARD OF TRADE
773 F.2d 1 (1985).

NATURE OF CASE: Appeal of summary judgment dismissing an antitrust action.

FACT SUMMARY: After losing an action for civil rights violations, Manego (P) filed an antitrust action based on essentially the same facts.

CONCISE RULE OF LAW: One may not bring an action subsequent to final judgment in another action which, although based on a different cause of action, involved essentially the same facts.

FACTS: Manego (P) sought and was denied permission to open a disco in the town of Orleans. The denial was based largely upon concerns that such a facility would negatively impact a nearby skating rink used by children and adolescents. Manego (P) sued various individuals and entities involved in the denial. Summary judgment was granted dismissing the action. Subsequent to this, Manego (P) filed an action based on the Sherman Antitrust Act, contending that a conspiracy to prevent him from competing with the rink, which had recently begun catering to adults, existed. The district court, holding that the matter was res judicata because of the prior suit, dismissed. Manego (P) appealed.

ISSUE: May one bring an action subsequent to final judgment in another action which, although based on a different cause of action, involved essentially the same facts?

HOLDING AND DECISION: (Bownes, J.) No. One may not bring an action subsequent to final judgment in another action which, although based on a different cause of action, involved essentially the facts. Under the doctrine of res judicata, a final judgment on the merits of an action precludes the parties or their privies from relitigating issues which were or could have been raised in that action. The standard is transactional. If the second action is based on the same transaction as the first, preclusion will exist. Here, while the causes of action are different, the underlying transaction is the same. Further, it is true that the defendants are not identical. This is of no moment; Manego (P) could have sued these defendants in the prior action, as the antitrust action could have been brought at this time. This being so, the summary judgment was proper. Affirmed.

EDITOR'S ANALYSIS: The standard used by the court here was borrowed from the Restatement (Second) of Judgments, which holds that subsequent claims, rights, or remedies which arise out of the same transaction as a prior action are precluded. The Restatement does not give a bright line definition of "transaction" but rather holds that a court should pragmatically weigh factors such as time, space, origin, and motivation.

[For more information on the res judicata doctrine, see Casenote Law Outline on Civil Procedure, Chapter 12, § I, Res Judicata Defined.]

RINEHART v. LOCKE
454 F.2d 313 (7th Cir. 1971).

NATURE OF CASE: Appeal from dismissal of an action for false arrest based on res judicata.

FACT SUMMARY: Rinehart's (P) action for false arrest was dismissed for failure to allege lack of probable cause. No leave to amend was granted.

CONCISE RULE OF LAW: The dismissal of a complaint for failure to state a claim, which does not specify whether it is with prejudice, is res judicata on a subsequent claim alleging the same facts.

FACTS: Rinehart (P) brought suit for an alleged false arrest. The action was dismissed for failure to state a claim since lack of probable cause was not alleged. No leave to amend was granted. Rinehart (P) did not appeal. Instead, a year later, he instituted a new suit based on the same cause of action but this time alleging lack of probable cause. Locke (D) moved to dismiss based on res judicata. The district court dismissed on this basis. Rinehart (P) appealed on the basis that a dismissal for failure to state a claim was not a judgment on the merits and that a dismissal, unless with prejudice, should not bar his claim.

ISSUE: Is a dismissal for failure to state a claim res judicata on a subsequent claim based on the same cause of action?

HOLDING AND DECISION: (Fairchild, J.) Yes. Rule 41(b) states that except for specific listed exceptions, all dismissals are on the merits. Under this rule, a dismissal of a complaint for failure to state a claim is a judgment on the merits and bars a subsequent claim. A plaintiff's only remedy is to request that the dismissal be made "without prejudice" or "with leave to amend." If this is refused, a plaintiff's only remedy is to appeal the decision. Since Rinehart (P) failed to do so, the dismissal (even though it was not stated to be "without prejudice") bars his subsequent claim. The decision of the district court is affirmed.

EDITOR'S ANALYSIS: It is discretionary with the trial court whether a case may be dismissed "with prejudice" where there is a failure to prosecute or to obey a court order. The reviewing court is somewhat hesitant to allow such a dismissal based upon an attorney's dereliction of duty. It will look for less drastic sanctions. Industrial Bldg. Materials, Inc. v. Interchemical Corp., 437 F.2d 1336 (9th Cir. 1970).

[For more information on the application of res judicata, see Casenote Law Outline on Civil Procedure, Chapter 12, § I, Res Judicata Defined.]

MARRESE v. AMERICAN ACADEMY OF ORTHOPEDIC SURGEONS
470 U.S. 373 (1985).

NATURE OF CASE: Appeal of dismissal of federal antitrust action.

FACT SUMMARY: A court of appeals gave preclusive effect to an antitrust action, holding that an earlier state action arising out of the same set of circumstances was res judicata.

CONCISE RULE OF LAW: A state court judgment's preclusive effect on a federal antitrust claim shall be governed by the law of the state in which the initial judgment was rendered.

FACTS: Marrese (P), denied membership in the American Academy of Orthopedic Surgeons (D), filed an Illinois state court action, alleging various violations of his common law rights. The action was dismissed. Marrese (P) then filed a federal antitrust action. The Academy (D) moved to dismiss on the grounds that the state action constituted res judicata. The district court denied the motion. The Seventh Circuit reversed, holding that as a matter of law the case was res judicata. Marrese (P) appealed.

ISSUE: Shall a state court judgment's preclusive effect on a federal antitrust claim be governed by the law of the state in which the initial judgment was rendered?

HOLDING AND DECISION: (O'Connor, J.) Yes. A state court judgment's preclusive effect on a federal antitrust claim shall be governed by the law of the state in which the judgment was rendered. The preclusive effect of such judgments is generally governed by the full faith and credit statute, 28 U.S.C. § 1738. The statute requires a federal court to look to the law of the state in which a judgment was rendered to determine the preclusive effect of the judgment. Comity and respect for state laws require this. The fact that the antitrust action could not have been brought in state court does not change this analysis. Unless an exception to § 1738 is found in the law upon which federal jurisdiction is predicated, § 1738 rules. Here, on remand, the district court is to apply the Illinois law regarding preclusion to the state action. Reversed.

CONCURRENCE: (Burger, C.J.) Where, as a review of Illinois law in this instance shows to be a possibility, the state law regarding preclusion is unclear, it may be appropriate to formulate a federal rule.

EDITOR'S ANALYSIS: The Court largely relied on a prior case, Kremer v. Chemical Construction Corp., 456 U.S. 461 (1982). The particular case enunciated the same rule but only as applied to issue preclusion. The Court extended it here to claim preclusion as well.

[For more information on intersystem preclusion, see Casenote Law Outline on Civil Procedure, Chapter 12, § III, Unique Problems of Inter-system Preclusion.]

LITTLE v. BLUE GOOSE MOTOR COACH CO.
Ill. Sup. Ct., 346 Ill. 266, 178 N.E. 496 (1931).

NATURE OF CASE: Appeal in an action for damages in tort for personal injuries and wrongful death.

FACT SUMMARY: A judgement was rendered for Blue Goose (D) against Little for negligence which became final. Little, and later his executrix (P), then sued Blue Goose (D) for personal injuries and wrongful death based on the same transaction.

CONCISE RULE OF LAW: A previous justice court judgment constitutes estoppel by verdict to a subsequent action, involving the same parties, issues, and transaction.

FACTS: A judgment in favor of Blue Goose (D) was rendered against Little in a justice court for negligently operating his vehicle. Because of a lack of prosecution, Little's appeal from the judgment was dismissed, but, during the pendency of that suit, he commenced an action for personal injury against Blue Goose (D). Little died, and his executrix (P) initiated a wrongful death action against Blue Goose (D) for negligence and willful and wanton negligence. A judgment for executrix (P) was reversed on appeal. The executrix (P) appealed.

ISSUE: Does a previous justice court judgment constitute an estoppel by verdict to a subsequent action involving the same parties, issues, and transaction?

HOLDING AND DECISION: (Per curiam) Yes. Where a former adjudication is a bar to a subsequent action, there must have been an identity of the parties and subject matter. Here, the issue of fact upon which both Little's and his executrix's (P) case was based was the negligence of Little as determined by the justice court. When the justice court judgment became final, it bound both parties. The fact that the executrix (P) charged Blue Goose (D) with willful and wanton negligence does not overcome the finding in the justice court that Little was negligent.

EDITOR'S ANALYSIS: Estoppel by verdict may be interposed as a defense whenever there is an identity between parties, subject matter, and transaction in a previous lawsuit where judgment was allowed to become final. The policy behind this is to protect the finality of prior judgments and to put an end to litigation.

[For more information on estoppel by verdict, see Casenote Law Outline on Civil Procedure, Chapter 12, § II, Collateral Estoppel or Issue Preclusion.]

COMMISSIONER OF INTERNAL REVENUE v. SUNNEN
333 U.S. 591 (1948).

NATURE OF CASE: Action in tax court challenging deficiency assessment made by the IRS.

FACT SUMMARY: Sunnen (P), having won a favorable determination in a prior year, sought to invoke the decision as res judicata to bar later challenges for other years where there was a complete identity of facts, issues, and parties.

CONCISE RULE OF LAW: Where two cases involve taxes in different taxable years, collateral estoppel will be confined to situations where the matter raised in the second suit is identical in all respects with that decided in the first proceeding and where the controlling facts and applicable legal rules remain unchanged.

FACTS: In 1928, Sunnen (P) had licensed his corporation to use his patents in exchange for a royalty. In various years following, Sunnen (P) assigned his interest in these agreements to his wife who reported this income on her income tax returns. In 1935, Sunnen (P) prevailed in a tax court proceeding brought by the Commissioner of Internal Revenue (D), who had contended that the income was taxable to Sunnen (P) himself. Later, the exact same action was brought by the Commissioner (D) against Sunnen (P) on the same issue, except this time for royalties paid in 1937.

ISSUE: Where two cases involve taxes in different taxable years, will collateral estoppel be confined to situations where the matter raised in the second suit is identical in all respects with that decided in the first proceeding and where the controlling facts and applicable legal rules remain unchanged?

HOLDING AND DECISION: (Murphy, J.) Yes. Collateral estoppel does apply in the income tax field but only insofar as it extends to any subsequent proceeding involving the same claim and the same tax year. Where a taxpayer secures a judicial determination of a particular tax matter which may recur without substantial variation for some years thereafter, a subsequent modification of the significant facts on a change or development in the controlling legal principles may make that determination obsolete, or erroneous, at least for future years. Permitting a taxpayer to invoke his decision in a single year for a number of years is unfair to other taxpayers causing inequalities in the administration of taxes, discriminatory distinctions in tax liability, and a fertile basis for litigious confusion. Tax inequality can result as readily from neglecting legal modulations by the Supreme Court as from disregarding factual changes wrought by state courts. This reasoning is particularly apposite here since, if Sunnen (P) had not had the benefit of the earlier decision, his claim, in view of recent legal developments in the tax field, would have failed if brought now for the first time.

EDITOR'S ANALYSIS: The Court's opinion here may be difficult to reconcile with its earlier decision in Tait v. Western Maryland Ry., 289 U.S. 620, 624, where it was said: "The scheme of the Revenue Acts is an imposition of tax for annual periods, and the exaction for one year is distinct from that for any other. But it does not follow that Congress, in adopting this system, meant to deprive the government and the taxpayer of relief from redundant litigation of the identical question of the statute's application to the taxpayer's status. . . . Alteration of the law in this respect is a matter for the lawmaking body rather than the courts. . . . It cannot be supposed that Congress was oblivious of the scope of the doctrine (of res judicata), and in the absence of a clear declaration of such purpose, we will not infer from the annual nature of the exaction an intention to abolish the rule in this class of cases."

[For more information on collateral estoppel, see Casenote Law Outline on Civil Procedure, Chapter 12, § II, Collateral Estoppel or Issue Preclusion.]

NOTES:

HARDY v. JOHNS-MANVILLE SALES CORP.
681 F.2d 334 (5th Cir. 1982).

NATURE OF CASE: Appeal of collateral estoppel order in action for damages for personal injury.

FACT SUMMARY: A trial court entered a collateral estoppel order regarding a failure-to-warn basis for products liability, although the jury in the prior action could have based its finding on one of several theories.

CONCISE RULE OF LAW: Collateral estoppel may not be applied when the fact finder based its decision on one of several possible bases.

FACTS: A class of plaintiffs sued various defendants for personal injury related to asbestos exposure. One theory of recovery was products liability based on a failure to warn. The plaintiffs moved for a collateral estoppel order based on a jury finding in a prior case that the same defendants had failed to warn of the danger of asbestos. However, it was unclear from the record of the prior case as to when the jury believed the duty to warn came into being. In the present action, warnings were placed by Johns-Manville (D) at various times from 1964 through 1969. The district court entered summary adjudication as to the failure-to-warn theory, and Johns-Manville (D) appealed.

EDITOR'S ANALYSIS: May collateral estoppel be applied when the fact finder based its decision on one of several possible bases?

HOLDING AND DECISION: (Gee, J.) No. Collateral estoppel may not be applied when the fact finder based its decision on one of several possible bases. Collateral estoppel may be applied only when there is an identity of issues. When the prior judgment is ambivalent, the doctrine is not to be utilized. Here, the jury in the prior action could have found that the duty to warn arose any time between 1963 and 1969. When it held the duty to have arisen is unclear from the record. Here, some defendants began issuing warnings as early as 1964. Therefore, it is possible that they fulfilled any duty to warn they may have had. This being so, collateral estoppel was incorrectly applied. Reversed.

EDITOR'S ANALYSIS: Most actions involve general verdicts without specific findings by juries. It is difficult to find an identity of issues in such situations. Collateral estoppel is usually more readily available when the prior case contained special interrogatories.

[For more information on collateral estoppel, see Casenote Law Outline on Civil Procedure, Chapter 12, § II, Collateral Estoppel or Issue Preclusion.]

HALPERN v. SCHWARTZ
426 F.2d 102 (2d Cir. 1970).

NATURE OF CASE: Appeal of order denying bankruptcy discharge.

FACT SUMMARY: A bankruptcy referee denied Halpern (P) a discharge in bankruptcy based on intent to defraud having been found earlier in the bankruptcy, although such intent was involved in only one of three possible bases for the prior decision.

CONCISE RULE OF LAW: When a prior judgment adjudicating one a bankrupt rests on two or more alternative grounds, it is not conclusive to discharge issues if less than all grounds in the bankruptcy adjudication involved such issues.

FACTS: Several creditors petitioned to put Halpern (P) into involuntary bankruptcy, alleging three different bases therefore. Only one of these involved an element of intent. The bankruptcy referee held all three bases fulfilled and held Halpern (P) bankrupt. Subsequently, Halpern (P) petitioned for discharge. Schwartz (D), the bankruptcy trustee, opposed this, contending that Halpern (P) had effected certain property transfers with the intent of defrauding creditors, a ground for denying discharge under 11 U.S.C. § 32(c)(4). The bankruptcy court held that the earlier finding of bankruptcy precluded litigation of the intent issue and denied the petition. Halpern (P) appealed.

ISSUE: When a prior judgment adjudicating one a bankrupt rests on two or more alternative grounds, is it conclusive to discharge issues if less than all grounds in the bankruptcy adjudication involved such issues?

HOLDING AND DECISION: (Smith, J.) No. When a prior judgment adjudicating one a bankrupt rests on two or more alternative grounds, it is not conclusive to discharge issues if less than all grounds in the bankruptcy adjudication involved such issues. It is established that, even if an issue was fully litigated in a prior proceeding, preclusive effect will not be given if the resolution of that issue was not necessary for the judgment below. This is based on the notion that if an issue is not necessary for the result in the first action, a party may not be motivated to fully litigate it. To subsequently consider it precluded would therefore work to the litigant's prejudice if it is determinative in the subsequent action. Here, the bankruptcy referee could have held Halpern (P) bankrupt with or without a finding of intent. In the present controversy, such a finding is necessary for Halpern (P) to lose. This being so, collateral estoppel on the issue of intent would be improper. Reversed.

EDITOR'S ANALYSIS: At first glance, it might appear that the rule established in this decision would effectively preclude the application of collateral estoppel whenever a prior decision is based on alternative grounds. This, at least theoretically, is not so. If an issue is a necessary element of each ground, then preclusion would be appropriate.

[For more information on collateral estoppel, see Casenote Law Outline on Civil Procedure, Chapter 12, § II, Collateral Estoppel or Issue Preclusion.]

BENSON AND FORD, INC. v. WANDA PETROLEUM CO.
833 F.2d 1172 (5th Cir. 1987).

NATURE OF CASE: Appeal of summary judgment dismissing antitrust action.

FACT SUMMARY: Benson and Ford (P), represented by the same attorney and having many of the same witnesses as a prior unsuccessful litigant against Wanda (D), was held subject to decisive issues subject to collateral estoppel.

CONCISE RULE OF LAW: An identity of legal representation and witnesses is not sufficient to permit issue preclusion.

FACTS: Shelby Gas filed an antitrust action against Wanda Petroleum (D). Wanda (D) prevailed on the merits. Subsequently, Benson and Ford, Inc., (P) filed a similar action. Benson and Ford (P) was represented by the same attorney as had Shelby and had essentially the same witnesses. Wanda (D) moved for summary judgment, contending that the relevant issues of liability were precluded from relitigation. The district court agreed, dismissing the action. Benson and Ford (P) appealed.

ISSUE: Is an identity of legal representation and witnesses sufficient to permit issue preclusion?

HOLDING AND DECISION: (Reavley, J.) No. An identity of legal representation and witnesses is not sufficient to permit issue preclusion. Because a litigant has a due process right to a full and fair opportunity to litigate an issue, preclusion may be asserted only against a party or privy to a party to a prior litigation. This has been held to exist when a nonparty who controlled the litigation has preclusion sought against it in a subsequent action. While no clear rule exists as to what constitutes "control," it is clear that the mere fact that representation and witnesses are the same for the subsequent litigant does not equal control. A nonparty has no control over a party's attorney, and that attorney's subsequent representation of the nonparty does not alter that fact. The same is true for witnesses. This being the case, an identity of parties did not exist in this action. Reversed.

EDITOR'S ANALYSIS: The most common situation of issue preclusion exists when a nonparty has succeeded a party. In the case of a corporate merger or consolidation, this is relatively easy to establish. It can be more problematic in the instance of an asset purchase.

[For more information on issue preclusion, see Casenote Law Outline on Civil Procedure, Chapter 12, § II, Collateral Estoppel or Issue Preclusion.]

LYTLE v. HOUSEHOLD MFG., INC.
494 U.S. 545 (1990).

NATURE OF CASE: Appeal from dismissal of a plaintiff's combined legal and equitable claims in an action seeking damages for discriminatory discharge.

FACT SUMMARY: After the district court dismissed Lytle's (P) § 1981 claim, then dismissed his Title VII claim after a bench trial, the court of appeals held Lytle (P) was collaterally estopped from litigating his § 1981 claim.

CONCISE RULE OF LAW: Where a district court erroneously dismisses a plaintiff's legal claims in an action combining both equitable and legal claims, collateral estoppel does not preclude relitigation of the same issues before a jury in the context of the plaintiff's legal claims.

FACTS: When Lytle (P), an Afro-American, asked to take a vacation day to see a doctor on Friday, he was told he would have to work on Saturday instead. Because he didn't report for work on either day, Lytle (P) was discharged in accord with company policy. He brought this suit, seeking relief under both Title VII and 42 U.S.C. § 1981 and alleging that he had been treated differently from white workers who had missed work. The district court dismissed Lytle's (P) § 1981 claims, conducted a bench trial on the Title VII claims, and entered judgment in favor of Household (D). The court of appeals affirmed, ruling that Lytle (P) was collaterally estopped from litigating his § 1981 claims. This appeal followed.

ISSUE: Where a district court erroneously dismisses a plaintiff's legal claims in an action combining both equitable and legal claims, does collateral estoppel preclude relitigation of the same issues before a jury in the context of the plaintiff's legal claims?

HOLDING AND DECISION: (Marshall, J.) No. Where a district court erroneously dismisses a plaintiff's legal claims in an action combining both equitable and legal claims, collateral estoppel does not preclude relitigation of the same issues before a jury in the context of the plaintiff's legal claims. Household (D) does not dispute that, had the district court not dismissed Lytle's (P) § 1981 claims, he would have been entitled to a jury trial on those claims. Furthermore, the purposes served by collateral estoppel of protecting parties from multiple lawsuits and conserving judicial resources do not justify applying the doctrine in this case. Relitigation is the only mechanism that can completely correct the error of the court below. Thus, the judgment is vacated, and the case is remanded.

EDITOR'S ANALYSIS: Lytle (P) requested a jury trial on all issues triable by jury. Only the trial court's erroneous dismissal of the § 1981 claims enabled that court to resolve issues common to both claims, issues that otherwise would have been resolved by a jury. Beacon Theatres v. Westover, 359 U.S. 500 (1959) emphasized the importance of the order in which legal and equitable claims joined in one suit would be considered.

[For more information on mutuality of estoppel, see Casenote Law Outline on Civil Procedure, Chapter 12, § II, Collateral Estoppel or Issue Preclusion.]

PARKLANE HOSIERY CO. v. SHORE
439 U.S. 322 (1979).

NATURE OF CASE: Review of order reversing denial of summary adjudication of issues in an action based on violation of securities laws.

FACT SUMMARY: Shore (P), representing a shareholder class in a derivative action, sought to use the result of a prior SEC enforcement action to preclude issue litigation regarding liability against Parklane Hosiery Co. (D).

CONCISE RULE OF LAW: A nonparty to a prior equitable action may assert collateral estoppel in a subsequent action at law.

FACTS: Shore (P) filed a derivative action against Parklane Hosiery (D), alleging fraud in a proxy statement. Concurrently, the SEC filed an enforcement action, seeking an injunction. The district court held the proxy statement to have been fraudulent and enjoined further such action. Shore (P) moved for summary adjudication, contending that liability had been determined in the SEC action. The district court denied the motion, but the court of appeals reversed. The Supreme Court granted review.

ISSUE: May a nonparty to a prior equitable action assert collateral estoppel in a subsequent action at law?

HOLDING AND DECISION: (Stewart, J.) Yes. A nonparty to a prior equitable action may assert collateral estoppel in a subsequent action at law. The old rule of mutuality for the application of collateral estoppel has been jettisoned. Now, collateral estoppel may be used defensively in most circumstances. Its use in an offensive capacity is suspect, however. The issue may have been minor in the previous action, and it would be unfair to allow the issue to be precluded in another action where the issue is vital. Also, the whole purpose of the preclusion doctrine is to avoid multiple litigation. The offensive use of preclusion may work against this, however, as it would permit a party to wait for the issue to be resolved, and then file its own suit. However, the best solution to this problem is to look at these factors in the context of each case. Whether the prior case was legal or equitable really is of no import. Here, Parklane (D) certainly had ample motivation to fully litigate the issue of fraud in the prior action. Further, it is unlikely that Shore (P) could have been a party to the SEC action. Since no policy reason for not permitting the offensive use of collateral estoppel exists, its use would be appropriate. Affirmed.

DISSENT: (Rehnquist, J.) The application of collateral estoppel in this action violates Parklane's (D) Seventh Amendment right to trial by jury.

EDITOR'S ANALYSIS: Mutuality was a requirement for any use of collateral estoppel for many years. The Supreme Court abandoned mutuality as a per se requirement in Blonder-Tongue Laboratories v. University of Illinois Foundation, 402 U.S. 313 (1971), which dealt with "defensive" collateral estoppel. As the present case illustrates, "offensive" use is still in a state of flux.

[For more information on the mutuality doctrine, see Casenote Law Outline on Civil Procedure, Chapter 12, § II, Collateral Estoppel or Issue Preclusion.]

NOTES:

UNITED STATES v. MENDOZA
464 U.S. 154 (1984).

NATURE OF CASE: Review of order precluding issue litigation in action seeking naturalization.

FACT SUMMARY: Mendoza (P), seeking naturalization, relied on an earlier action in which applicants similar to him had obtained naturalization.

CONCISE RULE OF LAW: Nonmutual offensive use of collateral estoppel may not be had against the federal government.

FACTS: Mendoza (P), a Philippine national, sought naturalization as a U.S. citizen under a certain statute. This was denied, the Government (D) contending that the statute did not apply to him. Mendoza (P) appealed, contending that a prior, successful action by individuals similarly situated to him precluded relitigation of his claim. The court of appeals agreed and ordered Mendoza (P) naturalized. The Government (D) petitioned for certiorari.

ISSUE: May nonmutual offensive use of collateral estoppel be had against the federal government?

HOLDING AND DECISION: (Rehnquist, J.) No. Nonmutual offensive use of collateral estoppel may not be had against the federal government. The federal Government (D) is situated sufficiently differently from private litigants to warrant disparate treatment. The Government (D) is by far the most frequent litigant in federal actions. To hold an issue decided in one action to be forever precluded from relitigation would thwart the development of important issues of law, as conflicts in the circuits, a common reason for grants of certiorari, would no longer occur. Further, it is natural and proper for successive executive administrations to take differing positions on issues, and the use of collateral estoppel against the Government (D) would hinder this. For these reasons, use of collateral estoppel in an offensive manner against the Government (D) cannot be allowed. Reversed.

EDITOR'S ANALYSIS: The Court did take some pains to prevent an overly expansive reading of the present action. Mutual collateral estoppel, either offensive or defensive, was not disapproved. Also, defensive collateral estoppel in an nonmutual situation was not mentioned, so an inference of its viability can at least be argued.

[For more information on the use of collateral estoppel against the government, see Casenote Law Outline on Civil Procedure, Chapter 12, § II, Collateral Estoppel or Issue Preclusion.]

NOTES:

NOTES